Engineering and Technical Education in India

About the Author

Pradeep Chaturvedi, the Chairman of The Institution of Engineers (India), Delhi State Centre is a Mechanical Engineer and an Energy and Environment Expert. Mr. Chaturvedi has been involved with sustainable development issues, mainly the energy policy and planning and implementation of environment friendly sustainable energy projects for over three decades in India and other Asian and Pacific countries. As a Member of the Perspective Planning Group of Planning Commission, preparing Development Vision 2020, he contributed 'India's Energy Vision 2020'. He has been actively involved with the formulation of Energy Conservation Act 2001 and the Electricity Bill 2001.

Mr. Chaturvedi has been involved with the Studies Programme of the World Energy Council since 1983. His understanding of energy issues of the South Asia Region, in the global context, has been widely appreciated.

Mr. Chaturvedi was deeply involved with the preparatory phase of the World Summit of Sustainable Development. He is also involved in the follow-up phase.

Mr. Chaturvedi is Vice-Chairman of the UNESCO sponsored World Renewable Energy Network; and Vice-Chairman of the World Environment Foundation, both based in UK; and President of the Bio Energy Society of India. He is also a Visiting Faculty at IIT, Delhi.

Mr. Chaturvedi has authored six and edited 25 books on Energy Management and Sustainable Development. These books are widely referred to understand the situation in the country.

Engineering and Technical Education in India

PRADEEP CHATURVEDI

CONCEPT PUBLISHING COMPANY, NEW DELHI-110059

ISBN 81-8069-039-3

First Published 2003

Published and Printed by
Ashok Kumar Mittal
Concept Publishing Company
A/15-16, Commercial Block, Mohan Garden
New Delhi-110059 (INDIA)

Phones : 25351460, 25351794
Fax : 091-11-25357103
Email : publishing@conceptpub.com

Preface

Liberalisation of the economy has given rise to a new culture which follows a course different from planned economy. The critical difference between planning and liberalization is that planning assumes that outcomes are predictable, while liberalization facilitates the unpredictable. It does so by unshackling the energy of innovation of millions of people unknown to planners, of letting them play around with ideas unthought of. Such unknown people and ideas have transformed other countries and may also transform India. It enables unknown to do the unthought of and become unstoppable.

The preparatory process for the World Summit on Social Development, coincided with the efforts of the Institution of Engineers (India), Delhi State Centre, launching a discussion on Technical Education in India, with a view to setting up appropriate capacity building programme leading to sustainable development of the economy. The scientific and technological community is expected to make a leading contribution to tackling major problems that include fighting against disease, population growth and urbanization, the digital divide, coping with climate change, confronting the water crisis, defending the soil, building a new ethic of global stewardship.

Implementing Agenda-21 during the next decade and beyond, will build on progress made during the past ten years in generating knowledge targeted to sustainable development objectives and in developing cleaner and more affordable technologies. However, enhancing the S&T community's capacity to contribute to sustainable development will require significant changes. The S&T community is committed to implement necessary changes and developing appropriate partnerships. These changes include, more policy relevant science, broad based participatory approaches and promoting gender equality in science.

It is now clear than ever that this challenge has thus far outstripped the capacities both of the S&T community and of society to forge effective and comprehensive responses. Nothing less than a new contract, between the S&T community and society is required.

Following crucial components of such a new contract were identified:

improving education and capacity building; bridging the north-south divide in scientific and technological capacity; clean technologies and sustainable production and consumption patterns; long-term perspectives and data needs; augmenting financial resources for S&T for sustainable development and governance for sustainable development. At the global level, these discussions were coordinated by the International Council for Science Union, ICSU, and the World Federation of Engineering Organisations, WFEO. As a member of the WFEO the Institution of Engineers (India), has also contributed significantly.

Whereas at the international level preparations are afoot for preparing for the World Summit on Social Development, the discussions organized by the Delhi State Centre also provided inputs to global discussions and national development

Awareness creation and technology assessment form an important component of the technological process. To achieve this objective the author was invited to speak on various engineering aspects that were relevant to growth of the sector.

The Book is a compilation of papers presented by the Author at various National and International Conferences; and also contains contributions of experts on Technical Education in India.

I hope the book will be found extremely valuable as a contribution of the Institution of Engineers (India), Delhi State Centre in its Platinum Jubilee Year.

PRADEEP CHATURVEDI
Chairman
The Institution of Engineers (India)
Delhi State Centre, New Delhi

New Delhi
December 23, 2002

Acknowledgments

I gratefully acknowledge the help and support of my colleagues at the Institution of Engineers (India), Delhi State Centre for motivating me to write this book and have it released on the occasion of the Annual Function on December 23, 2002. My special thanks to Shri V.K.Gupta, the in-coming Honorary Secretary of the Delhi State Centre for his persuasion to complete and publish the book.

Help and support of Shri Subhash Chander, Honorary Secretary, Delhi State Centre and Shri Praveen Singh, the Officer Administration, Delhi State Centre at different stages of preparation of papers and presentation is duly recognized. Secretarial assistance of Shri U.K. Bhalla is also duly recognized.

My grateful thanks to all the eminent personalities who presented papers at Discussion on Technical Education in India.

Shri Ashok K. Mittal, Managing Director, Concept Publishing Company deserves special thanks for his effort to publish this book at a very short notice.

My thanks also to various Institutions and personalities, who invited me to make these presentations during my tenure as the Chairman, The Institution of Engineers (India), Delhi State Centre.

PRADEEP CHATURVEDI
Chairman
The Institution of Engineers (India)
Delhi State Centre, New Delhi

New Delhi
December 23, 2002

Contents

TECHNICAL EDUCATION

FUTURE DIRECTIONS IN ENGINEERING

1

Challenges of Mechanical Engineering

I am privileged to participate in the 17th Convention of Mechanical Engineers being organised in the city of Indore—A city of historic and socio-economic importance. Indore has been a major trading centre—crucial for maintaining the supply of consumer durables in the heartland of the country. Emergence of major institutions of excellence in the education field, both in engineering education and management education; and establishment of centre of excellence like CAT have given a new dimension to the city. It is significant that such institutions have attracted best of the brains not only from within the country but even from outside. All credit goes to the visionary educationists, scientists, engineers and enterprising community of this city. Indore can proudly speak about its excellence in the intellectual field as well as socio-economic sector for its financial stability and self-sufficiency. The city can also be proud of educating Shri Digvijay Singh, Chief Minister of Madhya Pradesh, who with his engineering education has established new standards of governance. The Institution could not have hosted its first Convention of Mechanical Engineer in the New Millennium at any other better place in the country. On behalf of the President of the Institution, Shri H.P. Jamdar and my own personal behalf, I would like to thank the Director and Management of the SGS Institution of Technology and Science for hosting this Convention along with the Indore Local Centre of the Institution.

The topic of the National Seminar, namely "The Challenges for Mechanical Engineers at the Advent of Millennium" has gained a new dimension in the post-11th September 2001 global economic situation; and the post-ILO at Geneva and WTO round at Doha, both in

---

Chariman's Address at the 17th Convention of Mechanical Engineers organised by the Institution of Engineers (India), Indore Local Centre during November 2001 at Indore.

November, 2001. The 'concept of production' and the 'marketing strategies' are already being re-defined, and the shape of globalisation as dictated by the post-Second World War scenario is undergoing a serious shift. Environment, employment and poverty are now treated inseparable issues associated with the process of globalisation. At one time, it was considered that economic development, per say, should only mean enhancement of shareholder's interest. This is no more the case. The shareholder no doubt remains centre stage, but it is now necessary that other stakeholders be given equal importance. The overall strategy for corporate governance is now shifting to focus on poverty reduction, better employment opportunities and better quality of life, along with economic development. These two issues will not be separated as defined by WTO. The ADB Expert Consultation Group meeting at Tokyo, during November 11-15, 2001, has redefined corporate governance as controlled by three different groups rather than market driven forces alone. These include 'equity-based and market governed companies'; 'bank controlled companies' and 'family managed companies'. In the Indian context one more group, *i.e.* 'government controlled companies' also need to be added. Such a quick shift in concepts in the post-11 September 2001 scenario will send major corporates in a spin.

Also, the post-11 September scenario has thrown open new challenges to our country's engineers as well as new opportunities for the enterprising. The possibility of terrorist attack indicates that new approaches in the engineering sector are to be developed to counter these moves. In the post-Afghanistan war situation, the reconstruction phase will start sooner than later, where billions of dollars will be poured in the form of aid and loan in the South Asian continent. The opportunity lies now for the enterprising Indian organisations and professionals to have the vision and to conceptualise development strategies so that in the reconstruction phase Indian industry and their professionals have a bigger role. Either they can be the lead contractors or they can reap the benefits as sub-contractors. Whatever be the case, India has an opportunity to benefit from the post-Afghanistan war scenario. But, that can happen, if and only if, we plan our strategy right now. I am sure; many of the experts here have their ideas for the same.

We are meeting here at a crucial situation, when the role of engineering fraternity is seen more eminently for development of the country, which expects them to have the vision, translate that into plans, develop implementation strategies and implement the programmes. On the other hand the engineering fraternity also has the danger of losing out at policy-making level.

The shifting priorities on the global scene and enforcement of sanctions by USA and other developed countries have focused on mechanical engineering elements. Whether it is in terms of nuclear power, space or capital goods manufacturing, mechanical engineers have to show their innovative skills, evolutionary process, outstanding zeal and perseverance to find solution in a specific time frame. The eminent engineers who are being honoured today have time and again taken up the task to adequately deal with the challenges of sanctions imposed on the Indian economy.

Mechanical Engineering Concepts and Advances

It is customary for the Chairman deal with the recent advances in the mechanical engineering sector. I will reflect my views on the same.

Mechanical engineering has always been associated with manufacturing—which is as ancient as human civilisation. It gained significance, as it became technology when steam engine was invented and manufactured. The current globalisation process has focused on three elements — Technology, Management and Manpower. Technology, as applicable to manufacturing, is controlled by or evolved on the principles of mechanical engineering. Recent advances in communication and information technology have changed the total outlook and approach in product and process engineering. Though information technology is not an end in itself, it is serving as a very important tool in improving efficiencies of systems and dominating the decision making and improving efficiency of capital goods operation.

Industrial Revolution and Technology

Technology transfer played a central role in the industrial revolution but intellectual property protection was by no means the only route, nor was it always respected. Until the mid-19th Century the most important means of technology transfer was hiring skilled workers who brought needed technological knowledge. Skilled workers from industrially advanced countries were in high demand, resulting in government action. In 1719 French and Russian attempt to recruit

British workers—especially those skilled in wool, metal and watch making industries—prompted the British government to ban skilled worker's migration, making it punishable by fine or even imprisonment. Emigrant workers who failed to return home within six months of warning could lose their land, property and citizenship.

As technologies became embodied in machines, the focus shifted to controlling their export. In 1750 Britain banned the export of "tools and utensils" in wool and silk industries, then in 1781 widened that to "any machine, engine, tool, press, paper, utensil or implement whatsoever." But in response, entrepreneurs and technicians in Belgium, Denmark, France, the Netherlands, Norway, Russia and Sweden devised new ways to get the technologies, often with explicit state consent or even active encouragement, including offers of bounty for specific technologies.

By the mid —19th Century key technologies were too complex to acquire by hiring workers and importing machines, and licensing patents became increasingly important. Most of today's industrial countries introduced patents by 1850, followed by copyright and trade mark laws. But there were important exceptions. Swiss patent law was weak until 1907—when Germany threatened trade sanctions—and did not cover chemicals and pharmaceuticals until 1978. The United States, despite being a strong proponent of patent rights, did not recognise copyrights for foreigners until 1891.

Despite the emergence of international intellectual property rights among these countries, they continued to break the rules. In the late 19th Century German manufacturers found ways of infringing on British trade mark laws, producing counterfeit Sheffield cutlery with fake logos and placing the stamp of country of origin only on packaging, or hidden out of sight—as on the bottom of sewing machines.

Customised Production — Major Challenge

Globalisation of economy has exposed all the countries to the situation that has been experienced in the industrialised countries since 1980s. It is increasingly realised that vertically integrated global production is no more an effective approach. Changes in the corporate sector strategy are stimulated by demands for technology and the compulsions from the new markets that the earlier order had evoked. The conditions of competitiveness are radically altering.

The consumer preferences are shifting towards more specialised and customised products. Advantage of standardised mass production is being replaced by complex non-standardised production. Such a shift is necessitating integration of production ingenuity of all the constituents of the network. Insistence on quality is becoming ever more demanding and with that goes the difficulty of the manufacturing firms to attain quality in customised production. Realising the high cost of such production demands future strategies are requiring new approaches in production. Remember the present day demand is better quality accompanied by decreasing costs on customised production. That is the major challenge for mechanical engineers.

Responsiveness to Market Needs

Responsiveness to the market needs is the key to advantages that can be derived from customised products and market sensitive capabilities; their technological sophistication and inherent strength of competitiveness based on strong base of manpower and finance. Responsiveness requires well developed technological capabilities and social capabilities that underline the sensitivity of the corporate organisations to issues related to the impact of production and products on society as well as on the living environment.

New Directions in Mechanical Engineering on Quality Improvement

Mechanical engineering interventions like flexible manufacturing systems, computer integrated manufacturing systems and agile manufacturing along with concurrent engineering have been various concepts that have evolved in the recent past. These approaches have been rapidly bridging the gap with respect to global standards and quality to establish strong competitiveness.

Quality improvements in mechanical engineering practices are based on the global developments that have taken place during the last two decades. Emergence of the 20th Century witnessed two models of development—the first coming from the communist countries mainly the centralised or planned economy model based on self-reliance and import substitution; and the other based on the practice in the West European countries who worked on the concept of trade in technologies and products and therefore promoted the market concept. In the early 80s Mexico and other Latin American countries reached an economic chaos due to huge cumulative borrowing and inability to unburden their debts. That triggered massive support for the trade based market economy. The impact was so large that the centralised model of development promoted by the Soviet Union could not be sustained even in the Soviet Union.

At the end of World War-II, the Western world promoted the concept of market based economy and that gave birth to General Agreement on Trade and Tariff (GATT) to manage industrial and agricultural commodities to streamline the world trade, which was considered necessary and also sufficient for the developed poor. Subsequently it was realised that the intellectual property rights could not be retained, this resulted in the appearance of Trade Related Intellectual Property Rights (TRIPs) and Trade Related Investment Measures (TRIMs). That were brought in by magnifying the danger of piracy and reverse engineering. The disintegration of the Soviet Union helped in arriving the Marrakesh Agreement of 1994, when WTO came into being.

It has been projected that the WTO regime after being fully operational, by 2004, will be uniformly fair to all the countries. However, it can be so only if the industries are geared up to take advantage of emerging IPR regime and harness creativity to develop technologies, products and services. IPR has brought up several issues and new compulsions.

All sectors of mechanical engineering applications have to be governed by the changing regime and global market operation. Quality is and will remain the hallmark of competition. For Indian products to compete successfully continuous upgradation of quality will be desirable.

There have been mixed reaction to market economy propagated under the WTO regime as it gives an edge to those who are already into the system. Many a developing countries, including India, have opposed such a move. The movement raised by the Swadeshi Jagaran Munch in India is an example of the same. It is for every individual country to decide, whether they opt for market driven economy or not. In spite of public opposition by organisations who are outfits of different political parties different political parties in their regime have promoted the concept of market economy during the last ten years. Larger companies in the Indian market have opted to follow the market route for one simple reason that they are vying for the global markets.

The advent of the market economy in the early 90s also witnessed emphasis on ISO certification by the companies. An ISO 9000 certification was taken as a major step towards quality. Approval and anyone who received ISO 9000 certification was treated in a class. However, over the last decade the situation has changed and adoption of ISO 9000 has become the order of the day.

Industries of the 21st century are becoming intensely customer focused and adhering to the concept of total quality management. Techniques of quality management have already been integrated into the corporate management for the success in the market place. Quality goals are consumer driven rather than the producer thrust. In production networks of several companies that have transformed the operations the quality standards have been so rigidly followed that they are far better than what has been recommended under ISO. A number of Indian companies have recorded levels of quality perfection that surpassed those followed by the international or the multinational companies. The companies have evolved quality philosophy and integrated the same with the corporate strategies.

Value Addition through New Concepts in Mechanical Engineering

The market based economy and other important trends have been:

(i) The regional and global networks of production of high value added groups, shift in cross national transfers of mobile capital;
(ii) New forms of linkages between companies that include joint ventures, sub-contracting, licensing, cooperative, research agreements and second sourcing.
(iii) Many firms are involved in a complex web of agreements for cooperative research, production and marketing. This turnaround gives them a niche in international markets to regional networks.

Mechanical engineering interventions in the national development are extremely important both for retrieving the natural resources as well as producing manufactured goods. Various concepts in mechanical engineering like flexible manufacturing, computer integrated manufacturing and agile manufacturing have all emerged with relation to the demands of the customers and the efficiency improvement called by the market forces. Whereas the earlier advancements in manufacturing were mainly due to the evolutionary slow process, the advancements in the last two decades were mainly because of the widespread use of computers at different stages of manufacturing for example designing, planning and control.

Computer Integrated Manufacturing (CIM) is an interdisciplinary science applied to manufacturing. The USA used rigid automation practice, whereas Japan use flexible automation practice, which made them superior in manufacturing. The direct application of CIM is practiced where the computer or a network of computers monitor and control the hardware in a manufacturing plant, such as machine tools, inspection machines, robots and automated guided vehicles, which physically transform or transport or assemble components. The indirect applications include, computer aided design, inventory control, marketing and factory management.

The Agile Manufacturing Approach directs to discover and to codify guiding principles of manufacturing, which is viewed as broad based activity, ranging from product design to production, product use, maintenance etc. The Agile Manufacturing Approach is recognised as an interdisciplinary activity. It approaches holistically with a broad understanding of manufacturing that integrate key functions and disciplines involved in creating, designing, marketing, selling and servicing products. It encompasses not only the critical operations within a corporation, such as technology, product process engineering administration and marketing but also vendor, customer, community and the government. Agile manufacturing is basically the science of business system and is linked to management, technology and work force, making the system flexible enough for a manufacturer to switch over from one product to another product desired to produce in a cost effective manner within the framework of the system.

Integration of all such technologies into mechanical engineering process, mainly in manufacturing sector have called for continuous upgradation of quality and adherence to the highest level of internationally accepted quality approaches.

Emergence of ISO 9000 — 2000 specifications are giving rise to larger adherence to process and product quality rather than only the product quality. Recent advances in the global corporate sector are fast changing the quality and orientation of education as well as application of knowledge at each level.

The technological advances and their corresponding engineering applications have led to continuous improvement in the form of better performing materials, more efficient extraction methods, and new, more effective production technique. At the same time the knowledge of the detrimental effects of unwanted bi-products on the environment and corresponding investment to eliminate, treat or properly dispose of these materials has been emphasised. Most of these applications for sustainability of natural systems are linked to application of mechanical engineering in appropriate form and in the most efficient fashion.

Speed, imagination and excellence in execution are defined as the three attributes of a successful organisation. The new industrial age demands maximisation of profits that is maximising shareholder value while ensuring fairness to all stakeholders. Integration of artificial intelligence into the mechanical engineering processes are leading to options that will lead to the next industrial revolution and more sustainable quality of life.

Conclusion

I am sure that this Convention will deal with a number of important issues and will also lead to action plan that will help in building India's defence services and also will greatly help in supporting our socio-economic structure.

2

Molecular Nanotechnology

'Nanotechnology' is the word coined by Norio Taniguchi at the University of Tokyo, Japan. Nanotechnology is the rapidly emerging technology of building machines and mechanisms at the next level of precision and miniaturisation. It uses a basic unit of measure called a nanometer. Nanotechnology is gaining popularity and is used to describe many types of research where the characteristic dimensions are less than about 1,000 nanometer.

Manufactured products are made from atoms. The properties of those products depend on how those atoms are arranged. If we rearrange the atoms in coal we can make diamond. If we rearrange the atoms in sand (and add a few other trace elements) we can make computer chips. If we rearrange the atoms in dirt, water and air we can make potatoes.

Today's manufacturing methods are very crude at the molecular level. Casting grinding, milling and even lithography move atoms in great thundering statistical herds. We'll be able to snap together the fundamental building blocks of nature easily, inexpensively and in most of the ways permitted by the laws of physics. This will be essential if we are to continue the revolution in computer hardware beyond about the next decade, and will also let us fabricate an entire new generation of products that are cleaner, stronger, lighter, and more precise.

Nano scale science and technology involve building devices and structures at nano scale — the scale of atoms and single molecule. They can form gears, bearings, cantilevers, switches, machines, can direct electrons along one path rather than another, deviating from their pattern, design and habit. Nanotechnology lends a capability not only to image and view atoms, but also to move them that do the manual

---

Dr. S.C. Bhattacharya Memorial Lecture delivered at the 18th Mechanical Engineering Convention organised by the Institution of Engineers (I) during 9-10 November, 2002 at Rourkela.

and the intelligent routines and chores; nano wheels that rotate; processors that can be injected in the individual's blood streamas super-diagnostic probes, and devices of the size of a sugar cube that can store one netre resolution maps of the entire globe.

It's worth pointing out that the word "nanotechnology" has become very popular and is used to describe many types of research where the characteristic dimensions are less than about 1,000 nanometers. For example, continued improvements in lithography have resulted in line widths that are less than one micron: this work is often called "nanotechnology". Sub-micron lithography is clearly very valuable (ask anyone who uses a computer) but it is equally clear that lithography will not let us build semiconductor devices in which individual dopant atoms are located at specific lattice sites. Many of the exponentially improving trends in computer hardware capability have remained steady for the last 50 years. There is fairly widespread belief that these trends are likely to continue for at least another several years, but then lithography starts to reach its fundamental limits.

If we are to continue these trends we will have to develop a new "post-lithographic" manufacturing technology which will let us inexpensively build computer systems with mole quantities of logic elements that are molecular in both size and precision and are interconnected in complex and highly idiosyncratic patterns. Nanotechnology will let us do this.

Molecular nanotechnology or molecular manufacturing will have the following objectives:

- Get essentially every atom in the right place.
- Make almost any structure consistent with the laws of physics that we can specify in molecular detail.
- Have manufacturing costs not greatly exceeding the cost of the required raw materials and energy.

There are two more concepts commonly associated with nanotechnology:

- Positional assembly,
- Self-replication.

There is no single method that can simultaneously serve all the three objectives. However, this seems difficult without using some form of positional assembly (to get the right molecular parts in the right places) and some form of self-replication (to keep the costs down).

The need for positional assembly implies an interest in molecular robotics, *e.g.* robotic devices that are molecular both in their size and precision. These molecular scale positional devices are likely to resemble very small versions of their everyday macroscopic counterparts. Positional assembly is frequently used in normal macroscopic manufacturing today, and provides tremendous advantages. Imagine trying to build a bicycle with both hand tied behind your back! The idea of manipulating and positioning individual atoms and molecules is still new and takes some getting used to. We need to apply at the molecular scale the concept that has demonstrated its effectiveness at the macroscopic scale: making parts go where we want by putting them where we want!

The requirement for low cost creates an interest in self-replicating manufacturing systems, studied by von Newmann in the 1940s. These systems are able both to make copies of themselves and to manufacture useful products if we can design and build one such system the manufacturing costs for more such systems and the products they make (assuming they can make copies of themselves in some reasonably inexpensive environment) will be very low.

Molecular Nanotechnology

Molecular nanotechnology is the name given to a specific sort of manufacturing technology. As its name implies, molecular nanotechnology will be achieved when we are able to build things from the atom up, and we will be able to rearrange matter with atomic precision. This technology does not yet exist, but once it does, we should have a thorough and inexpensive system for controlling of the structure of matter.

Other terms, such as molecular engineering or molecular manufacturing are also often applied when describing this emerging technology.

The central thesis of nanotechnology is that almost any chemically stable structure that is not specifically disallowed by the laws of physics can in fact be built. The possibility of building things atom by atom was first introduced by Richard Feynman in 1959 when he said: "The principles of physics, as far as I can see, do not speak against the possibility of manoeuvering things atom by atom."

Scientists have recently gained the ability to observe and manipulate atoms directly, but this is only one small aspect of a growing array of techniques in nano scale science and technology. The ability to make commercial products may yet be a few decades away. But theoretical and computational models indicate that molecular manufacturing systems are possible — that they do not violate existing physical law. These models also give us a feel for what a molecular manufacturing system might look like. Today, scientists are devising numerous tools and techniques that will be needed to transform nanotechnology from computer models into reality. While most remain in the realm of theory, there appears to be no fundamental barrier to their development.

Achieving the Precise Control

Using macro-manufacturing techniques as a guide, we know that managing fleets of nano machines is no insignificant task. To name just a few essential requirements: we need a location for storing our atom inventory, a method for delivering an atom or molecule from inventory to the manufacturing floor, machines for assembling the various parts; and a way for controlling these processes, to ensure that the right quantity of parts is in the right place at the right time. By creating systems that work together to ensure each atom is properly placed, we will be able to manufacture products of high quality and reliability.

Upon considering these issues, K. Eric Drexler proposed a device called an "assembler", which at first might be little more than a submicroscopic robotic arm. Assuming this arm can be built and is controllable, we should be able to use it to secure and position compounds in order to direct the precise location at which chemical reactions occur. This general approach should allow the construction of large, atomically precise objects by initiating a sequence of controlled chemical reactions.

In order for this to function as we wish, each assembler will require a process for receiving and executing the instruction set that will dictate its actions. We have already created a system that does just that: the computer. Integrating computer technology with nanotechnology gives us a model that will allow the kind of manufacturing proposed. In time, molecular machines might even have onboard, high speed RAM and slower but more permanent storage. They should have communications capability and power supply. In the case of the assembler, we might also develop interchangeable tips that can be placed at the ends of the assembler's arms to allow for expanded functionality.

It would take a lone assembler an eternity to build anything we might hold in our hands as atoms are so small; and so we must think of a large network of assemblers working together to build our products. Networking machinery is something that we humans have learned how to do, and our understanding of the issues involved is becoming more sophisticated every year. If a computer network is reasonable guide, there is a vast potential for interconnectivity among nanotechnological devices.

The Need to Develop

Ignoring for the moment that scientists are a curious lot, always pushing the envelope of what can and cannot be done, precision has been mentioned as a benefit of molecular machines and is one of the key to understanding why we would want to develop this technology.

In this application, precision means that there is a place for every atom and every atom is in its place. Schematics will be detailed, and there will be no unnecessary parts anywhere in the design. We will use machines of precision to create products of equal precision. With this precision, we should be able to recycle all of the waste products produced by the manufacturing processes and put them to good use elsewhere. Manufacturing will also become less expensive as a result.

Technology has never had this kind of precise control; all of our technologies today are bulk technologies. We take a lump of something and add or remove pieces until we're left with whatever object we were trying to create. We assemble our objects from parts, without regard to structure at the molecular level. Precise atomic-level fabrication has previously only been seen in the growth of crystals or in living biological organisms like the ribosome, which assembles all the proteins in living creatures, or DNA, which carries the instructions for creating a living being. If we incorporate similar processes during our development of nanotechnology, we will begin to gain a degree of complexity and control over systems that previously only evolution and nature have had.

Additional benefits arise when we consider the size of devices that we will be able to create. Once we are working on the atomic scale, we can create machines that will go places about which we could once only dream. More information will be packed into smaller and smaller spaces, and we will be able to do much more with much less. Nanotechnology promises unprecedented and efficient control over our environment, but taking advantage of anticipated developments requires forethought and planning. This is a primary aspect of Foresight's mission, and we continue to explore the costs and the benefits of developing nanotechnology.

How will Nanotechnology Improve our Lives?

One of the first obvious benefits is the improvement in manufacturing techniques. We are taking familiar manufacturing systems and expanding them to develop precision on the atomic scale. This will give up greater understanding of building things, and greater flexibility in the types and quantity of things we may build. We will be able to expand our control of systems from the macro to the micro and beyond, while simultaneously reducing the cost associated with manufacturing products.

Nanotechnology is expected to touch almost every aspect of our lives, right down to the water we drink and the air we breathe. Once we have the ability to capture, position, and change the configuration of a molecule, we should be able to create filtration systems that will scrub th toxins from the air or remove hazardous organisms from the water we drink. We should be able to begin the long process of cleaning up our environment.

Space will also open up to us in new ways. With the current cost of transporting payloads into space being so high ($20,000/kg), little is being done to take advantage of space. Nanotechnology will help by allowing us to deliver more machines of smaller size and greater functionality into space, paving the way for solar system expansion. Some have suggested that application of medical nanotechnology might even go so far as to allow us to adapt our bodies for survival in space or on other worlds. While this is certainly a long way off, it provides a glimpse of the thorough control that nanotechnology may provide.

Taking all of this into account, it is clear that nanotechnology should improve our lives in any area that would benefit from the development of better, faster, stronger, smaller, and cheaper systems.

Precautions for Safe Development?

While nanotechnology will facilitate control over the structure of matter, we must ask ourselves who will control nanotechnology? The chief danger may not be a devastating accident, but instead, an abuse of power. We live in a competitive world, and one that is accelerating towards the development of molecular nanotechnology.

This concern about control issues encourages us to argue against secrecy. Combating the dangers will be greatly aided if we all have access to information about progress in the laboratory. If we reduce the number of projects being developed in a military black box, we will probably increase the number of people working on nanotechnology. Having more people involved in the field will mean that we are better able to defend ourselves in an emergency. We might see increases in the number of additional projects working on medicine, manufacturing and the environment. Openly focusing on projects that aid people should go a long way to ensure that information remains available to the public.

We must also remember that there are dangers from both accidents and deliberate misuse. Much can be done to prevent accidents through the promotion a consistent ethical system and a system of accountability for those who develop and employ new technology. Trust will remain a central issue as nanotechnology research comes closer to deployment in the commercial world.

There are those who propose that trust is in short supply and that development guidelines should take into account that there will always be subversive elements. In this case, steps can be taken to prevent the abuse of nanotechnology through the application of, say, exotic environments, whereby a machine will only operate under specific laboratory conditions; and if applied, a machine released into the "wild" would cease to function.

Irrespective of trust issues, there are also concerns that replication errors may arise. We must work towards the creation of systems that reproduce information with as few errors. Some suggest that it is also a good idca to design systems to limit internal evolution.

Computer systems continue to advance as well, with the development of faster smaller, and cheaper systems that have greater capacity. Assuming that security system also see improvement, then these should be applicable to molecular machines, once they are developed. These improvements will also impact our ability to model new molecular devices, and help stabilise design parameters before the machines are actually built.

Development in nanotechnology is expected to continue at an accelerating pace, given that funding for these types of research is increasingly available. While estimates range from 15-30 years, there is no question that nanotechnology will arrive in the not-too-distant future.

During the last half century the electronic components and computers have grown more and more powerful with the shrinking dimensions of transistors which is approaching 100 nm with about a billion tiny devices working together on a single processor. The laws of quantum mechanics and limitations of materials and fabrication techniques restrict further reduction below 100 nm. Thus it is imperative to look for entirely new concepts to overcome limitations. This has given tremendous boost to development of nanotechnology and molecular devices. It is expected that nanotechnology is going to bring another technological revolution which will again change the way we live, communicate and think. The other promising area is Micro Electro Mechanical Systems (MEMS) and Nano Electro Mechanical Systems (NEMS).

The technology trend has rapidly shifted from giant machines to miniaturised devices and today we are at the threshold of entering system on chip and molecular devices. Today's computer power is achieved by machining bulk material into submicron tailored components, but nature has created millions of species under harsh varying condition utilising limited number of elements available to us using entirely reverse concept, *i.e.* starting from molecular/cellular level to create micro-organism to huge plants and whales. Scientists around the globe are trying to understand how things can be manufactured or synthesised using concept of self-assembly which nature has perfected in millions of years. Nanotechnology addresses the problem of material synthesis, starting from atom upward and drawing on the theory and perception of self-assembly. It is visualised that manipulation of atoms and molecules in appropriate fashion results into micro-electronic devices and circuits.

The topic of Nanotechnology is very often discussed under the following sub-heads:

- Nanotechnology Overview
- Micro-Electro-mechanical Systems

- Nano Electronics
- Bio Nanotechnology
- Nano Materials and Characterisation

Conclusion

Various experts and the technology futurists who have devoted sufficient time thinking about nanotechnology have made a few conclusions that may be of interest. Firstly, nanotechnology will progress at the same rate as the technology in general, there would be no such thing as "a microscopic self-contained universal assembler; secondly, automated systems always exist in a larger context which is not automated and their products are not free; thirdly, whatever capability AI has at any given time, humans assisted by computers would have already reached that point and moved ahead; and fourthly, making things with atomic positioners would be as expensive as making them with biotechnology and bulk technology.

There is no dead-end in science or in technology. Every possible step in the direction of technological development throws open new challenges along with the possibilities and the contribution to the society. It is left to the human ingenuity to explore and find solutions to most difficult problems in the world. The cost reductions make technology acceptable at a faster place and its use multiplies manifold. Maybe the engineering fraternity will contribute its might to open new avenues through better use of nanotechnology in future.

3

E-Manufacturing and Economic Development in India

Introduction

India's march into globalisation, a decade back, projected the need that overall improvement in business ethics is brought into our production and marketing systems. There is absolutely no possibility of facing global challenge with outdated methodologies, processes and tools of management. The overall business environment has to be taken into consideration. As IT has started playing its role in business management, it has also played a significant role at the shop floor production centres.

Companies today — including old-line manufacturers — are driven by shareholders and financial analysts to improve bottom-line performance. Market validations like: meeting or exceeding earnings, forecasts and the Return-On-Net Assets (RONA), are here—figures that, if met, can send company stock soaring. The financial and accounting shifted from an activity to each element, and accordingly in plant activity each element was accounted.

For today's manufacturing companies, what matters most is not growing sales. It's how efficiently a company can operate as an organisation. And Chief Financial Officers have found a religion of operational excellence. Whether it's Lean, Six Sigma, or any variety of home grown initiative, successful companies today leave no stone unturned to squeeze the excess. By cutting the "fat", streamlining internal processes and leveraging technologies like the internet, a company can overall be better, faster, and cheaper than the

---

Invited Lecture at International Conference on e-Manufacturing organised by the Institution of Engineers (India), M.P. State Centre during November 17-19, 2002 at Bhopal.

competition—and maintain the confidence of stock exchange experts and investors.

Manufacturing Asset Management

People, products, and processes make up the manufacturing assets of any organisation. And asset management maximises the return on those assets in a manufacturing environment.

The Enterprise Resource Planning (ERP) system in the front office of the enterprise has become the financial backbone for many corporations. But these systems were originally intended to be something much more encompassing of an enterprise, structure around the top down master scheduling systems for all classes and operations throughout the company.

ERP systems especially have brought marked efficiencies to closing a company's financial books every month and tracing human resources. Where they have been less than successful, however, has been in integrating with the plant system. ERP systems have had a tendency to assume that plant floor operations have infinite capacity, not adequately planning around variables, such as maintenance or unpredicted shut downs, or that supplies were always on time, not acknowledging that both supply and demand can be highly variable. Because of these limitations most companies have not made the investment or have under invested, to tightly couple plant floor manufacturing directly with ERP systems. Thus, one of the greatest challenges facing the true effectiveness of enterprise level systems has been the ability to couple it to the reality of the plant floor—in other words linking the shop floor to the top floor.

Proactive planning around assets has historically been pragmatic, at best. Assets have been assumed as a necessary evil by many manufacturers. Other parts of the business look at the plant operations as unavoidable costs, especially in terms of assets. The plant floor operation is more concerned with product quality and less with operational efficiencies, and did not place heavy emphasis on asset management, either. The focus rather was meeting production goals.

Thus, it will be observed that e-manufacturing became important as one time efficient management of meeting production goals and fulfilling sales needs totally overtaken by modern concepts of asset management and financial returns and investments on the processes.

The management of assets on the plant floor requires tight coupling with the broader supply chain. The flow of primary materials into the factory, management of inventory and stock for maintenance and supply and delivery of finished goods to distributors and customers has been complex and pragmatic. For each entry and exit point a customary supply strategy managed the floor of that particular good in or out of the plant.

Traditionally, the plant floor has been viewed as an island in isolation of other elements within the supply chain and the organisation. The role of the plant floor was only to manufacture a quality product and make sure that it was in stock and ready for sale. The plant engineers focused their time and talent within the walls of the factory floor, mainly to optimise production within a given process, improve yield, heighten product quality, and increase productivity. The focus was to look at the raw materials into the production process, and ensure that consistently high quality goods were available in stock at all times. Speed, efficiency, flexibility, productivity, cost savings, yield and productivity around a given element of the plant were of utmost importance, but rarely was a broader views of these parameters taken, beyond the plant was to the broader supply chain.

The technology employed to achieve these high levels of quality and productivity created an immense amount of information about that little performance of the enterprise. Rarely was it effectively consolidated and communicated for use in the rest of the enterprise. Traditionally, that information remained within the lower walls of the factory floor, primarily used to drive the local behaviour of the plant. In some cases, manufacturing execution systems (MES) were deployed to provide a higher-level view of production. But these systems were often too monolithic to deploy and inflexible to operative to be truly effective.

Break Down Maintenance Affect Production

It is also important to note that despite infinite assumptions, plants themselves are not utopian. With machines and lines working in some cases up to 24 hours day, seven days a week, they are prone to wear, tear and breakdowns. Any shut downs to a production line are expensive. It was observed that in US the average loss for a discrete manufacturer could run around US $ 1200 per hour. And, with the lack of asset management programmes or supply chain efficiency precious hours can pass from the time machine breakdown to the time a replacement arrives for servicing.

Let this statement not be misunderstood as if the plant floor efforts did not take care of their machines. Traditionally, plant engineers do schedule preventive maintenance on their lines to catch problems before they occur. The difficulty in doing such maintenance on a particular line, was again the time required for the maintenance. And when production demands for the plant floor was high, it was hard to justify the time to stop for a system check. The "if it is not broke, don't fix it" mentality ruled the floor.

So in a historical context, information technologies arrived on the plant floor, bringing the potentials for high levels of quality to finish goods and improve process yield, but all optimised within the four walls of the plant. At the same time, little was done to leverage plant floor data for enterprise level decision. Furthermore, the management of assets and supply were fragmented. Maintenance was mostly reacted, production focused on build to stock, and processes were optimised for long production runs with little need to change quickly, all these were costly and did not fit into new financial concepts.

India's March into Globalisation and Internet Intervention

India entered the globalisation era in 1990s, and opened its economy. That provided an opportunity to look outward and adopt new technologies and processes to become globally competitive.

Also in the late 1990s two phenomena emerged that shook the old ways of running plants to their foundations:

(i) The Internet as a commerce tool and technology enabler
(ii) A very fickle consumer

A great booster/catalyser for e-manufacturing was the Y2K syndrome. Over the last decade of the last millennium, the evaluation of manufacturing technology included the introduction of contemporary information technologies, such as the PC and open standards on the factory floor networking with concerns such as the scramble to ensure Y2K readiness. Thus, whereas the Internet intervention into business gave larger options for the buyer—new IT inventions were evolved for shop floor. During that time, manufacturers evolved the application of information technology from relatively passive data collection and reporting role to control and diagnostic applications. This reflected that the IT is not new to the plant floor, it took its natural place in the course of business; information technology was never the cure-all solution of any business process, rather it shared another tool that enables the solution.

The 'customer rules' is a traditional misnomer in business that has existed with the underlying assumption: consumer will buy what they are told that they can't live without. In the past the average consumer would tolerate any inundation of commercials and market techniques. Warehouses were stocked with high quality goods ready to go. In other words, optimise yield and have products ready and waiting for the buyers.

But the consumer has changed over the past 20 years and is not as easily swayed by sale speeches or propaganda. Instead, the customer really does rule—and with an iron hand controlling a mouse. The current consumer mindset is one of control, and it is enabled by the power of the Internet as a buying tool and information source: "I can order something the way I want — via the Internet, in a store, or some other way". I can request my own features for that product and I expect to be delivered when I need it. If not, then I will go somewhere else to get what I need. The Internet enables the average consumer to shop more aggressively and select from wider options. And this means that manufacturers can't assume that products sitting in stock will meet the needs of fickle consumer. The ability to shop on line has been the catalyst of e-business. Companies have scrambled to create e-based channels to interact and sell goods to consumers. And the pressure from stock exchange for traditional manufacturing companies to sit up and take notice of the Internet further intensified by the race to sell on-line to consumers.

Thus, e-business and e-manufacturing were linked. This situation offered following opportunities:

(i) Make manufacturing most cost effective.
(ii) Make manufacturing more favourable to custom-built and responsive to customer.

e-Manufacturing: A Strategy to Take the Friction out of the Enterprise

Certain principles were thrown open in view of the integration of information technology with the factory floor practices and despite some limits of information transparency today via this technology, there are excellent foundation in place for many manufacturers to adopt e-manufacturing strategy.

Basic questions asked include:

(i) What does an e-manufacturing strategy look like?
(ii) How does it work?

Consider an example of a limit switch. A limit switch is nothing more than a regular on/off switch with an "arm" hanging on it. This limit switch sits on a conveyor line. Each time a box approaches on the line, it pushes the arm out of the way, and the switch goes "on". As the box passes by, the arm snaps back, and the switch goes "off".

This switch is embedded with intelligent technology and is plugged into a communications network on the plant floor. This switch also is wired back to a plant floor controller, which houses the production programme for the conveyor line. The controller's programme for that switch is to ask it a basic question: Are you "on", or "off"? And so each time a box hits the limit switch, a message shoots to the controller, which then sends an instruction to the conveyor line, telling the line which way to send each box. The box quickly diverts in an assigned direction, and the limit switch snaps back, waiting for the next box to approach.

But the switch can provide far more information than "on" or "off". It can tell the controller and communications network that its arm is over-travelling or under-travelling — moving too far in either direction when a box passes by. It can tell how fast the arm snaps back, or if it doesn't snap back at all. In any of these cases there is a likelihood that something is starting to go wrong — either with the switch or the conveyor line — that could cause a future lag in production on the plant floor. The data is there — it just has'nt been traditionally pulled from that limit switch.

With a predictive maintenance system in place, however, the data warning of that switch's problems can be driven directly into the plant's condition monitoring programme—well before the switch breaks. A work order can be quickly created for an engineer to assess the problem. The engineer then can place an online order for a supplier to deliver and install a new limit switch within 24 hours. At the same time, the programme also can schedule a repair or replacement on that switch using information from the on-line plant schedule to determine the opportune time to access the machine. The new switch can be delivered by the supplier and installed before the first switch breaks down. There is little more than a hiccup in the production line.

This has direct relationship in narrating the process of e-manufacturing. Traditionally, a manufacturer did not get the warning information from something as nebulous as a limit switch and considering the production demands on the plant. Pro-active schedule of maintenance was a luxury. Largely, reactive measures, when a switch would break involve down time of the line, a paper based work order system, a varied stock of supplies to deal with the problem, and little, if any connection to front office procurement. The end result was lost revenue from lost production.

E-manufacturing, on the other hand, includes the ability to monitor the plant floor assets and leverage the internet to schedule maintenance and order supplies quickly and easily. It also provides the front office with a transparent view of the health and flow of its plant floor assets, helping to streamline supply and subsequent costs. In the end, it creates a highly integrated — and highly flexible — system that provides a complete view of the entire enterprise, up, down and sideways.

Having an e-manufacturing strategy means that the company is e-business ready. But this extends beyond the ability to connect on-line with potential buyers of goods. Since price pressures won't go away, manufacturing plants will be still expected to deliver enhanced products and ever lower prices. To be e-business ready, a company's manufacturing enterprise must be able to build-to-order and maintain non-stop operations. To achieve this, four competencies are required to any manufacturer.

Design: The ability to rapidly deploy and reconfigure manufacturing production capacity based on demand for goods. Rapidly changing consumer demands are forcing companies to accelerate and streamline the design and deployment of production processes. Rapid new product introductions in response to changing market demand is a critical competitive advantage and a key to growth. Having a design competency which ensures new products are not only launched on time, but that those launches are cost effectively executed is a key to translating that top-line growth into bottom-line results.

Operate: Optimisation of process yield and consistency throughout the enterprise. Plant productivity has always been a focus in manufacturing. As manufacturers consolidate through acquisitions and have new facilities to operate worldwide, they must further figure out how to get products made with consistent quality and efficiency at each manufacturing location. This is where initiatives like lean manufacturing drive out excess, achieving non-stop operations for maximum efficiency and throughput of production and where techniques like Six Sigma reduce variability in processes to ensure peak quality.

Maintain: Efficient management of all company assets — materials, processes, and employees — to ensure non-stop operations, and optimum asset productivity. Without such a solid, efficient foundation, it is not possible to withstand the rigors of this fast paced environment, where growth and profits are demanded simultaneously.

Synchronise: Tight coupling of a manufacturing operation into the greater supply chain, both upstream and downstream. This fourth competency is best achieved only after the other three competencies (Design. Operate, Maintain) are firmly in place. Only then is the plant truly ready to the fully coupled into an e-commerce driven supply chain.

E-manufacturing requires a new approach to manufacturing and distribution systems – throughout the Design, Operate, Maintain, and Synchronise competencies. It is enabled through full integration between manufacturing control systems and enterprise applications using commercially developed, off-the-shelf information technologies. Moreover, an e-manufacturing strategy provides direct information exchanges between manufacturing and Customer Relationship Management (CRM) systems and supply chain management systems (ARC Advisory Group, August 2000). Finally, it requires a complimentary set of process optimisation methodologies, be it for designing, operating, maintaining, or synchronising the manufacturing operation.

The example of the limit switch is only to explain the e-manufacturing strategy that works. At even greater level, e-manufacturing is a necessary part of an e-business strategy for companies that manufacture a product line and transform their business into e-business enterprises.

How to Excel in Design, Operate, Maintain and Synchronize Modes

Manufacturers can achieve the promise of e-manufacturing through Design, Operate, Maintain, and Synchronise competencies that drive build-to-order processes and non-stop operations. There are four enablers which will speed any company to reap the benefits of e-manufacturing.

- Integrated control and Information — a contemporary. information architecture with associated integration management services;
- Manufacturing information management/seamless integration of business and production systems — electronic management of products and orders on the manufacturing floor — bringing visibility to customers, partners, and the enterprise.
- Asset management and reliability-centered maintenance — tools, methodologies, and services for increasing overall asset utilisation with minimising unplanned maintenance and unexpected downtime.
- E-Fulfilments and e-procurement solutions — direct transfer of customer order details to manufacturing personnel and equipment, configuration options, as well as tight electronic connections to suppliers and partners to optimise inbound supply chain in the face of changing demand.

The following sections reveal how these four enablers bring optimum benefit to any manufacturer.

Following are a few points on how these four enablers bring optimum benefit to any manufacturer.

Working Together Seamlessly in a Typical Plant Environment

- The convergence of controlled disciplines continues to lead manufacturers toward integrated solutions that reduce integrated costs, and ultimately, create greater plant-wide productivity through a tightly integrated system. The design cycles are shortened, speeding time to market of new goods. The benefits of the architecture itself are measurable, software training and programme time work. The total integration of multiple controlled disciplines, all but eliminates challenges in making systems work together. Flexibility also comes in with infinitely expandable, communications system. No additional programming is needed to integrate networks.

- Networks must deliver an efficient means to exchange data for precise control, while supporting non-critical systems and device configurations at start-up and during run time. Networks must also provide the critical links for collecting data at regular intervals for analysis. An integrated architectural benefits from a common set of advanced network services and interfaces optimise for real-time control. Configuration and collection of data, with seamless communications up and down the architecture, allowing access to any part of a system from any location.
- The ability for a company to view plant information from anywhere in the world, and at any stage of production, completes an integrated architecture, a transparent view of the factory flow, provides integration benefits, like common user experience across the operator interface environment; configuration tools for open and embedded control applications; improve productivity through the ability to be used technology throughout the plant; and overall reduce cycle costs relating to training, upgrades and maintenance.

The four enablers of Design, Operate, Maintain, and Synchronise competencies for a complete e-manufacturing strategy (integrated architecture, manufacturing information management, asset and reliability centered maintenance, and e-procurement) have several common characteristics. First, foundations are in place today for any of these best practices to occur, in nearly every manufacturing facility. Second, the Internet is a great facilitator of the technologies and processes needed to seamlessly link these enablers together. And third, these enablers don't have to happen all at once; a manufacturer can find a starting point that best suits its current business model, and build the strategy from within overtime.

No Manufacturer is too Small: The Roadmap for an e-Manufacturing Strategy

The single biggest roadblock to both optimisation and collaboration for e-manufacturing is a lack of integration. Most plants are still make-to-stock using in-house proprietary systems for plant-floor control, which offer little information visibility. The survivors will be lowest cost producers that make precisely what customers want. That means making-to-order, going beyond just-in-time manufacturing, and adopting collaborative e-manufacturing approaches. Collaboration means companies and their supply chain partners must function as a single, highly optimised entity, not a bunch of divisions or departments.

For manufacturers, the advantages of adopting an e-manufacturing strategy are real and timely. But entering the world of e-business for gains in operational efficiencies truly involves a fundamental evolution of a company's strategic direction and operations. Managers must approach e-business with care, yet with speed and decisiveness.

This can be a scary proposition for any manufacturer, particularly those that are feeling the pressures to be faster, better, and cheaper. But the ability of manufacturers to proactively consider the benefits of e-manufacturing, and look within for potential starting points, will likely provide a competitive edge as the pressure to implement e-business increases.

It would be ideal if a manufacturer could achieve an e-manufacturing environment overnight. Unfortunately, it doesn't work that way. Today, though, there are hundreds of examples in which manufacturers have started down the road to e-manufacturing by focusing on one competency — either through integrated architecture, shop-floor-to-floor information management, asset management, or supply chain efficiencies via e-procurement. These companies carefully evaluated the need, implemented a working solution, measured the effectiveness, and then took on another competency in their enterprises.

It is necessary to follow certain common guidelines when considering the potential investments and resulting benefits from an e-manufacturing approach:

(i) *Accept the Internet:* All parties in the company must recognise the organisational change required to adopt an e-manufacturing strategy — and the greater influence of the Internet and of customer demand.

(ii) *More than ever, engineers have an important place in decision-making process:* Plant engineers bring expertise in plant floor processes as well as the information available and required for seamless integration.

(iii) *Build an internal team, and draw the company's roadmap for e-manufacturing:* Draw from various departments and functions within the organisation, and discuss the common and specialised benefits each would receive from information transparency.

(iv) *Find a company leader to serve as champion:* Whenever, possible, secure the CEO as the e-manufacturing mouth piece of the enterprise.

(v) *Take one step at a time on the roadmap*: Don't attend to do everything at once. Focus on actions that have the highest immediate impact.

(vi) *Measure the success and failure of the roadmap*: Put matrix in place to determine the real savings and efficiencies from a transparent enterprise.

(vii) *Evaluate your traditional channels — and listen to their needs:* Analyse the ways the company works with customers, suppliers, distributors and others to determine their effectiveness and find ways to streamline relationships and processes.

(viii) *Build on your existing foundations, and on your incremental success along the way:* An e-manufacturing strategy will help your organisation embrace information transparency that will foster operational excellence.

(ix) *Get help from an expert:* Outsourcing to a supplier to provide the planning, technology, services and support for integrated architecture, manufacturing information management, asset and programme management, and supply chain will prove to be worthwhile.

Is e-Manufacturing Suitable for India?

India having been credited for the largest software manpower can adopt and transform the business environment fastest by moving to e-manufacturing. The rapid industrial growth and induction of modern capital equipment in major manufacturing sectors, in mid-1990s provided an opportunity to move in this direction. Some front-runners took the lead but the off-and-on growth pattern, of later 1990s, followed by recession put a brake. The cost of such interventions had to be justified through very high levels of production that were not achieved.

The labour laws also did not allow the industrialists to adopt most cost-effective measures. Labour laws presently have a bias for larger employment and support employment generating technologies rather than employment reducing technologies.

Thus, India's march into e-manufacturing will be slow — but, is unavoidable as India has to face global competition and grow its exports. Whereas, employment generating manufacturing systems are required, so are higher growth rates desirable for higher employment generation in other sectors.

4

Quality Management in Mechanical Engineering

Introduction

Mechanical engineering has always been associated with manufacturing — which is as ancient as human civilisation. It gained significance as it became technology when steam engine was invented and manufactured. The current globalisation process has focused on three elements — Technology, Management and Manpower. Technology, as applicable to manufacturing, is controlled by or evolved on the principles of mechanical engineering. Recent advances in communication and information technology have changed the total outlook and approach in product and process engineering. Though information technology is not an end in itself, it is serving as a very important tool in improving efficiencies of systems and dominating the decision making and improving efficiency of capital goods operation.

Industrial Revolution and Technology

Technology transfer played a central role in the industrial revolution but intellectual property protection was by no means the only route, nor was it always respected. Until the mid-19th century the most important means of technology transfer was hiring skilled workers who brought needed technological knowledge. Skilled workers from industrially advanced countries were in high demand, resulting in government action. In 1719 French and Russian attempts to recruit British workers—especially those skilled in wool, metal and

---

Paper presented at the Seminar on Mechanical Engineering organised by the Institution of Engineers (India), West Bengal Centre during August 2001 at Kolkata.

watchmaking industries — prompted the British government to ban skilled worker migration, making it punishable by fine or even imprisonment. Emigrant workers who failed to return home within six months of warning could lose their land, property and citizenship.

As technologies became embodied in machines, the focus shifted to controlling their export. In 1750 Britain banned the export of "tools and utensils" in wool and silk industries, then in 1781 widened that to "any machine, engine, tool, press, paper, utensil or implement whatsoever." But in response, entrepreneurs and technicians in Belgium, Denmark, France, the Netherlands, Norway, Russia and Sweden devised new ways to get the technologies, often with explicit state consent or even active encouragement, including offers of bounty for specific technologies.

By the mid-19th century key technologies were too complex to acquire by hiring workers and importing machines, and licensing patents became increasingly important. Most of today's industrial countries introduced patents by 1850, followed by copyright and trade mark laws. But there were important exceptions. Swiss patent law was weak until 1907 — when Germany threatened trade sanctions — and did not cover chemicals and pharmaceuticals until 1978. The United States, despite being a strong proponent of patent rights, did not recognise copyrights for foreigners until 1891.

Despite the emergence of international intellectual property rights among these countries, they continued to break the rules. In the late 19th Century German manufacturers found ways of infringing on British trade mark laws, producing counterfeit Sheffield cutlery with fake logos and placing the stamp of country of origin only on packaging, or hidden out of sight — as on the bottom of sewing machines.

Customised Production — Major Challenge

Globalisation of economy has exposed all the countries to the situation that has been experienced in the industrialised countries since 1980s. It is increasingly realised that vertically integrated global production is no more an effective approach. Changes in the corporate sector strategy are stimulated by demands for technology and the compulsions from the new markets that the earlier order had evoked. The conditions of competitiveness are radically altering.

The consumer preferences are shifting towards more specialised and customised products. Advantage of standardised mass production is being replaced by complex non standardised production. Such a shift is necessitating integration of production ingenuity of all the constituents of the network. Insistence on quality is becoming ever more demanding and with that goes the difficulty of the manufacturing firms to attain quality in customised production. Realising the high cost of such production demands future strategies are requiring new approaches in production. Remember the present day demand is better quality accompanied by decreasing costs on customised production. That is the major challenge for mechanical engineers.

Responsiveness to Market Needs

Responsiveness to the market needs is the key to advantages that can be derived from customised products and market sensitive capabilities; their technological sophistication and inherent strength of competitiveness based on strong base of manpower and finance. Responsiveness requires well developed technological capabilities and social capabilities that underline the sensitivity of the corporate organisations to issues related to the impact of production and products on society as well as on the living environment.

New Directions in Mechanical Engineering on Quality Improvement

Mechanical engineering interventions like flexible manufacturing systems, computer integrated manufacturing systems and agile manufacturing along with concurrent engineering have been various concepts that have evolved in the recent past. These approaches have been rapidly bridging the gap with respect to global standards and quality to establish strong competitiveness.

Quality improvements in mechanical engineering practices are based on the global developments that have taken place during the last two decades. Emergence of the 20th Century witnessed two models of development — the first coming from the communist countries mainly the centralised or planned economy model based on self-reliance and import substitution; and the other based on the practice in the West European countries who worked on the concept of trade in technologies and products and therefore promoted the market concept. In the early 80s Mexico and other Latin American countries reached an economic chaos due to huge cumulative borrowing and inability to unburden their debts. That triggered massive support for the trade based market economy. The impact was so large that the centralised model of development promoted by the Soviet Union could not be sustained even in the Soviet Union.

At the end of World War-II, the Western world promoted the concept of market based economy and that gave birth to General Agreement on Trade and Tariff (GATT) to manage industrial and agricultural commodities to streamline the world trade, which was considered necessary and also sufficient for the developed poor. Subsequently it was realised that the intellectual property rights could not be retained, this resulted in the appearance of Trade Related Intellectual Property Rights (TRIPs) and Trade Related Investment Measures (TRIMs). That were brought in by magnifying the danger of piracy and reverse engineering. The disintegration of the Soviet Union helped in arriving the Marakesh Agreement of 1994, when WTO came into being.

It has been projected that the WTO regime after being fully operational, by 2004, will be uniformly fair to all the countries. However, it can be so only if the industries are geared up to take advantage of emerging IPR regime and harness creativity to develop technologies, products and services. IPR has brought up several issues and new compulsions.

All sectors of mechanical engineering applications have to be governed by the changing regime and global market operation. Quality is and will remain the hallmark of competition. For Indian products to compete successfully continuous upgradation of quality will be desirable.

There have been mixed reaction to market economy propagated under the WTO regime as it gives an edge to those who are already into the system. Many a developing countries, including India, have opposed such a move. The movement raised by the Swadeshi Jagaran Munch in India is an example of the same. It is for every individual country to decide, whether they opt for market driven economy or not. In spite of public opposition by organisations who are outfits of different political parties the concept of market economy has been promoted by different political parties in their regime during the last ten years. Larger companies in the Indian market have opted to follow the market route for one simple reason that they are vying for the global markets.

The advent of the market economy in the early 90s also witnessed emphasis on ISO certification by the companies. An ISO 9000 certification was taken as a major step towards quality. Approval and anyone who received ISO 9000 certification was treated in a class. However, over the last decade the situation has changed and adoption of ISO 9000 has become the order of the day.

Industries of the 21st Century are becoming intensely customer focused and adhering to the concept of total quality management. Techniques of quality management have already been integrated into the corporate management for the success in the market place. Quality goals are consumer driven rather than the producer thrust. In production networks of several companies that have transformed the operations the quality standards have been so rigidly followed that they are far better than what has been recommended under ISO. A number of Indian companies have recorded levels of quality perfection that surpassed those followed by the international or the multinational companies. The companies have evolved quality philosophy and integrated the same with the corporate strategies.

Value Addition through New Concepts in Mechanical Engineering

The market based economy and other important trends have been:

(i) The regional and global networks of production of high value added groups, shift in cross national transfers of mobile capital;
(ii) New forms of linkages between companies that include joint ventures, sub-contracting, licensing, cooperative, research agreements and second sourcing;
(iii) Many firms are involved in a complex web of agreements for cooperative research, production and marketing. This turnaround gives them a niche in international markets to regional networks.

Mechanical engineering interventions in the national development are extremely important both for retrieving the natural resources as well as producing manufactured goods. Various concepts in mechanical engineering like flexible manufacturing, computer integrated manufacturing and agile manufacturing have all emerged with relation to the demands of the customers and the efficiency improvement called by the market forces. Whereas the earlier advancements in manufacturing were mainly due to the evolutionary slow process, the advancements in the last two decades were mainly because of the widespread use of computers at different stages of manufacturing for example designing, planning and control.

Computer Integrated Manufacturing (CIM) is an interdisciplinary science applied to manufacturing. The USA used rigid automation practice, whereas Japan use of flexible automation practice, which made them superior in manufacturing. The direct application of CIM is practiced where the computer or a network of computers monitor and control the hardware in a manufacturing plant, such as machine tools, inspection machines, robots and automated guided vehicles, which physically transform or transport or assemble components. The indirect applications include, computer aided design, inventory control, marketing and factory management.

The Agile Manufacturing Approach directs to discover and to codify guiding principles of manufacturing, which is viewed as broad-based activity, ranging from product design to production, product use, maintenance etc. The Agile Manufacturing Approach is recognised as an interdisciplinary activity. It approaches holistically with a broad understanding of manufacturing that integrate key functions and disciplines involved in creating, designing, marketing, selling and servicing products. It encompasses not only the critical operations within a corporation, such as technology, product process engineering administration and marketing but also vendor, customer, community and the government. Agile manufacturing is basically the science of business system and is linked to management, technology and work force, making the system flexible enough for a manufacturer to switch over from one product to another product desired to produce in a cost effective manner within the framework of the system.

Integration of all such technologies into mechanical engineering process, mainly in manufacturing sector have called for continuous upgradation of quality and adherence to the highest level of internationally accepted quality approaches.

Emergence of ISO 9000 : 2000 specifications are giving rise to larger adherence to process and product quality rather than only the product quality. Recent advances in the global corporate sector are fast changing the quality and orientation of education as well as application of knowledge at each level.

The technological advances and their corresponding engineering applications have led to continuous improvement in the form of better performing materials, more efficient extraction methods, and new, more effective production technique. At the same time the knowledge of the detrimental effects of unwanted bi-products on the environment and corresponding investment to eliminate, treat or properly dispose of these materials has been emphasised. Most of these applications for sustainability of natural systems are linked to application of mechanical engineering in appropriate form and in the most efficient fashion.

Speed, imagination and excellence in execution are defined as the three attributes of a successful organisation. The new industrial age demands maximisation of profits that is maximising shareholder value while ensuring fairness to all stakeholders. Integration of artificial intelligence into the mechanical engineering processes are leading to options that will lead to the next industrial revolution and more sustainable quality of life.

REFERENCES

1. Singh, D.V., *Industries of the Future,* Dr. S. P. Luthra Memorial Lecture, XVI National Convention of Mechanical Engineers, Roorkee, September 29-30, 2000.
2. Chowdiah, M.P., *Manufacturing: Global Scenario*, 11 Engineering Congress, Bangalore, December 20-24, 1996.
3. Human Development Report 2001, UNDP.

5

Role of Metal-based Industry in Development and Security

Introduction

Materials and their machining has been the starting point for mechanical engineering interventions in economic development. Men's quest to control the earth, space and undersea required materials that could last and withstand extreme environmental conditions. Machines are also similarly required to work much below the freezing point on one hand, and to extremely high temperature on the other. Technological advancements in materials and manufacturing processes are making possible to design and fabricate systems to respond to such intricate needs. In order to meet such diverse needs and remain a leader in technology, a nation should engage itself in latest research and development activities.

Role of Engineering Industry in Economic Development

Engineering industry remains at the heart of the 'old economy'. It is the only sector credited with having developed forward and backward linkages with almost every sector of the economy. It is the backbone of the manufacturing sector. The industry is reeling under the impact of a liberal import regime aided by lower duty structure. While awaiting revival, several segments of the engineering industry have taken up the task of improving their competitiveness in terms of technology, design, cost quality and productivity.

Metal-based industry is not uniformly spread over India. South India has traditionally focused on metal-based industry. A CII Study,

---

Chairman's Address at the All India Seminar on Materials and Machining organised by Institution of Engineers (India) on January 16, 2002 at New Delhi.

released in November 2001, has reflected that in the manufacture of metal products, Maharashtra, Karnataka and Tamil Nadu, together accounted for 50.3 per cent of gross output and 55.7 per cent of the value added in 1997-98. During the year, in the manufacture of machinery other than transport, the three states together shared 49.1 per cent of value of output and 48.6 per cent of the value added.

Although the contribution of service sector has gone up considerably during the post-1992 era; the traditional engineering industry-dominant states did not lose interest in this sub-sector. Additionally, the expansion of automobile industry in Haryana, saw expansion of engineering industry in that state. In the manufacture of transport equipment and parts, the three states of Maharashtra, Haryana and Tamil Nadu together accounted for 57.6 per cent of the value of output and 59.6 per cent of value added during 1997-98.

Government's focus on infrastructure sector will continue importance of engineering industry. The increasing flow of public and private investments in the Tenth Five Year Plan (2002-2007) into power, transportation, logistics and automobile sectors will promote larger investments for upgradation and creation of new capacities in engineering industry.

The post-11 September, 2001 scenario has forced Indian companies to look for domestic market and focus on non-IT export market. Both the cases require greater reliance on engineering industry. The ILO discussion at Geneva, in November 2001, focused on economic development based on employment creation. That can best be done through engineering industry. Also, the WTO discussion at Doha, in November 2001 has focused on internalising environment issues in trade agreements. Something that the government of India has also willingly accepted. Whether we decide to introduce 'environmentally clean technologies' or 'end-of-the pipe cleaning-up technologies', the engineering industry will have an important role. New materials, alloy metals and new machining processes will take to market place to meet this challenge.

The general observation of experts is that the growth of engineering industry in states of Tamil Nadu, Maharashtra and Karnataka has been mainly due to their focus on technical education and the work culture that promoted quality.

The strength of the engineering industry has been development of its forward and backward linkages with almost every sector of the economy, which is also the backbone of manufacturing.

Technology Revolution and Globalisation

The technology revolution and globalisation are creating a network age — and that is changing how technology is created and defused. Its impact on the engineering sector is pronounced, and efficiency of virtually every engineering sector is dictated by information technology. Computers have become internal parts of mechanical devices. These have become tools to perform controlled operations. R&D activities are required to integrate machines with transducers and sensors and design software for effective control of machines/systems.

The industrial age was structured around vertically integrated organisations with high costs of communication, information and transportation. But, the network age is structured along horizontal networks, with each organisation focusing on competitive niches.

Technological development also followed evolution of low cost raw materials and automated machining operations. Materials and machining both go hand in hand to provide the best of technological output. Availability of one is not sufficient to provide products of required quality. Unfortunately the developing countries, and that includes India, lack in materials, both in quality and characteristics, as well as in machines. Borrowing a technology from other nations is mostly an expensive proposition. The onset of the economic reforms in 1992 gave a false feeling that technologies of all kinds, of the latest generation, are available off-the-shelf in the market place. The reality was otherwise. The developed countries would not provide current technology to the other country.

In the post-1992 era, the Department of Science & Technology established an important project of 'Technology Mission 2020'; identifying R&D needs to achieve national development goals in 2020. That study also focused on materials need in different sectors.

New Concept in Development of Technology for Materials and Machining

Some of the concepts introduced recently include the following:

Concurrent Engineering is a manufacturing philosophy, which involves managing product development process with the aim of getting new product with the highest quality at the best competitive price in the least time to the market. In other words, concurrent engineering is a systematic approach towards integrated, concurrent design of products and their processes, including manufacturing and support. This approach is intended to cause development from the outset, to consider all arrangements of the project lifecycle from conception to disposal, including quality, cost, schedule, and user requirements. This definition places extreme value on the team work; and recognises that concurrent engineering will fail if the organisation, at all levels does not embrace the norms of team working and does learn to live by them each day. The next important value, that he embedded in the definition is the focus on customer.

Product Development Life (PDL) Cycle approach requires carrying out many steps from market study, product design conceptualisation, and analysis to prototype manufacturing, testing, product manufacturing. Conventionally design of machines carries equipment and component in isolation. Manufacturing aspects were looked in production sections after receiving the detailed drawings. In case some changes were required due to manufacturing or machining constraints, the production section referred back the design to the designer for modification.

Following this approach every stage in PDL cycle is performed sequentially. New concepts in product development enable an engineer to perform various steps simultaneously. Such an approach will make product development cost effective.

Application of *smart structure technology* to various physical systems are evolving actively to control vibration, noise, aeroelastic stability, damping shape and stress distribution. Application range from space systems, fixed-wing and rotary-wing aircraft to automotive, civil structures and machines. Much of the early development of smart structures methodology was driven by space applications such as vibration and shape control of large flexible space structures, but now wider applications are envisaged in aeronautical and other systems. Embedded or surface-bonded smart actuators on an airplane wing or helicopter bladed with induced alternation of twist/camber of airfoil (shape change), that in turn will cause variation of the distribution and may help to control static and dynamic aero-elastic problems.

A smart structure involves distributed actuators and sensors, and one or more micro-processors to analyse the responses from the sensors and use distributed parameter control theory to command the actuators to apply localised strains to minimise system response. A smart structure has the capability to respond to changing external environmental (such as loads or shape change) as well as to a changing internal environment (such as damage or failure). It incorporates smart actuators that allow the alternation of system characteristics (such as stiffness or damping) as well of system response (such as strain or shape) in a controlled manner. Many types of actuators and sensors are being considered, such as piezoelectric materials, shape memory alloys electrostrictive materials, magnetostrictive materials, electro-rheological fluids and fiber optics. These can be integrated with main load-carrying structures by surface bonding or embedding without causing any significant changes in the mass or structure stiffness of the system.[1]

Manufacturing/Machining Process

A number of manufacturing processes have evolved recently. Some of these are elaborated below:

Cellular Manufacturing: Cellular Manufacturing is midway to flexible manufacturing system. FMS — a fully automated system that is still not adopted easily in a medium scale industry. It was identified that in current global and competitive buyer markets, manufacturing just cannot survive with fixed automation. Flexible automation has to take its final shape. Present global need is to manifest the vital mid-volume and mid-variety area of manufacturing and for that the only answer is flexible automation. There are 30 different types of flexibilities, associated with flexible automation. Out of these there are 5 fundamental flexibilities, *viz.* Machine, Product, Process, Routing and Volume flexibilities.

The recent trend of medium size Indian industries is towards the use of Cellular Manufacturing (CM) system. In such a system, there are different types of cells, viz. Manual Machine Cell, CNC Machine Cell, Mixed CMC and Manual Machine Cell, Flexible Automated Cell and Super Cell. Cellular Manufacturing is the application of Group Technology (GT) philosophy in which similar parts are identified and grouped together to take advantage of the similarities in the part-geometries and operation processes in manufacturing.[2]

Rapid Prototyping: Rapid Prototyping (RP) refers to a set of modern technologies that automate the processes for fabricating 3D solid objects from materials. Such processes generate 3D solid objects by laser driven solidification curing, fusing or cutting of special polymers and powders guided by 3D design made by engineers on ordinary desktop computers.[3]

Laminated Object Manufacturing Laminated: Object Manufacturing, LOM, is one of the Rapid Prototyping Technologies, that creates 3D objects from 3D models, created on ordinary Desktop computers. In LOM a laser cuts a pattern, representing a cross section of a desired object, in a sheet material, pre-quoted with adhesive. A new piece of material lay over and is bonded to it. Laser cuts another pattern and the process is repeated. Currently the most common material used is polyethylene quoted paper. An application of heat in each layer melts the polyethylene, causing it to fuse in the previous layer. The object built in this material have a resemblance with wood.[4]

Electrical Discharge Manufacturing: The primary and secondary processing technologies for Metal Matrix Composites, MMCs, have yet to become adequately mature. Since these materials contain abrasive particles of ceramic it becomes difficult to machine them using traditional methods. Rapid tool sub-surface damage and high cost are the major issues associated with traditional machining of them. In view of this Electrical Discharge Machine (EDM) is found to show a promise to be an effective technique in machining these materials in many applications.[5]

Abrasive Water Jet Machining: The newest addition to the family of non-traditional manufacturing processing is Abrasive Water Jet Machining (AWJM). The process is based on the principle of water jet machining to create a unique process that relies on the erosive action of an abrasive laden water jet for application to cutting and drilling hard materials and for general cleaning. The technique is one of the recently introduced machining methods in which an abrasive, such as garnet, aluminum oxide, or silicon carbide is accelerated by a thin high velocity water jet, and directed to an abrasive water jet nozzle at the material to be cut. More work is needed to develop models where both the water phase and abrasive phase of the jet contribute to material remover.[6]

Advancement in Materials and Machining Crucial for Defence Applications

Whereas the superiority in optical glass was advantageous for the Germans during World War-I, communication systems have controlled the World War-II. However, it was ultimately the man, material(metal) and metal engineering based hardware that decided on the victory in the War.

With serious threats from terrorist groups and neighbouring countries, the defence preparedness is a matter of national concern. It has been observed that in the wartime situation we have to rush for import of equipment at the last minute. Defence preparedness therefore desires a focus on specific material and manufacturing processes of the highest order.

Ongoing war in Afghanistan has demonstrated the technological advantage of fighting the war in tough terrains and extreme environment using highly developed warplanes, weapons and communication media. Quite often it is said that war gives birth to new materials and technologies and philosophy of decision-making. This development, during the peacetime, becomes available to common citizen for general use.

The concern for technology for the defence applications has received the highest appreciations. The Prime Minister, Shri Atal Behari Vajpayee, while addressing the Senior Commanders of Armed Forces on 26th November, 2001 in New Delhi, emphasised on constantly upgrading the technical and human capability to anticipate and counter threats to India's security. He said, "The revolution in technology has completely transformed the conduct of offensive and defensive military operations in these times. The military strategists should factor these developments into their long term defence planning". The Prime Minister called on DRDO to prepare itself for such an action.

Subsequently, the Defence Minister, Shri George Fernandes in his address to Officers of the Ordnance Factories said (on November 29, 2001) "the level of technologies in the Indian Ordnance factories is very poor".

Both these statements coming from the top level of governance indicate that there is a realisation that we need to have the latest version of technology for our defence preparedness. That is the concern of all Indians.

The Institution, therefore, considered appropriate to focus on materials and machining process as applicable to defence services as the main focus of the Seminar.

Role of Private Sector and Public Sector Industries

The concept of privatisation was seen as overall solution for all ills.

However, government policies and market have not allowed the engineering industry to grow systematically. The national goal of development and security desires that the growth of public sector and private sector should go hand-in-hand.

REFERENCES

1. Jain, S.C., *Present Scenario in Mechanical Engineering R&D and Education: Challenges Ahead*, 17th National Convention of Mechanical Engineers, IE(I), November 26-27, 2001, India.
2. Rajayaguru, K.B., *Cellular Manufacturing: A Leaner Cell Concept and Case Study*, 17th National Convention of Mechanical Engineers, IE(I), November 26-27, 2001, India.
3. Rajayaguru, K.B., *Manufacturing Flexibility: The Master Key for All Manufacturing System*, 17th National Convention of Mechanical Engineers, IE(I), November 26-27, 2001, India.
4. Joshi, Durgesh, *Development and Implementation of Low Cost Laminated Object Manufacturing*, 17th National Convention of Mechanical Engineers, IE(I), November 26-27, 2001, India.
5. Brahmankar, P.K., *Investigation on Electrical Discharge Machining of Metal Matrix Composites*, 17th National Convention of Mechanical Engineers, IE(I), November 26-27, 2001, India.
6. Chhabra, R., *Models for Material Remover in Abrasive Water Jet Machining*, 17th National Convention of Mechanical Engineers, IE(I), November 26-27, 2001, India.

6

Globalisation, Corporate Governance and Professional Institutions

Introduction

Corporate Governance, the present buzzword has taken over the economic growth of developing countries like India. Corporate Governance is taking a new dimension as the developing countries make a massive thrust to become a global business players.

Corporate governance has been a concern of globalised economies for more than one hundred years, as is evident from the following quote from Abraham Lincoln:

> "I see in the near future a crisis approaching that unnerves me and causes me to tremble for the safety of my country...corporations have been enthroned and an era of corruption in high places will follow, and the money power of the country will endeavour to prolong its reign by working upon the prejudices of the people until all wealth is aggregated in a few hands and the Republic is destroyed."
>
> *US President, Abraham Lincoln, Nov. 21, 1864 (letter to Col. William F. Elkins) Ref: "The Lincoln Encyclopedia", Archer H. Shaw (Macmillan, 1950, NY).*

The 'economic reforms era' of the last decade of the millennium has also focused national attention on corporate governance. It was expected that the era of government administered corporates will be over, and the corporate governance will really have a chance to mature and will allow the market forces to play their assigned role. As the

---

Paper presented at the First World Congress on Corporate Governance organised by Insititute of Directors during June 1-2, 2002 in New Delhi.

government administered implementation strategies have still not been diluted and replaced by facilitation strategies the government's hold on new corporates continues. The corporate governance is still an academic exercise that is discussed but not practiced. The democratically elected Parliament, that decides country's policies, will not allow a revolutionary change in the economic sector of the country. Whatever changes will come around will be slow — whether gradual or erratic. However, to prepare the new actors and players in the economic field, it is quite appropriate to develop the skills of the manpower that will have faith in corporate governance in the new millennium.

Understanding of Corporate Governance

The concept of corporate governance is to include the very fundamentals on how the companies function in its day-to-day dealing with:

(i) with customers;
(ii) with traders;
(iii) with suppliers;
(iv) with shareholders;
(v) with government; and
(vi) with public

The corporate governance requires more internal discipline over external accountability. The internal discipline implies that the quality of its management has to be of a high order to be able to exercise that discipline in the organisation. By this one would expect that a good management will lead a company being a corporate citizen. It may soon be that in the open market economy survival may be at stake if the issues of corporate governance are not given due importance.

The basic issue that directly impinge on good management — whether in the public or private sector — relate to ethics and values which too have direct linkage with good governance.

It would be relevant to discuss the three issues of globalisation, corporate governance and professional societies separately before projecting as to how they are interlinked.

Globalisation of Indian Economy

The concept of globalisation of economy was introduced in India in the last decade of the millennium. Proponents of the concept, who strongly believe that India can earn its position in the global economy and earn the foreign exchange necessary for building India's socio-economic structure, had lot to talk about and convince the policy makers and the general public. An equally strong opposition has been critical of following the path of globalisation as that aims at removing subsidies, correcting prices and shifting the balance in favour of large and modern companies. The critics also firmly believe that an approach to globalisation results in loss of employment opportunities, and weakening the local manufacturing and R&D base, thereby demolishing the self-reliance of the country. Liberalisation and globalisation as a process of change do not in themselves guarantee growth and economic development at desired levels.

Liberalisation has given rise to a new culture which follows a course different from planned economy. The critical difference between planning and liberalisation is: planning assumes that outcomes are predictable, while liberalisation facilitates the unpredictable. It does so by unshackling the energy of innovation of millions of people unknown to planners, of letting them play around with ideas unthought of. Such unknown people and ideas have transformed other countries and can also transform India. It enables unknown to do the unthought of and become unstoppable.

A look at the economic growth of the country would indicate that India's exports have grown as a result of opening up of the economy. With increasing globalisation, rapid export growth has become important for economic growth more than ever. Openness and trade expansion is the buzz word. The strategy for development is now to focus on export led growth through optimal utilisation of comparative advantage *vis-a-vis* rest of the world.

With the opening up of the economy, a compositional change has been witnessed in the export basket. Some products like gems and jewellery, marine products, engineering goods and chemicals have been gaining in importance as compared to the traditional products like plantation, agriculture and allied products, ores and minerals.

There have also been certain new directional trends. Major export markets for India are USA, United Kingdom, Germany, Hong Kong, UAE and Japan. An analysis of the trends in the share of our major export destinations during the 1990s reveals that our exports to USA has been exhibiting a positive growth trend and its share has increased from 15 per cent in 1990-91 to 26.1 per cent in 1999-2000.

The whole approach to globalisation of Indian economy and its impact on Indian efforts at innovation, environment management and poverty alleviation need a total dispassionate study.

Globalisation in Post — 1945 Economy

Globalisation is not new, but the present era has distinctive features. Shrinking space, shrinking time and disappearing borders are linking people's lives more deeply, more intensely, more immediately than ever before. The phenomena of globalisation can be traced to over thousand years when countries started trading with each other. The earlier concept of globalisation was restricted to three basic elements: physical capital in terms of plant and machinery; labour and technology. The concept continued well into 1960s. Then new theories in economics got prominence, and new interpretation of globalisation of economy emerged. 1960s saw the emergence of information technology and its integration with capital market. This combination brought forth a new process of globalisation, and the movement is often termed as financial capital. Thus, globalisation starts with the concept of 'financial capital' in terms of capital invested in the capital market—mainly foreign direct investments in emerging markets.

The post-1945 era realised the need for economic interdependence. The leaders chose a course of openness and cooperation. The United Nations, the Bretton Woods institutions and the General Agreement on Tariffs and Trade (later incorporated into the World Trade Organisation) and a host of other organisations were established, whose job was to make the overall systems work. In the industrialised countries, domestic support for open market was secured by constructing social safety nets and providing adjustment assistance to adversely affected groups and industries. The situation, as it existed immediately after the second world war, was well served by the older concept of globalisation.

The Secretary General, UN commented on status of globalisation as:

> "The crux of today's problem, where globalisation has to support build up of economies of a large number of independent developing

countries, is that while the post-war multilateral system made it possible for the globalisation to emerge and flourish, in turn, it has progressively rendered its designs antiquated. Simply put, our post war institutions were built for an inter-national world, but we now live in a global world. Responding effectively to this shift is the core institutional challenge for world leaders today.

The post-war institutional arrangements were premised on a world made up of separate national economies, engaged in external transactions, conducted at arm's length. Globalisation contradicts each of these expectations. It is hardly surprising, therefore that the trade regime is under such stress — it increasingly deals with traditionally "domestic" matters rather than border barriers. Thus, calls for a new financial architecture are so insistent."

Does Globalisation Offer Opportunities to Millions of Poor?

In a country with 350 million below poverty line, living in less than US $ 1 per day, it is but obvious to ask the question about the benefit to the poor. The indicative results of various surveys have not shown immediate benefits to the poor. The obvious issue is whether globalisation of economy is wrong or the approach adopted in our country is wrong ?

The era of globalisation is opening many opportunities for millions of people around the world. Increased trade, new technologies, foreign investments, expanding media and internet connections are fueling economic growth and human advance. More than $ 1.5 trillion is now exchanged in the world's currency markets each day and nearly a fifth of the goods and services each year are traded. Globalisation is far beyond just the flow of money and commodities. It is growing interdependence of the world's people. Globalisation is a process integrating not just the economy, but culture, technology and governance. People everywhere are connected — affected by events in far corners of the world. Global markets, global ideas and global solidarity can enrich the lives of people everywhere, greatly expanding their choices. The growing interdependence of people's lives calls for shared values and the shared commitment to the human development of all.

Globalisation can become an effective tool to offer growth opportunity to millions of poor. But, not by excluding them from the markets. This will be feasible only through inclusive globalisation, where the poor have a role to play.

The enormous potential of globalisation needs to be tuned to eradicate poverty in the 21st Century — to continue the unprecedented progress in the 21st Century. UNDP identifies that : "to achieve this the challenge of globalisation in the new century is to find the rules and institutions for stronger governance to preserve the advances of global markets and competitions, but also to provide enough space for human, community and environmental resources to ensure that globalisation works for people — not just for profits."

Globalisation has to evolve with:

(i) *Ethics:* less violation of human rights, not more.
(ii) *Equity:* less disparity within and between nations, not more.
(iii) *Inclusion:* less marginalisation of people and countries, not more.
(iv) *Human Security:* less instability of societies and less vulnerability of people, not more.
(v) *Sustainability:* less environmental destruction, not more.
(vi) *Development:* less poverty and deprivation, not more.

The opportunities and benefits of globalisation need to be shared much more widely. If global opportunities are not shared better, the failed growth of the last decades will continue. More than 80 countries still have per capita incomes lower than they were a decade ago; while 40 countries have sustained average per capita income growth of more than 3 per cent a year since 1990, 55 countries, mostly in Sub-Saharan Africa and East Europe and the Commonwealth of Independent States, have had declining per capita incomes. Many people are also missing on employment opportunities. Inequality between countries has also increased. The income gap between the one-fifth of the world's people living in the richest countries; and the one-fifth in the poorest was 74 to 1 in 1997 up from 60 to 1 in 1990, and 30 to 1 in 1960. These are the signs that often carry the governments in developing countries to think away from globalisation.

Observations on Threats Created by Globalisation

Globalisation has also created new threats, mainly in the following categories:

(i) Financial volatility and economic insecurity.
(ii) Job and income insecurity.
(iii) Health insecurity.
(iv) Cultural insecurity.
(v) Personal insecurity.
(vi) Environmental insecurity.

Threats perceived from globalisation can be practically tackled and overcome for new measures in corporate governance are established and implemented.

Critical Ingredients

(i) Expanding access to the opportunities of globalisation.
(ii) Inequalities increase — like for example introduction of knowledge based industries will help technologically up to date skilled man power in comparison to conventional manpower. The disparity increases — it does not start with globalisation but only gets exacerbated.
(iii) Major source of income — inequalities within countries is gender discrimination in:
  - Wages,
  - Property rights,
  - Access to education.

  Globalisation may be having some positive impact.
(iv) Economic, success of globalisation will depend on 'good governance' to be appropriately supported by 'good corporate governance'.

Corporate Governance

Increased trade and foreign direct investment, increased financial flows and the role of global markets and firms operating worldwide create both important opportunities for, as well as threats to, sustainable development. On the one hand, they may lead to positive developments such as technology transfer; decreased pressures on the local, regional and even global environment; and enhanced social development. On the other hand, they may lead to undesirable developments such as: increased pressures on the local environment; overexploitation of natural resources; the loss of valuable skills and techniques (notably in agriculture); the deterioration of the social fabric; and the impoverishment of certain groups in society. Thus, globalisation in itself is neither good nor bad. The challenge is to minimise the "bad" and maximise the "good". This implies many trade-offs, notably with respect to inter-generational and intra-generational equity and national and international equity.

For globalisation to be a success all the issues outlined by UNDP have to be taken into consideration, *i.e.* ethics; equity; inclusion (of poor); human security; sustainability; and development. These issues if addressed properly can lead to good corporate governance.

The Corporate Accountability Project in USA has identified characteristics of 'corporates'.

- Of the world's 100 largest economies, 51 are now global corporations.
- The richest 1 per cent of Americans own 40 per cent of all US assets.
- The combined assets of 358 billionairs equal the combined assets of almost half the world's population.
- The courts have given corporations the basic constitutional rights of persons, but workers lose those rights on entering the workplace.
- The corporate share of taxes paid has fallen from 33 per cent in the 1940s to 15 per cent in the 1990s. Individuals' share of taxes has risen from 44 to 73 per cent.
- The new World Trade Organisation effectively gives corporations veto power over our US environmental and labour laws, weakening your right to protect ourselves and our land by our legislation.

If this is the situation in USA, then similar observations may also be valid for India.

Globalisation is taking place and offers significant opportunities for further development. On the other hand, this process alone is not sufficient to ensure sustainable development, since the latter is dependent on balanced policies. There are important trade-offs such as those between the rapid pace of trade and investment liberalisation and the need for adjustment periods to avoid disruptive social, economic and environmental developments. In this respect, much attention is to be given to the effects of higher degrees of specialisation and concentration of certain economic activities at local levels (including the depletion of natural resources and irreversible damage), and measures to reconcile these developments with well-balanced policy objectives. All these aspects are best covered under corporate governance.

India also set-up Kumaramangalam Birla Committee to present a framework for corporate governance. It was realised that besides the government administered framework, it was necessary to promote a market regulation framework. The government should only have a catalytic and promotional role in supporting India's economy to globalise. Since a number of multi-national companies are now operating in India who may or may not have similar understanding nor follow the same route of the governance, the role of corporate governance is likely to be more relevant in times to come.

In a number of discussions on the corporate governance, the role of financial institutions and the role of Board of Directors has been a major focus. While these two bodies no doubt have a major role to play in ensuring good corporate governance, there are a number of other relevant issues that need to be covered. Some of these are as follows:

Information Sharing

Basic and the most fundamental requirement is to bring around transparency in governance which can only be achieved through Acts on Information. It may call for certain changes in the Right to Information Act and Official Secrets Act. Whereas the public demand is transparency in government's operations. The reason given here is that as the government is dealing with public money, it should be more transparent. In the context of corporate governance, same logic is being applied on a broader platform. Most of the privately managed companies have a vide shareholder base, directly or through investments or through mutual funds, and there are a large number of people interested in functioning of the companies. The need for transparency in operation of the companies is becoming as important as that for the government.

What all is required in information sharing: The most fundamental is the Annual Report which can be shared with the shareholders and the public. Subsequently other elements involved the methodology of operation, technical trouble shooting, cost of operation, etc. Sharing of the maximum possible information will certainly evoke more confidence in the working and will also improve the performance of the organisation. Some of the reasons for not parting the information in government are covered under 'security', and in case of private companies, it is covered under 'competitive advantage/company interest'.

Awarding of Contracts

Awarding the contracts and management of suppliers is one area where greater transparency is required at all levels. The Chief Vigilance Commissioner of India has taken a decision that for major contracts the government has to provide absolute transparency in awarding the contracts. While companies following ISO 9000 norms have evolved certain procedures others have still not evolved any such thing. Getting competitive quotations from suppliers regularly needs to be practiced since this will offer the best price for the component and also lead to weeding out the inefficient companies. The Board of Directors can appoint independent agencies reporting directly to the Board or by auditing the transactions relating to contracts.

Customer Service

A basic concept in market economy is the customer satisfaction — or in other words making products customer friendly. The general tendency is to face the customer complaint by a certificate issued by a research lab or an administrative order (mostly by the public sector companies). This attitude takes no where, especially in the new competitive world. Service-after-sale is one reason that foreign and multinational companies are strengthening their foothold.

Some of the companies are becoming responsive, but that is only a part of the solution. The work ethics and values inculcated by the top management/board will to a large extent determine the altitudes of the rank and file. The management needs to imbibe value system that will promote good governance.

Company Resources and Workers Rights

An observation in USA, as mentioned in 4.0 above, states "the courts have given corporations the basic constitutional rights of persons, but workers lose those rights on entering the workplace." Such a situation in USA brings about better floor discipline and productivity. At the same time the workers are protected by other social safety nets.

Emerging labour laws in India may also see a replication of the same. In the absence of other supporting laws, it will be difficult for Indian workers to protect their interests. The management will have to carefully select strategies so that the workers are not deprived of their rights.

Associated with this will be the issue of use of company resources. Large amounts of public funds will be used and therefore involvement of labour in Board decision making process can be useful.

Training and Education

This sector is important as the paper deals with the role of professional institutions in globalisation and corporate governance.

The education and training programmes are required to be developed and introduced in 'corporate governance'. The threats of rapid globalisation can be best averted by sharpening skills of people who matter in governance of such large corporates within the Code of Ethics, suited to Indian economy. No such 'Code of Ethics' exists in India, but is certainly under evolution. Training and education programme has to be developed within the broad framework of ethics expected for corporates.

The Price Waterhouse Survey of Public-Listed Companies in USA stated that 62 per cent of the respondents put education about existing rules at the top of the list of matters requiring improvement. The thrust of training and education would not only be focused on the introduction of the Code and the accompanying regulatory reforms but also on the existing regulatory framework as they affect corporate participants involved in the governance of companies.

Target Participants

The primary issue involved is: 'To whom should training and education be targeted?'

The Corporate governance is not about government regulation — it is about directors, officers and shareholders being responsible for their company's fate. Although regulators and the judiciary have a role to play in providing the legal, regulatory and enforcement framework for the governance of companies, it is ultimately the company directors, company advisers and the shareholders who determine the equilibrium between management flexibility and controls.

Therefore the training needs of the following are to be recognised:

- directors, both executive and non-executive;
- company secretaries;
- audit committees; and
- shareholders/investors, both individual and institutional.

Training and education for the target participants would focus on the following areas:

- their general duties, obligations, responsibilities, rights and liabilities under laws, both common law and under statutes, rules, regulations and guidelines;
- the application of the code; and
- where necessary, industry and company specific information.

Role of Professional Institutions

Professional institutions perform two major functions:

(i) First, and foremost, they promote the advancement of their profession.
(ii) Second, they protect the professional interest of their members and their image in society.

The professional institutions also have a responsibility to ensure that their members follow a strict code of ethics in their professional dealings with the society at large and offer the highest quality of service to their clients.

The emerging global economy is based on 'information' and 'knowledge' where professional engineers have an important role. Therefore, the Institution of Engineers (India), a corporate professional body of over 4,00,000 engineers can contribute a great deal. The Institution was set-up under the Royal Charter in 1920, and has a strict Code of Ethics for professional engineers.

Subsequently other professional institutions have also been established and have their own guidelines on ethics for engineers.

Consulting Engineering Association of India is another apex body of engineers and represents the major engineering consultants. The Association has a membership open only to such individuals and organisations who are already a member of another professional society. Thus with the spirit of professional intitutionalism was doubly ensured. To keep the best spirits of his professional activities, it has a code of ethics which calls for ensuring professional service safeguards to enhance health, happiness and safety of the society; uphold the principles of environmentally sustainable development; act with fairness and justice with clients in all matters pertaining to contracts and service; and not indulge in any corrupt practices. The consulting engineers that contribute significantly to a wider economy are already contributing the corporate governance and uphold the best professional practices.

The third important engineering institution is Indian National Academy of Engineers. The Academy also has a code of ethics that makes it mandatory for all members to develop the best practices in science of engineering and hold the educational and business ethics.

Thus it will be observed that the professional engineering institutions have a direct role assigned to them within the Constitution framework to directly undertake activities that will help to promote corporate governance of the highest order.

Currently the Ministry of Human Resources Development is considering setting up the Engineering Council of India. The main function of the Engineering Council of India will be to grant appropriate certificate of competency to practice as 'Professional Engineers', to develop the profession of engineering and to regulate the profession through a 'Code of Ethics'. In furtherance of the these functions of the profession, it will be ensured that only a 'Professional Engineer', either working individually or in an organisational set-up will approve designs/drawings/reports.

Integration of Professional Institutions with Corporate Governance

The Board of Directors or the Management has to realise the importance of such engineering institutions, mainly in the emerging knowledge based economy. Role of engineers is of paramount importance and therefore with their integration with corporate governance, the country can really march towards globalisation of its economy.

Conclusion

The fear of corruption in high places exist only because of lack of understanding of existing norms and professional approach in corporate governance. Involvement of professionals in corporate governance will create an environment of confidence in various stakeholders and also develop practices that will be fair, transparent and acceptable.

7

Information Technology for Poverty Alleviation Through Good Governance

The Institution of Engineers, Bangladesh has chosen a topic which is most appropriate for the South Asia and the South-East Asia region that houses most of the global poor. It is a co-incidence that I venture to write this paper after listening to the legendry figure Prof. Mohammed Yunus of Bangladesh this morning (on February 2, 2001) at the Micro Credit Summit, asking for appropriate regulations through good governance. Prof Mohammed Yunus has shown the way to the world as to how small amounts can bring around big changes in the lifestyle of the poor in the rural areas. His movement of Grameen Bank has given a new orientation to the approach for poverty alleviation through self-help and small credits. The example was followed in different countries in different forms. The micro credit scheme promoted by him to launch a cellular telephone all over Bangladesh gave an income generation opportunity to rural families by running public call office and earn their livings and an access to the common man to the modern mean of communication at a reasonable price. Solar photovoltaic panels are used for electricity generation which is stored in batteries and used to recharge cellular phones. The rural poor did not have to be literate or educated to use a sophisticated IT tool, to become a part of local, national, regional and global market. The tremendous power that the cellular phone provided to the rural poor and thereby a tool for poverty alleviation is the best example I can quote while making a presentation in Bangladesh.

Its amazing to notice also another effort of the Grameen Bank to set up computer training centre on Kutubdia Island, which has for the first time provided an opportunity to masses to learn computer. The

---

Paper presented at the 45th Annual Convention of the Institution of Engineers (Bangladesh) during February 2001 at Dhaka.

electricity is again provided by solar photovoltaic systems. Grameen Bank provides loan for setting up such a centre. Twenty more such centres are being set up under similar arrangement. This will be a beginning for providing computer literacy and thereby prepare the masses to work efficiently. On the other hand the government will have properly trained manpower to establish transparent and efficient official systems.

I think my tribute to Prof. Mohammed Yunus will be the appropriate beginning to my Paper for the 45th Annual Convention of the Institution of Engineers, Bangladesh.

Bangladesh has the rich tradition of acquiring information, storing it and retrieving it in the most appropriate fashion. Records of most of the geological surveys were housed in Bangladesh and provided insight for deciding strategies for development. Khulna lies in the richest mangrove area of Sunderbans and provides an opportunity for income generation and living to the poor during its plantation and growth as well as by its use. Mangroves is an eco-system that becomes a part of the life of common man. Countries like Thailand, Singapore and Malaysia who had earlier cleared mangroves are now replanting the same. The richness of biodiversity in this region and as a part of life of the common man is significant in this region.

South Asia Characteristics

The South Asia region has been termed as the poorest with the following characteristics:

The South Asia Human Development Report, 1999 specifies: "The main reasons for South Asia's deprivation are not just economic. These problems go hand in hand with social and political factors rooted in governance. South Asia remains a region divided — between the hopes of the rich and the despair of the poor. A region where the richest one-fifth earns almost 40 per cent of the income, and the poorest one-fifth makes do with less than 10 per cent. A region where today begins with the struggle of survival for 515 million poverty ridden destitute and tomorrow threatens the future of 395 million illiterate adults. At the threshold of the twenty-first century, this is the South Asia that we live in."

According to South Asia Development Report, 1997 : South Asia covers over one-fifth of the humanity and this population of 1.2 billion is growing rapidly. Its share in world population is 22 per cent and inhabits nearly 40 per cent of the world's absolute poor. More people are born in South Asia every year (27 million) than the total population of all the Scandinavian countries (Denmark, Finland, Norway and Sweden). As a matter of fact the South Asian population exceeds the total population of 50 of the smaller UN Member countries.

In the global context, the South Asia region has begun to lag behind all other regions of the world, both in its income and in human development levels. South Asia is by now the poorest region in the world—its per capita income of US $ 309 is much below US $ 555 for Sub-Saharan Africa and is only one-third of US $ 970 for all developing countries.

Adult literacy rate of 48 per cent lags behind 58 per cent achieved in Sub-Saharan Africa and 98 per cent in East Asia (excluding China). South Asia also experienced an increase in its share of the world's illiterate adult population, from 32 per cent in 1960 to 46 per cent in 1993, demonstrating that adult literacy in this region increased at a much slower pace than in other regions and also that the school education was not on a desired level.

The extent of human deprivation in South Asia can be summed up as follows:

(i) Over 515 million people live in absolute poverty.
(ii) 260 million people lack access to even rudimentary health facilities.
(iii) 337 million people are without safe drinking water.
(iv) 830 million people have no access to basic sanitation.
(v) 395 million adults are unable to read and write.
(vi) 600 million people have no proper shelter.

The potential for economic growth, employment and income generation in the rural areas is centred around agricultural development, which is the source of primary food production and the base for allied activities, such as cottage and small scale industry, and off-farm village enterprises. In the face of growing population and declining land-human ratio the enhancement of agricultural productivity and other income generating activities through the introduction of modern technologies and inputs is, therefore, a major policy objective in all countries. This is accompanied by efforts to improve the quality of life in the rural areas to infrastructure development, such as access roads and communication facilities, and the provision of social amenities in the form of health care, education and water supply, among others.

The South Asia Development Report, 1997 identified following three major actions:

(i) South Asian States need to redirect their policies. They must refocus their efforts towards the core human development concerns.
(ii) Existing state institutions should be revitalised.
(iii) New partnerships between the state and society have to be forged for any major turn around.

The Human Development Report is quite emphatic that good governance is a must for the development of South Asia. Its relationship with or dependence on IT needs to be looked into. Before moving to that stage the need of globalisation of economy and impact of knowledge on economy need to be studied.

Globalisation of Economy

Globalisation of the economy in the whole region has been tried by all the member countries in one form or the other. The responses to the efforts had been proportionate to the infrastructural capabilities.

The post-1945 era realised the need for economic inter-dependence. The leaders chose a course of openness and cooperation. The United Nations, the Bretton Woods institutions and the General Agreement on Tariffs and Trade (later incorporated into the World Trade Organisation) and a host of other organisations were established, whose job was to make the overall systems work. In the industrialised countries, domestic support for open market was secured by constructing social safety nets and providing adjustment assistance to adversely affected groups and industries. The situation, as it existed immediately after the Second World War, was well served by the older concept of globalisation.

Globalisation is not new, but the present era has distinctive features. Shrinking space, shrinking time and disappearing borders are linking people's lives more deeply, more intensely, more immediately than ever before. The phenomena of globalisation can be traced to over thousand years when countries started trading with each other. The earlier concept of globalisation was restricted to three basic elements: physical capital in terms of plant and machinery; labour and technology.

The concept continued well into 1960s. Then new theories in economics got prominence, and new interpretation of globalisation of economy emerged. 1960s saw the emergence of information technology and its integration with capital market. This combination brought forth a new process of globalisation, and the movement is often termed as financial capital. Thus, the present day globalisation starts with the concept of 'financial capital' in terms of capital invested in the capital market—mainly foreign direct investments in emerging markets.

The Secretary General, UN commented on status of globalisation as:

> "The crux of today's problem, where globalisation has to support build up of economies of a large number of independent developing countries, is that while the post-war multilateral system made it possible for the globalisation to emerge and flourish, in turn, it has progressively rendered its designs antiquated. Simply put, our post war institutions were built for an inter-national world, but we now live in a global world. Responding effectively to this shift is the core institutional challenge for world leaders today."

In the region with 500 million below poverty line, living in less than US $ 1 per day, it is but obvious to ask the question about the benefit to the poor. The indicative results of various surveys have not shown immediate benefits to the poor. The obvious issue is whether globalisation of economy is wrong or the approach adopted is wrong ?

Globalisation is also perceived to have created following threats:

(i) Financial volatility and economic insecurity.
(ii) Job and income insecurity.
(iii) Health insecurity.
(iv) Cultural insecurity.
(v) Personal insecurity.
(vi) Environmental insecurity.

Role of Knowledge in Development

The speed and extent of development depends on the availability of material, technology and financial resources, but in its essence development is a human process that has emerged by the response of people to their external environment. Whereas the 1960s saw the emergence of information technology its role in economy grew fully only by the end of the century. The 'industrial age' really transformed into 'information era'.

Knowledge contributes to develop in following ways:

(i) As a productive resource;
(ii) As an essential input for education, scientific research and industrial technology;
(iii) As a catalyst for social change and economic development; and
(iv) As a basis for civilisation and cultural values that promote social integrity and harmony, which is the essential foundation for development.

In earlier stages of development, land and minerals constituted the principle resources for development. Technology was rudimentary. Human beings were valued mainly for their physical labour. Today, information and knowledge have become increasingly important inputs to the development process. All economic activities are becoming more knowledge intensive. By one recent estimate, 50-60 per cent of all industrial output is based on information. The phenomenal growth of employment opportunities in the US has been driven by the rapid expansion of services. The four most important sectors — financial services, insurance, health and education — are especially knowledge intensive. This shift from material to knowledge based resources open vast opportunities for developing countries to accelerate the pace of development. The characteristics of knowledge differ greatly from those of material and financial resources. Knowledge expands as it is shared rather than being consumed. Knowledge is not lost when it is freely given away. Knowledge is readily transportable at rapid speed and at very low cost.

The knowledge gap in this information age becomes a serious handicap even for countries endowed with manpower and know-how of information technology. The task of harnessing available knowledge for development is complicated by the fact that the rate of global knowledge generation is growing exponentially and old knowledge is quickly superseded or nullified by new knowledge which generates more and better results, faster and at lower cost. Humanity's knowledge base, which has been accumulating slowly over centuries, is now doubling every three to five years. The concept of quality improvement and manufacturing cost leading to 'incremental improvement in product performance' has been replaced by the concept of 'evoluation of new product'.

Not only knowledge is much more available, it is also much more essential for the globally competitive world. The common man also needs knowledge and practical skills to perform even routine functions such as operating sophisticated machinery and appliances, complying with laws, interacting with government departments, benefiting from modern medical technology, etc. The countries in South Asia have a vast rural and poor population. This region has not been able to take total benefit of the IT revolution due to knowledge gap.

Knowledge Gap — A Hindrance

It is pertinent to look at the knowledge gap and its impact on progress of literacy, education, application of technology, R&D and the growth of communication systems.

Literacy comes first. In India there are over 300 million illiterate forming almost 30 per cent of the population. For these people the traditional avenues of knowledge dissemination through education and printed information are ruled out. These people form a vulnerable group and are likely to be marginalised in the new economy.

Education is the second yardstick of measuring the knowledge gap. Education is a primary and most effective means so far evolved for transmitting practical useful knowledge from one generation to another. Education is a process of passing on to future generations in a concentrated and abridged form the essence of knowledge accumulated by past generations. The higher percentage of school dropouts make it necessary to entrust the needs of large illiterate population. The South Asia region needs a strategy to develop innovative approach to enhance knowledge acquisition among such population.

Research and Development activities directly reflect the rate of knowledge generation. The capacity of a country to adapt and fully harness the global advances depends to a significant extent on domestic R&D activity. The recent decreasing investments on R&D suggests the increasing knowledge gap resulting from inadequate knowledge generation.

Application of technology is the fourth route to estimate country's knowledge gap. The empirical studies and field research conducted in

India by California Agricultural Consulting Services indicated that knowledge accounts for more than 50 per cent of the difference in productivity on American and Indian farms.

Knowledge dissemination grows through the system of formal education and through a variety of informal channels. The media is the most prominent where the rate of literacy and education are low. Unfortunately, the circulation of newspapers, internet penetration and the IT infrastructure are still at a very low level in South Asia as compared to other countries. Taking India as an example, its IT infrastructure will be as figured in the table below:

2000	*2008*	*2016*
PCs	4.3 million	20 million
Internet subscribers	1.0 million	35 million
Internet users	3.7 million	100 million
Cable TV subscribers	37.0 million	70 million

The words 'knowledge, information and data' are often used interchangeably. But, a true understanding of the role of knowledge in development requires that an offer is made to make the distinction between its ascending and descending levels or grades. In the ascending phase that deals from experience to knowledge, raw data is distilled into information and ideas. The raw, unprocessed physical facts or data is the lowest level. At the next higher level these facts get categorised and organised as information. At a higher level organised facts are processed and distilled into ideas, concepts and theoretical propositions that provide a perspective which reveals their significance and physical skills that express in action.

Good Governance and IT

Various measures indicate that knowledge gap in India is indeed great; and very great will be the benefits of implementing the strategies of close that gap. The measures also reveals that India has substantial media infrastructure that is not being effectively utilised for knowledge dissemination. That can happen only through good governance by using IT as a tool.

Increased dependence on trade and foreign direct investment, increased financial flows and the role of global markets and firms operating worldwide create an opportunity for development, but only for those that have the means for good governance as well as good corporate governance. IT couid help in bringing better transparency in its decision — making; in financial disclosures and in speedy flow of information and thereby action based on this information.

Good governance along with good corporate governance utilising the IT tools have been observed to help and support development of the poor at a faster rate as they are also made a part of the whole development process.

Role of Professional Institutions

Professional institutions perform two major functions:

(i) First, and foremost, they promote the advancement of their profession.
(ii) Second, they protect the professional interest of their members and their image in Society.

The professional institutions also have a responsibility to ensure that their members follow a strict code of ethics in their professional dealings with the society at large and offer the highest quality of service to their clients.

The emerging global economy is based on 'information' and 'knowledge' where professional engineers have an important role. Therefore, in India the Institution of Engineers (India), a corporate professional body of over 4,00,000 engineers can contribute a great deal. The Institution was set-up under the Royal Charter in 1920, and has a strict Code of Ethics for professional engineers. Similar institutions in other countries can also work effectively.

Conclusion

Involvement of professionals in governance will create an environment of confidence in various stakeholders and also develop practices that will be fair, transparent and acceptable and favourable for uplift of the poor by appropriate use of IT tools.

8

Quality of Life for the Poor and Digital Revolution

Quality was considered to be an approach to attaining higher productivity. It is no longer so. Quality is now considered a commonplace activity. The premium attached to quality is slowly vanishing. Higher price tag for better quality is no longer the call for consumer durables or any other items. Quality has to be in-built if the product is to survive market competition. Product and productivity have to show rising trends. Increasing competition results in better quality at lowering price the need of the hour. Only such institutions and business houses can be successful who attain this goal.

This has been the impact of pace of technology innovation and information technology. Launched as the preserve of the higher-level resource intensive enterprises information technology tools have become accessible for development of the poorest of the poor. These tools are effectively employed to improve the quality of life of the poor. Thus, information technology is playing an important role in improving quality of products and life style — and both to serve the poor. All that we need is to empower the poor to use theses tools effectively. The poor do not have to be highly educated. They need functional skills.

I wish to focus here on a technological shift that is already transforming social and economic life: the digital revolution. Fundamental changes are occurring in the communications and information industries, and at near-lightning speed.

The advent of information and communication technology has created seemingly limitless opportunities for improving productivity and efficiency in support of economic growth and poverty reduction. For example, information technology can reduce transactions costs

---

Paper published in Quality Time dated May 2002.

for the rural poor and small farmers. The speed and reduced cost of information search and dissemination can revolutionise the delivery of human resource and support services and thus work in favour of agricultural and rural development. A consensus exists that information technology has huge potential economic payoffs.

Its actual utilisation to advance the cause of rural development, however, entails substantial requirements in term of human capital and physical infrastructure. Recent literature on the observed patterns and variations in economic growth, existence of externalities and poverty traps may have important relevance in this regard. Evidence suggests that the application and adoption of information and communication technology may be characterised by increasing returns but they require a minimum quantum of inherent human capital and physical outlay, before sustainability can be achieved. Access to the technology is not possible below this quantum.

Given the prevailing initial conditions of a lack of overall human asset and physical infrastructure in rural areas, there is real danger that the advent of information and communication technology can create a technology divide between the rural poor and the non-poor. Such a situation can extend to income groups, areas, or regions within or even across countries, where great disparity exists in the ability to afford the initial human and physical requirements to gain access to the modern technology and enjoy the increasing benefits it can offer.

Therefore, the poor entities who are constrained by lack of necessary resources face the threat of being left farther and farther behind with the passage of time. Without the initial means to cross the threshold, the poor and trapped. In contrast, the rich can easily exploit such up-to-date technology and derive increasing and continuous returns from it, thereby enhancing their further investment in its even newer and better generations. This situation means that the rich is getting richer, while the poor remains poor, depending the inequality that the information technology could otherwise bridge.

This issue merits urgent and careful attention by governments, considering its strategic implications to the success or failure of agricultural and rural development efforts. Existence of externalities makes public sector intervention necessary so that widespread and equitable adoption of information and communication technology can be achieved. Appropriate public policies and resources must be mobilised to tackle the quantum requirements for an equitable access to and distribution of growing benefits that can be derived from the revolution in formation and communication technology.

To fully appreciate how the digital revolution can stimulate economic growth and development, we need to grasp several of its core features. First, it has created a brand new economic sector that simply did not exist before. As the countries at its forefront devote ever larger shares of their economies to this sector, a high-value space is opened up for others to occupy, and so on successively throughout the world economy. This, indeed, is how the so-called emerging economies first 'emerged' when other sectors were vacated. Globalisation facilitates such shifts.

Second, the capital that matters most in the digital revolution increasingly is intellectual capital. Hardware costs are declining. The shift from hardware to software as the cutting edge of the industry helps to overcome what has been a major impediment to development — the shortage of finance. It also improves the chances for poor countries to leapfrog some long and painful stages in the development process. Clearly, the requisite intellectual capital is not universally available, but it is far more widespread in the developing world and in the transition economies than is finance capital.

Third, the digital revolution, besides creating a new economic sector, is also a means to transform and enhance many other activities. Mauritius, for example, uses the Internet to position its textile industry globally. The UNCTAD Trade Point Programme allows participants to trade products on-line. The Governmental of Mali has established an intranet to provide more effective administrative services. And there are many other opportunities: for telemedicine and distance learning: for "virtual" banking coupled with micro credit; for checking weather forecasts before planting and crop prices before harvesting; for having the world's largest library at your fingertips; and so on. The information technology sector, in short, can transform many if not most other sectors of economic and social activity.

Finally, the core product in this sector — information — has unique attributes, not shared by others. The steel used to construct a building, or the boots worn by the workers constructing it, cannot be consumed by anyone else. Information is different. Not only is it available for multiple uses and users, it becomes more valuable the more it is used. The same is true of the networks that link up different sources of information. We in the policy-making world need to understand better how the economics of information differs from the economics of inherently scarce physical goods — and use it to advance our policy goals.

9

Information and Communication Technologies (ICTs) Crucial for SMEs

Introduction

'Digital Divide' is caught in debate in the developing world and considered an important element in their slow progress. The longer globalising industries are able to grow and employ people who are experts in information technology. But, the smaller ones who provide larger employment opportunities do not have such access.

In both developed and developing countries there is still considerable skepticism as to whether providing access to Information and Communications Technology (ICT) can play a significant role in reducing poverty.

The Secretary General of the United Nations talked of the digital divide between developed and developing countries in his Millennium Report to the UN General Assembly, in September 2000. The divide is not only in the digital field but is all over in the basic human needs like, primary health care, basic education, family planning, nutrition, shelter, water and sanitation. The Information and Communication Technologies cannot itself bring an end to world poverty, but is one of the tools that can solve the global problem. Entering into the ICT age is extremely important for achieving quality of life and quality in production for small and medium enterprises. For most of humanity, the information age rhetoric is still a far cry from reality. In a world where 80 per cent of internet users live in the richest nation, and half the people of the planet never made a telephone call, bridging the digital divide will be an immense task. It will require nothing less than a digital Marshall Plan for the 21st Century.

Paper published in Quality Times dated August, 2001.

Mr. Marla Mallouch Brown, Administrator, UNDP says. "Certainly ICT cannot by itself bring an end to world poverty. ICTs are simply tools. And no single set of tools can solve a global problem with such multiple and complex causes.

But while ICTs are not a magic bullet, they do provide powerful ammunition in the fight against poverty. As with all tools, the usefulness of ICTs depends upon how they are employed. And there is now a body of cost-effective, country-differentiated and empowerment-oriented solutions, which use digital opportunities to address basic development goals. New technologies offer potent support to efforts to address the divides in health care, human rights and education.

In the area of health, ICTs are being used in developing countries to facilitate remote consultation, diagnosis and treatment. Across sub-Saharan Africa, for example, the Internet is used to monitor daily cases of meningitis and to help coordinate mass vaccination programmes when threshold levels are reached.

As for education, many organisations and vocational training facilities are employing ICT for distance learning and to train workers and even teachers in any array of functional areas. And through ICT, curricula can be developed collaboratively, and educational materials can be distributed and updated more cheaply.

In terms of political empowerment, ICTs can provide poor people, and the intermediaries who work with them, with new vehicles for voicing their concerns, organising popular movements, and making governments accountable. For instance, last year in Yugoslavia, local non-governmental organisations (NGOs), including student groups, used the Internet to rally and organise support for the overthrow of Slobodan Milosevic.

ICT can also help create jobs. The tremendous distance of developing countries from the major corridors of trade and from the major markets of the world has been a primary driver of the inequality in economic development that exists globally. ICT can make those distances much less significant. And for some countries, such as India, ICT may offer major economic opportunities.

So I am convinced that ICT can help us reach the targets established by world leaders at September's Millennium Summit, including the goal of halving poverty by 2015."

This is not just the wishful thinking. The inference is borne out of synthesis of world leaders at the UNDP platform, and their firm belief that the industrial development route and trade alone can solve the poverty problem.

Before I deal with how IOD's activities are linked to ICTs and quality, let me give some details on ICT and Employment.

ICT and Employment

(i) While 70 per cent of the European Union's (EU) workers are involved in Technology-intensive occupation, over half the world's population has yet to make a phone call.

(ii) In early 2001, some 160 million younger workers were unemployed, two-thirds in Asia.

(iii) About 500 million workers earn too little to keep their families above the US$1 a day poverty line.

(iv) Barely 6 per cent of the world's people are Internet users. And 88 per cent of them are in industrialised countries.

(v) Two phones per person are the norm in the industrialised world. In Africa there are fewer than 14 million phones for a population of over 700 million.

(vi) Over the last 4 years in India, an estimated 250,000 jobs for women were created in the mobile telephony sector.

(vii) In the Caribbean, some 5,000 women found new work in the data processing industry during the 1990s.

(viii) About 75 per cent of all Internet information is produced in just one language: English.

(ix) There is a glaring gender-related digital divide in developed and developing countries: 38 per cent of Internet users in Latin America are women, 25 per cent in the EU, 19 per cent in Russia, 18 per cent in Japan and 4 per cent in the Middle East.

[*Information drawn from the World Employment Report 2001, published by the International Labour Organisation. The Report deals with work life in the information economy.*]

At root it will demand the marriage of socio-economics of development with the new socio-economic of digital networks, both still highly controversial areas in their own right. Today, the disconnect between the ICT and development sector is a serious cause of concern.

Global Commitment to ICT

Realising this fact two separate task forces have been set up at the global level. The G-8 Digital Opportunity Task Force (DOT Force) and the United Nations ICT Task Force represent a commitment of the world's most powerful economic trade grouping and the most representative international organisation to address the issue of the global digital divide.

Certain pre-requisite have been identified as following actions:

(i) In the areas of policies, we need to move much faster in promoting increased competition in the ICT sector.
(ii) We need to modify wider commercial course and regulations to prepare for cross border e-applications.
(iii) In the area of programmes, we must incorporate ICT as a major piece of development portfolio.
(iv) It is necessary to fully integrate programmes with policy measures and ensure that they are innovative, well matched to local needs, and address market failures, poverty alleviation and social exclusion.
(v) Policies that increase creative cooperation between sector such as public-private partnerships are necessary for effective spread and optimal use of ICT as an enabler for development.

The Way Ahead

There is still a long way before fundamental ICT policies or programmes become operative. New evidence and innovative strategic frameworks may well be needed to convince the leaders of developed and developing countries of the urgent need to integrate ICT in the development policies. In other words the case for ICTs must be made compelling enough to illicit the political will to get the job done.

Two issues need special attention:

(i) Global governance of the Internet; and
(ii) The future of official development assistance in relation to ICT.

Developing countries are already woefully under-represented in the debate on global governance. The notion of operating the Internet in the future as a private non-profit cooperation based in the United States, functioning under US Law, is plainly unacceptable to developing countries. Here the United Nation's ICT Task Force could play a vital role in promoting the Internet as a global public good.

In terms of ODA, most major donor nations are currently struggling with how to incorporate ICT into their broader development strategies. The ODA debate is moving towards understanding ICT as a development objective in tandem with clean water, basic health and primary education.

That relates directly to the G-8 Digital Opportunity Task Force (DOT Force). Representing a new structure of global governance based on the notion of inclusion, and comprising all stakeholders-private sector, developed and developing countries government, non-profit organisations, and multilateral institutions.

The DOT Force report would be delivered to leaders at the G-8 Summit at Genoa, Italy at its meeting during July 20-22, 2001. The Report is likely to contain few major ideas that will help mobilise support for sustainable projects on the ground. To support this work the Digital Opportunity Initiative, a public-private partnership between the United Nations Development Programme (UNDP), Accenture and the Markale Foundation, has provided a innovative framework which position ICT as an enabler for achieving development goals and helping developing countries to be critical players in the new global network economy.

How Does it Take Shape and Relevance to India?

In the last 4-5 years, the Application Service Provider (ASP) Model has taken shape and gained significant importance. It provides immense opportunities for customers, service providers and software lenders. ASPs renting software through the Internet are trying to find solutions through IT implementation. Being quick to respond to the situation and low cost for the infrastructure, either in terms of accessing the solutions or providing information, ASP makes a sensible proposition to SMEs. In India, SMEs play a significant role contributing to almost 50 per cent of its industrial production and about 40 per cent of its exports. This sector is growing at a rapid pace. Whereas the larger organisations with their well established manpower base and financial infrastructure have better capability to access international funding and more informed decisions regarding large scale IT investment, the smaller businesses do not have this kind of a facility and are very often not able to take advantage of IT interventions. The experts are of the opinion, that despite there being the right reasons to invest in IT, adoption of IT in the SME segment has been low primarily due to the high cost of deploying and maintaining a state-of the art infrastructure.

It has been observed that the SMEs need an IT solution that is cost effective, scalable and flexible to the needs of a growing business and can keep pace with the rapid developments in the IT Industry. ASPs provide an opportunity for an SMEs to out source product and services and also to end to end implementation. This results directly in cost reduction for the SMEs.

Effective use of IT by SMEs has already shown results.

IOD Has an Opportunity

The Institute of Directors with its networking arrangements with SMEs in India and in other neighbouring countries is an ideal institution to develop its linkage with the UNDP's ICT Task Force and the G-8's DOT Force and become a partner in the Global Initiative the SMEs still lack the financial resources, manpower and a proper understanding of the possible benefits by effective and speedy implementation of ICTs in their operations. The Institute of Directors can launch major awareness programme for the benefit of its members to take maximum advantage of the emerging Information and Communication Technology Age.

10

Infrastructure Development and Poverty Reduction in Globalised Indian Economy

Introduction

The concept of globalisation of economy was introduced in India in the last decade of the second millennium. Proponents of the concept, who strongly believe that India can earn its position in the global economy and earn the foreign exchange necessary for building India's socio-economic structure, had lot to talk about and convince the policy makers and the general public. An equally strong opposition has been critical of following the path of globalisation as that aims at removing subsidies, correcting prices and shifting the balance in favour of large and modern companies. The critics also firmly believe that an approach to globalisation results in loss of employment opportunities, and weakening the local manufacturing and R&D base, thereby demolishing the self-reliance of the country. Liberalisation and globalisation as a process of change do not in themselves guarantee growth and economic development at desired levels.

Liberalisation has given rise to a new culture, which follows a course different from planned economy. The critical difference between planning and liberalisation is: planning assumes that outcomes are predictable, while liberalisation facilitates the unpredictable. It does so by unshackling the energy of innovation of millions of people unknown to planners, by letting them play around with ideas unthought of. It enables unknown to do the unthought of and become unstoppable.

A look at the economic growth of the country would indicate that India's exports have grown as a result of opening up of the economy.

Paper presented at the International Conference on Infrastructure Development organised by DFID, UK during December 2001 at Kolkata.

With increasing globalisation, rapid export growth has become important for economic growth more than ever. Openness and trade expansion is the buzzword. The strategy for development is now to focus on export led growth through optimal utilisation of comparative advantage *vis-a-vis* rest of the world.

The Secretary General, UN, in his Millennium Report, commented on status of globalisation as:

> "The crux of today's problem, where globalisation has to support build up of economies of a large number of independent developing countries, is that while the post (second world) war multilateral system made it possible for the globalisation to emerge and flourish, in turn, it has progressively rendered its designs antiquated. Simply put, our post-war institutions were built for an inter-national world, but we now live in a global world. Responding effectively to this shift is the core institutional challenge for world leaders today.
>
> The post-war institutional arrangements were premised on a world made up of separate national economies, engaged in external transactions, conducted at arm's length. Globalisation contradicts each of these expectations. It is hardly surprising, therefore that the trade regime is under such stress — it increasingly deals with traditionally "domestic" matters rather than border barriers. Thus, calls for a new financial architecture are so insistent."

Does Globalisation Offer Opportunities to Millions of Poor?

Human development is about much more than the rise or fall of national incomes. It is about creating an environment in which people when develop their full potential can lead productive, creative lives in accord with their needs and interests. People are the real wealth of the nations. Development is thus about expanding the choices people have to lead lives they value. And it is thus about much more than economic growth, which is only a means — if a very important one — of enlarging people's choices.

Inequality can exacerbate the effects of market and policy failures on growth and thus on progress against poverty. That makes inequality a special problem in poor countries, where imperfect markets and institutional failures are common. For example, where capital markets are weak, poor people, lacking good collateral, will be unable to borrow.

Their potential to start small businesses will be limited—reducing overall growth and limiting opportunities for poor people. Though growth is not always sufficient to advance human development and reduce income poverty, the experiences of China, the Republic of Korea and other countries of East Asia suggest that it makes a big contribution. Finally, there is the arithmetic reality. Even if there is growth and poor people gain proportionately from that growth, the same growth rate buys less poverty reduction where inequality is high to start with.

Concentration of income at the top can undermine the kinds of public policies—such as support for high-quality universal public education—that are likely to advance human development. Populist policies that generate inflation hurt poor people in the long run. Artificially low prices for water and sanitation mean that bankrupt public utilities never expand to poor neighbourhoods. Support for industrial subsidies or cheap loans for large landowners may also reduce growth. Developing and implementing good social policies is especially difficult where inequality takes the form of concentration at the top combined with substantial poverty at the bottom.

These disparities should come as no surprise. After all, electric power generation and grid delivery were first developed in 1831 but are still not available to a third of the world's people. Some 2 billion people not have access to low-cost essential medicines (such as penicillin), most of which were developed decades ago. Half of Africa's one year-old have not been immunised against diptheria, pertussis, tetanus, polio and measles. And oral rehydration therapy, a simple and life-saving treatment, is not used in nearly 40 per cent of diarrhoea cases in developing countries.

In India, a country with 350 million below poverty line, living in less than US $ 1 per day, it is but obvious to ask the question about the benefit to the poor. The indicative results of various surveys have not shown immediate benefits to the poor. The obvious issue is whether globalisation of economy is wrong or the approach adopted in our country is wrong?

The era of globalisation is opening many opportunities for millions of people around the world. Increased trade, new technologies, foreign investments, expanding media and internet connections are fueling economic growth and human advance. More than $ 1.5 trillion is now exchanged in the world's currency markets each day and nearly a fifth of the goods and services each year are traded. Globalisation is far beyond just the flow of money and commodities. It is growing interdependence of the world's people. Globalisation is a process integrating not just the economy, but culture, technology and governance. People everywhere are connected — affected by events in far corners of the world. The biggest example is of the Post-11th September world. The bombing of World Trade Centre in New York has affected the whole world.

Observations on Threats Created by Globalisation

Globalisation has also created new threats, mainly in the following categories:

(i) Financial volatility and economic insecurity.
(ii) Job and income insecurity.
(iii) Health insecurity.
(iv) Cultural insecurity.
(v) Personal insecurity.
(vi) Environmental insecurity.

Increased trade and foreign direct investment, increased financial flows and the role of global markets and firms operating worldwide create both important opportunities for, as well as threats to, sustainable development. On the one hand, they may lead to positive developments such as technology transfer; decreased pressures on the local, regional and even global environment; and enhanced social development. On the other hand, they may lead to undesirable developments such as: increased pressures on the local environment; over-exploitation of natural resources; the loss of valuable skills and techniques (notably in agriculture); the deterioration of the social fabric; and the impoverishment of certain groups in society. Thus, globalisation in itself is neither good nor bad. The challenge is to minimise the "bad" and maximise the "good". This implies much trade-offs, notably with respect to inter-generational and intra-generational equity and national and international equity.

To attain maximum benefit from globalisation of economy it is necessary that the government support the infrastructure development. If the process of globalisation has to be poor inclusive then the infrastructure development should also be with the involvement of the poor.

Power and Transport Infrastructure

Power Sector

Energy and transport are major constraints on any effort to achieve a significant acceleration on the growth of GDP in the 10th Five Year Plan Period. To add to the present employment potential it is necessary to attain a GDP growth rate of over 8 percent that will require the industrial growth rate to be over 10 per cent. This will place heavy demand on the generation and distribution of electric power and also transportation. The government is totally dependent on building of the infrastructure in the electric power and transportation sector. Since these are non tradable services, the necessary expansion in supply must come from increased domestic production. Further, more in a globally competitive environment, the quality of these services in terms of both price and reliability are as important as availability, and India faces serious problems on both counts. Unless these problems are speedily resolved, India will not be able to compete effectively in the increasingly integrated international economy. High cost of power makes Indian products non-competitive.

The Ministry of Power has developed a strategy or a blue print for power sector development and has demonstrated its determination to transform the sector. Various positive initiatives have already been taken and a historic legislation introduced in the Parliament. A coherent blue print has been prepared by listing the problems and issues hampering development of the power sector and designing strategies to resolve each of these problems. Reform of the distribution sector is the key. A number of ground level strategies for reforming this sector have been prepared:

(i) Building of the national grid;
(ii) Repairs and maintenance of plants to increase their efficiency;
(iii) Capacity addition of 1,00,000 MW in the next ten years;
(iv) Emphasis on utilisation of the hydro potential;
(v) Demand side management;
(vi) Research and development; and
(vii) Capacity building through training.

Involvement of common man can be useful in decentralised power generation systems and the energy efficiency measures, mainly the demand side management.

Transport Sector

Railways

The other area for implementation is the transport sector. Considering India's size and geographic resource endowment, it is natural that railways should have a lead role in the transport sector — not to mention other considerations, such as greater energy efficiency, eco-friendliness and relative safety. However, Indian Railways has experienced a continuous decline in its position relative to the road transport system. The most important policy distortion is the skewed tariff policy, which overcharges freight movement in order to subsidise ordinary passenger traffic. This is accompanied by an investment strategy, which has placed excessive emphasis on opening new lines for passenger traffic and not enough emphasis on expanding capacity in areas where there is potential commercial traffic. The net result has been an alarming deterioration in the financial condition of the railways and an inability to undertake the investment needed to improve railway transport services. The heavy cross subsidisation of passenger fares is economically irrational and cannot be justified on social grounds since the beneficiaries of the subsidy are not the poor.

If the provision of rail transport services, which lacks consumer focus at present, is to be replaced by a system, which provides services in line with consumer needs, it will require restructuring of Indian Railways. It should concentrate on its core function that is running of transport services on commercial lines, while spinning off non-core/ peripheral activities, such as manufacturing units, into individual corporations. These can remain in the public sector for the time being, but should function like any other public sector unit on commercial accounting principles. That will allow Railways to offer better service to the poor.

Greater emphasis has to be made on completion of existing projects, and a proper privatisation of all on-going projects has to be made to ensure that the resources are not spread too thinly across projects. Capacity on the saturated high density corridors needs to be augmented particularly on the golden quadrilateral by undertaking doubling, opening up of alternative routes through new lines etc. The programme of containerisation needs to be accelerated, not only to promote inter-modal transport but also as a strategy for increasing its own market share and catering to high value traffic.

Roads

Our road network is not up to the requirement of a rapid growth in an internationally competitive environment in which Indian industry must compete actively with other developing countries. Improvement in the national highway network should have high priority in the Tenth Plan. Competition of the ongoing work on the Golden Quadrilateral and the related North-South corridor projects must have top priority in the Tenth Plan. More generally, the existing deficiencies in the road network should receive higher priority than the extension of the network itself. In the longer run, it may be necessary to plan and take preliminary action for expressways to be built in future on those sections where they can be commercially justified.

There are a number of areas of concern, which affect the efficiency of road transport operations. These include the need for rationalisation of road transport taxation structure, which may support cost-effective road transport system, restraining of overloading of trucks, control of encroachments and promoting road safety. Particular emphasis needs to be given to removing all unnecessary policy and procedural hindrances to greater private participation in road transport operations, particularly in rural areas, without compromising on road safety considerations.

Rural road connectivity is an extremely important aspect of rural development. Substantially enhanced rural road accessibility should be achieved in the Tenth Plan by linking up all villages with all-weather roads through he Prime Minister's Gram Sadak Yojana. The need is for linking of villages and habitations with all-weather roads. However, while constructing rural roads, connectivity of public health centres, schools, market centres, backward areas, tribal areas and areas of economic importance should be given priority.

What can be done to have Poor Friendly Globalisation?

The foregoing discussion makes it evident that economic development or infrastructure creation for economic development does not necessarily mean reaching benefits to the poor. It can, on the other hand, give rise to inequalities that are not conducive to poverty reduction.

It is now imperative that:

(i) Globalisation of Indian economy needs to evolve its own Model that should have the common man as the main beneficiary.

(ii) Infrastructure creation for economic development should also involve the poor so that they get employment and income in this phase.

(iii) Infrastructure development for economic development and social development are complementary and should not be seen as separate entities.

Model for Globalisation of Indian Economy

The cost-effective economic development model of globalisation, based on existing international norms and oriented to foreign exchange earning through higher exports, has not been totally or absolutely fruitful. The Secretary General of the United Nations had already pointed out to this effect in his Millennium Report to the UN General Assembly in September 2000. The happenings after September 11, 2001 have changed the overall global scenario of equations and understanding. An overall economic recession and state of uncertainty has drastically reduced imports by leading economies. This has resulted in shrinking of exports from India. Thus, export growth itself may not be sufficient, though inevitable, to keep our economy growing. Thus drop in exports and loss of employment in industry and agricultural have gained a threatening dimension.

It is, therefore, necessary that large industries develop satellite small and medium size industries in semi-urban and rural areas aimed at *distributed* 'production centres' and 'employment opportunities'. This will result in decentralised area development and higher employment opportunities. Distributed incomes also lead to growing purchasing capacities and consumption patterns resulting in better quality of life for the poor. Another advantage of such an approach is that production facilities under a large industrial centre, requiring high technical competence and skill, when distributed into smaller units, can be controlled by smaller number of technically competent group leaders assisted by the work force that can be trained out of the local manpower. The technology in that case will not become alien to the poor but include the poor into the process of globalisation.

The poor will benefit at the time of creation of infrastructure for industry and agriculture; as well during the actual production cycle. Whereas they will have better income and purchasing power, they will also be benefited by the area development due new infrastructures creation.

Poor in the Infrastructure Creation

India has large programme for the core sector development, of which energy and transport open opportunities for involving the poor in creation of such infrastructure and also in maintenance and operation of the infrastructure.

The national quadrilateral and supporting arterial road infrastructure opens large opportunities for providing income and employment to the rural poor in its course. The unskilled labour can be appropriately trained and utilised.

The rural road building programme can be directly linked to rural development schemes, which will be mainly under the direct control and supervision of district, block and village level panchayats. Food for work programmes of the rural development can link road construction, which also ensures the food security for the poor. It is necessary that while core sector roads construction work be undertaken it is linked to various schemes of poverty alleviation so that there is a dual benefit of construction of roads in time as well as reduction in poverty. As most of this work is under government's direct funding, it will result in most cost effective utilisation of public funds.

Complementarity in Infrastructure for Social Development and Economic Development

There are three fundamental requirements for achieving reduction in poverty — growth, equity and security. The livelihoods of poor people have to be at the center of any strategy for poverty reduction. People's own experience of poverty is important. Poverty in the wider context includes — food security, unemployment, housing, and vulnerability. Growth is essential for poverty reduction. Globalisation, which is model for economic development, creates significant opportunities for the poor people, faster in open economies rather than closed economies. This benefits poor people and does not systematically increase inequality. For developing countries to attain better economic standard, it is necessary that they have a more effective participation in global trade and negotiations. Recent research highlights that countries with more equal distribution are able to convert a given level of growth into greater poverty reduction. This in other words means that availability of social infrastructure; better education level, health standards etc. can also be conducive to better economic development. Access to education, health, information, transport and financial services are all important.

The infrastructure for economic growth will have any meaningful application when that is supported by corresponding growth of social infrastructure. Once the poor is included in the process of economic development in the process of globalisation with equity, the possibility of social development also exist.

It is, therefore, important to note that the process of infrastructure creation for faster growth of economy will always be conducive to social development of the people.

Conclusion

Global markets, global ideas and global solidarity can enrich the lives of people everywhere, greatly expanding their choices. The growing interdependence of people's lives calls for shared values and the shared commitment to the human development of all.

Globalisation can become an effective tool to offer growth opportunity to millions of poor. But, not by excluding them from the markets. This will be feasible only through inclusive globalisation, where the poor have a role to play.

The enormous potential of globalisation needs to be tuned to eradicate poverty in the 21st Century — to continue the unprecedented progress in the 21st Century. UNDP identifies that "to achieve this the challenge of globalisation in the new century is to find the rules and institutions for stronger governance to preserve the advances of global markets and competitions, but also to provide enough space for human, community and environmental resources to ensure that globalisation works for people — not just for profit."

11

Role of TQM in Knowledge Economy to Improve the Quality of Life

Introduction

Development is the process by which human beings become aware of opportunities and challenges, formulate responses, make decisions, and initiate organised actions. This process follows the sequence from knowledge to inspiration to action. Human beings acquire knowledge, they become aware of opportunities and challenges. When that knowledge matures, they acquire a motivation or inspiration to transiate that knowledge into action.

The age of knowledge based developing economy brings to reality faster development to countries that have manpower equipped to handle data, information and knowledge. "Innovation" has replaced "improvement" and therefore the revolutionary process means new products and not improved products.

In earlier stages of development, land and mineral constituted the principle resources for development. Technology was rudimentary. Human beings were valued mainly for their physical labour. Today, information and knowledge have become increasingly important inputs to the development process. All economic activities are becoming more knowledge-intensive. By one recent estimate, 50-60 per cent of all industrial output is based on information. Modern manufacturing industries depend as much for their success on the management of information relating to quality, cost and scheduling as they do on the management of production processes. The service sector, which is the greatest source of new jobs and economic growth in the world economy,

---

Paper presented at the World Congress on Total Quality organised by World Quality Council during January 2001 at Mumbai.

is essentially knowledge-based. In the USA, the percentage of the workforce engaged in manufacturing is now the same as it was in 1850. The phenomenal growth of employment opportunities in the USA has been driven by the rapid expansion of services. The four most important service sectors—financial services, insurance, health and education—are especially knowledge-intensive.

Impact of Globalisation

Globalisation of national economies in developing countries have helped a number of them to develop and fulfil the objective of meeting the basic needs of its population. Globalisation has been made possible by the progressive dismantling of barriers to trade and capital mobility, together with fundamental technological advances. The benefits of globalisation are plain to see: faster economic growth, higher living standards, accelerated innovation and diffusion of technology and management skills, new opportunities for individuals and countries alike.

Few people, groups or governments oppose globalisation as such. They protest against its disparities. First, the benefits and opportunities of globalisation remain highly concentrated among a relatively small number of countries and are spread unevenly within them. Second, in recent decades an imbalance has emerged between successful efforts to craft strong and well-enforced rules facilitating the expansion of global markets, while support for equally valid social objectives, be they labour standards, the environment, human rights or poverty reduction, has lagged behind.

Such an impression exists when globalisation is seen as a means for just creating bigger markets. The economic fears cannot be supported from the more complex fabric of social and political life. To survive and thrive, a global economy must have a more solid foundation in shared values and institutional practices — it must advance broader, and more inclusive, social purposes.

The global communication revolution has created new expectations that humanitarian suffering will be alleviated and fundamental rights vindicated. The communication revolution is being felt in other ways too. The Internet is the fast growing instrument of communication in the history of civilisation, and it may be the most rapidly disseminating tool of any kind ever. The convergence of information technology, the internet and e-commerce may well become as transformative as the industrial revolution. Perhaps most important, these technologies enable people to be connected directly who otherwise might remain divided by distance, culture and economic stratification, potentially creating, thereby, a better understanding of who we, the peoples, are. But none of these possibilities exists for those without infrastructure or lacking in capital or because regulatory environments stand in the way.

TQM and Quality of Life

"TQM is very often understood as a technique, whereas it is a philosophy of managing an enterprise. TQM is defined as an approach towards transformation of an enterprise by focusing on quality through the involvement of all its members and aiming at success through customer satisfaction with a view to creating value for all its stakeholders including the society at large", says Dr. Madhav Mehra, Chairman, World Quality Council. Transformation from the 'industrial age' to 'knowledge era' called for pivotal role of TQM. The rapid pace at which global transformations are taking place, leave no opportunity for marginal improvements in products and techniques through improved methods of quality management. Gone are the days of incremental improvements and we are in the era of rapid transformation in the whole system.

Major problems facing the large poor, mainly rural, population are those associated with poverty and underdevelopment. Underdevelopment in turn includes: drinking water, sanitation, education, healthcare, poor rural infrastructure, and poor nutritional intake.

The quality of life of the common man can be significantly improved by introducing TQM practices for higher education and training and TQM practices for health/sanitation/water supply and rural infrastructure. Also building a TQM conscious private/public sector can help in community development.

TQM can impact social and economic activities and lead to better quality of life. Mr. Claude Fussler, the Eco-Development Guru mentions, "Good multinationals will certainly like to transfer best of the technologies and manage their operations most efficiently to the advantage of recipient countries. As the corporate management is now including corporate social responsibility also, it is but natural that the management tools that improve efficiency and thereby financial reforms, must also have a positive impact on poverty alleviation. The

TQM concept needs to be applied to provide best products and services and means to improve individual rural incomes and overall regional wealth."

TQM in Knowledge Economy

The shift from material to knowledge-based resources opens up vast opportunities for developing countries to accelerate the pace of development. The characteristics of knowledge differ greatly from those of material and financial resources. Knowledge expands as it is shared rather than being consumed. Knowledge is not lost when it is freely given away. Knowledge is readily transportable at rapid speed and very low cost.

Development depends on four knowledge processes:

- Knowledge generation and acquisition through scientific discovery. R&D and transfer of technology.
- Knowledge adaptation through innovation to particular fields, needs and operating environments.
- Knowledge dissemination through formal and informal channels from knowledge developers and adapters to those responsible for applying the knowledge in society.
- Knowledge application through skilled action in fields, factories, classrooms, hospitals and every other field of activity to achieve practical results.

TQM has very specific role in all the sectors of knowledge, as applicable to economy. The effectiveness of economic development can only be improved only when TQM is applied in the new concept.

India's Knowledge Gap

Prof. Gary Jacob has reflected the knowledge gap in India as follows: As a result of impact of knowledge on economy, the role of global knowledge generation is growing exponentially and old knowledge is quickly superseded or nullified by new knowledge, which generates more and better results, faster and at a lower cost. Whereas the global knowledge base is now doubling every 3-5 years, India's knowledge gap has become a challenge to development.

Literacy

Literary rates in India have doubled over the past four decades. This impressive progress is diminished by the fact that the starting rates were extremely low. This will leave approximately 300 million illiterate adults in the country, 30 per cent of the entire population. For these people, the traditional avenues of knowledge dissemination.through education and printed information are ruled out. Innovative approaches will be needed to increase knowledge dissemination to this group.

Education

Education is the process of passing on to future generations in a concentrated and abridged form the essence of knowledge accumulated by past generations. In spite of significant progress in reducing school dropouts, 31 per cent of children still dropout before completing the 5th grade and 70 per cent dropout before completing high school. Therefore, apart from addressing the needs of a large illiterate population, India's knowledge strategy must also develop innovative approaches to enhance knowledge acquisition among the large community of school dropouts.

R&D

Estimates of R&D activity can only be taken as crude indices of the knowledge gap, but the figures do suggest that knowledge generation in the country is not keeping pace, even proportionately, with the global knowledge revolution. R&D expenditure in different countries is given below:

Country	*Exp in US $*	*Exp. As per cent GNP*
Japan	825	3.0 %
USA	568	2.9 %
Korea	146	2.1 %
India	2.4	0.8 %

Two points are important to note about India's performance. First, atomic energy, space and defence research account for 71 per cent of all government spending on science and technology, which means that relatively little is left for investment in agriculture, energy, telecommunications and other crucial sectors. Second, R&D expenditure in India's fast growing IT sector is currently 3.1 per cent suggesting a strong correlation between investment in R&D and economic growth.

There are other indicators that also suggest an increasing knowledge gap resulting from inadequate knowledge generation.

- India's share of global scientific output in 1998 was only 1.58 per cent of the world's total.
- India's annual output of scientific papers has declined from 13,000 in 1981 to 12,000 in 1998, while world output has risen from 4 lakh to 7.6 lakh per year.
- India's share of global scientific citations in 1997 was only 0.7 per cent of the world's total.
- India's rank on the Science Citation Index has fallen from 8 to 13 since the early 1980s.

Knowledge generation directly impacts national development when it results in new and improved, patentable industrial processes. Every year more than 500,000 new patent applications are filed globally. Of these, China accounts for 96,000 and Korea accounts for 72,000, while India accounts for only 8,000. Korea produces nine times as many patents as India with only twice India's total investment in R&D, suggesting that not only the quantum of investment but the management of R&D activities is a critical determinant of knowledge generation.

Application of Technology

A fourth way to estimate the country's knowledge gap is to examine the extent to which commercially viable technology is being applied in the country. Since agriculture is still the largest source of employment in India, the application of technical knowledge in this field can be a useful index of knowledge dissemination through agricultural education, agricultural extension services and other delivery systems. The agricultural productivity in India differs vastly from that in USA and other developed countries. Reasons for this are many.

According to empirical studies and field research conducted in India by California Agricultural Consulting Services, knowledge accounts for more than 50 per cent of the difference in productivity on

American and Indian farms. To test this conclusion, CACS has conducted experiments in which the knowledge available to Californian farmers has been provided to Indian farmers. Without any change in the size of the land holdings or quality of inputs, productivity on the Indian farms rose by 100 to 200 per cent. While this data can only be taken as indicative, it illustrates the enormous potential for accelerating India's development by closing the knowledge gap.

A critical review of the above mentioned facts lead to a new role for TQM to improve effectiveness of knowledge creation, transfer and its acquisition. TQM practice in education, R&D and mass communication section can greatly enhance India's capacity to access knowledge.

Conclusion

Knowledge, which includes information and data, is playing an important role. The quality fraternity has to change, and change fast to catch up with the knowledge economy. Quality should not be just looked at as conformance of requirement, nor should it be taken to be a tool for satisfying customer needs. Quality provides means for anticipating customer needs and exceeding them before the competition catches up. Quality is creating products and services, which is different. In a global economy, which is led by service sector contributing upward of 50 per cent of GDP. The knowledge based system and appropriate means for TQM have to be developed. The process of incremental improvement is now being replaced by innovation.

12

Engineering Education by IE (I)

It is for the first time that since its inception in 1992 the IEI Convocation is being organized in the city of Delhi. It is also a happy coincidence that the 10th IEI Convocation is being organized in this historic city during the Platinum Jubilee year of the Delhi State Centre of the Institution of Engineers. Needless to say, organising the Convocation brings significance to AMIE Certificate, as it represents public acceptance of the courses offered by us.

Let me give a brief background to AMIE education. The Institution was set up as an outcome of the Report of the Industrial Commission in 1916-18. As India embarked on its industrial development, the status of the engineering profession became a matter of higher importance and received public prominence in the Report of Industrial Commission. The Chairman of the Commission, Sir Thomas Holland, was then the Commerce Member of the Government of India. There were signs and endeavours to advance an industrial society in India to safeguard and assure the status of the profession. Subsequently, an Organizing Committee for the proposed Indian Society of Engineers was formed on January 3, 1919 with Sir Thomas Holland, as Chairman. The Institution was formally incorporated in the Presidency of Madras on September 13, 1920 under the Indian Companies Act of 1913. The Institution was formally inaugurated at an impressive ceremony in the Hall of Asiatic Society of Bengal on February 23, 1921, by His Excellency Lord Chelmsford, Viceroy of India. In his inaugural address Lord Chelmsford said "The Institution has taken upon itself the great social responsibility of ensuring promotion of professional education among the youth of the country. This moulding of the youth, would be the greatest responsibility of the Institution." That was the understanding on the day of the founding of the Institution.

Welcome Address at 10th IEI Convocation and Technicians'/ Students' Convention, October 26, 2002 at New Delhi.

The Institution continued its journey as a qualifying body and learned society.

The rules and syllabi of the Institution examinations were first drawn up in 1924. In 1927, the Council announced the first list of accepted qualifications for exemptions from Sections A and B of the Associate Membership Examination. In 1928, the Council established the Examinations Committee, which was later re-named as Education, Examinations and Accreditation Committee. This Committee is responsible for the conduct of examinations, and draws up rules and syllabi and recommends them to the Council.

The examination for Corporate Membership was introduced in August 1928, when only four candidates appeared in Part A and only one in Part B. The preliminary examination (now called studentship examination) was held for the first time in 1931. There were no major changes during the next 20 years except that the number of subjects in part B were progressively increased to cover more fields. A complete revision of the examination and the syllabi took place in 1962, when entry examinations for Corporate members either written or oral or both called Section-C were introduced. The programme for laboratory experiments was introduced as an additional subject in Section-B from 1977. In 1992, the Council approved of a restructure of syllabi compatible with the requirement of the profession on the changing global scenario. The changed syllabus has given emphasis on training in the basic and common principles of design, production process and management etc.

The quality of the AMIE education was recognized by the Public Service Commission when it approved AMIE qualification equivalent to degree for all jobs in the government service. The Ministry of Education approved AMIE qualification.

It will be observed that the Institution, which came into existence as an outcome of the Industrial Commission (1916-18), launched its AMIE examinations in 1928 and launched a formal Convocation Ceremony in 1993. It took 65 years after the Institution had launched its Examination system that a Convocation was organized. The first Convocation was held on October 16, 1993 at Ranchi, with His Majesty, Governor of Bihar, Dr A.R. Kidwai as the Chief Guest. Prof. V.C. Kulandai Swamy, Vice-Chancellor of Indira Gandhi National Open University, delivered the Convocation address.

The Institution, realizing the significance of making its actions transparent and improving its outreach decided to hold public

Convocation, so that wider awareness of the AMIE qualification is created.

The Contribution of AMIE students is significant in the Government sector, mainly Defence, Railways, CPWD and Public Sector Undertakings.

The AMIE students have risen to high positions in such sectors. Over the last 5 years, the AMIE students contributed significantly towards the UPSC Administrative Service Examinations and the Engineering Service Examinations. It was observed that for the year 1999-2000, AMIE students contributed to about 25 per cent of those elected under the Indian Engineering Service Examinations.

Whereas the acceptability of AMIE students has been highly established in the government sector, the corporate world has still to realize the significance of AMIE education. With an effort to improve our out reach to the corporate world the Delhi State Centre has taken initiative of organizing On-Campus Interviews for the passing out students for the year 2001-2002. We personally feel that the process will certainly continue on a permanent basis. Our grateful thanks to eight forward looking enterprises, and their CEOs, who will be conducting on campus interviews tomorrow at the Institution of Engineers.

There are certain requirements in the corporate world that differ from those in the government sector. These changes have come in mainly due to globalisation of economy. The industry now needs persons with experience and with a mind set that can be made adaptable in different changing environment. Moving from one country to another or from one region to another is a frequent demand of the industry. The industry no more wants to know the number of years of experience in a particular sector; but would rather be interested in knowing the competence on latest developments. There is an old English saying: "You have not had 30 years' experience. You have had one year's experience thirty times". These words from the English Novelist, J.L. Carr points to a new thinking in the corporate world. In the present, ever changing techno-managerial scenario, such claims of long years of routine experience do not make much sense. What is relevant today is exposure to the latest technology and their applications. Often the work environment may not provide the right opportunity to learn the emerging trends, and therefore, will require other means to acquire the new knowledge. Professional societies like the Institution of Engineers will play a significant role. AMIE students trained in the

IEI environment will be better oriented to professional competence building than those from other formal sectors of engineering education.

As for the Delhi State Centre we have adopted to this thinking. Our Honorary Secretary is an AMIE Graduate, and was just 40 years when he took over as Honorary Secretary. Our incoming Honorary Secretary is also an AMIE graduate.

The industries are becoming more and more inter-disciplinary in nature and thereby requiring its employees to gain experience in other sectors and faculties of engineering. The AMIE route provides an opportunity for the existing professionals to improve and upgrade their qualifications in other branches of engineering.

Our effort is to give a clear message to the corporate world that AMIE students are as competent and suitable for the corporate world as they are suitable for government jobs. With this focus, in the recent past we have had number of discussions with ASSOCHAM and FICCI and many other major corporate giants. They have all found this interaction useful. Encouraged by the results of the initiatives we have made efforts to project strongly our intention to attract the corporate world. To make this message loud and clear we have invited, Shri Subir Raha, Chairman and Managing Director, ONGC to preside over the function. You are all aware, Shri Raha has brought a turn around in ONGC in a very short span of time.

Recognising importance of the Convocation, Shri Raha has also sponsored today's function, making bonds between IEI and ONGC much stronger. We have also invited Shri Yogendra Prasad, Chairman and Managing Director, National Hydro Electric Power Corporation to preside over the valedictory function.

Association of Corporate World with the Convocation Session, Valedictory Session and On Campus interviews reflects their confidence in IEI education system. Probably we are projecting this confidence for the first time in Delhi.

On this occasion, we have also undertaken a few other first time activities that include organizing a quiz competition for the students. It will be held tomorrow morning at the Institution premises. Also the entertainment programme this evening is being organized by students and not by any commercial troupe. The exhibition of equipment and technical books, inaugurated yesterday, is being organized for three days.

13

Globalisation and Strategy for Manpower Development in Construction Industry

Introduction

Globalisation of Indian economy has offered an opportunity for the Indian industry to exploit global markets. It has also thrown open a number of challenges, of which the most important is the process of restructuring of manpower. The process has converted India's protected seller's market into buyer's market, wherein the buyer can now demand quality at a price that is globally competitive. Opening up of economy to international competition; adoption of global standards; and disappearance of protected domestic markets is a major move forward. Such a change was not acceptable readily to all the sections in India. This calls on the technical education and training agencies to prepare for new challenges.

Changing Pattern of Economy

The agricultural economy of India in 1951 observed contribution from agriculture to be 62 per cent of GDP; manufacturing to be 22 per cent and service sector less than 20 per cent. But by March 1999 the contribution of agriculture has gone down to under 25 per cent, industry 25 per cent and service 52 per cent. It is expected that the service sector would exceed its contribution to 60 per cent of GDP. While this change is also reflected in the employment pattern of urban population, the rural employment continues to be primarily in the agriculture sector. Because of no expansion of the agriculture sector, the need for acquiring new skills is growing very fast in the rural sector.

Paper presented at the Seminar on Mechanical Engineering organised by the Institution of Engineering (India) West Bengal Centre during August 2001 at Calcutta.

Role of Construction Industry

A survey of Indian economy, released by the Confederation of Indian Industries in January 2000, reflected that IT, cement, steel, and automobile sectors are on the growth path — as indicated in the performance statistics from April to November, 1999. It can be inferred that construction industry — activities relating to housing and infrastructure — is growing and will continue to grow. Recovery of economy points out that in future 'quality construction' needs to be promoted.

The construction sector is one of the most complex, dynamic and dis-organised sector in our economy. This sector, by virtue of its forward and backward linkages, caters to all infrastructural activities — agricultural, industrial and service sector. The annual value of construction is in the range of Rs. 1500 billion. Three factors, namely, the resilience of the economy, large scale improvements in the basic infrastructure facilities and the massive capital and resource inflow point to a tremendous spurt in industrial activities.

Experts points out "all the antiquated concepts and practices are expected to make a hasty retreat. A new order is emerging. The construction sector too is having a break from the past. Some of the important trends forming part of the new order lead to challenges and threats to the existing stakeholders and new entrants." Dr. T.N. Subbarao has defined these challenges as follows:

(i) Flotation of mega projects involving huge project outlay.
(ii) Innovative contract procedures.
(iii) Adherence to schedule completion time.
(iv) Predominance of BOT projects and associated policies and procedures.
(v) Competition against vertically integrated and resourceful MNCs.
(vi) Lower margins caused by competition.
(vii) Induction of hi-tech equipments and improved methods of construction.
(viii) Uncertain environment.
(ix) Organisational transformation.

Solutions for all of them can be found out. One element is important to all — and that is manpower.

Human Resource Requirement in the Construction Sector

The transformation of the Indian economy is an important and dynamic change necessary for the very survival of the construction industry. Those who will change with time will continue to find their place in the Indian and global construction industry and others will either remain only builders or perish. The leaders will certainly will have to change at a very fast pace. The work force in the construction industry will have to be carefully chosen and special courses for education and training will have to be conducted. The importance of manpower development becomes important when we consider 30 million of working population is engaged in construction industry in India. Still more significant is the point that the majority of them are illiterate and unskilled. Skill building and developing them to reach international standard is the major challenge to this sector. They are mostly from the rural background with high illiteracy rate.

The Indian construction industry has more than 28,000 registered construction companies of which majority are involved in housing construction and maintenance works and bidding contracts worth value less than Rs. 100 million. According to Mr. A. Ramakrishna of Larsen and Toubro Limited, "The number of players were involved in executing, high value contracts with turnkey capabilities are very low in the order of less than 200 including those with joint venture partners."

Studies have shown that about 40,000 civil engineers are employed by the private sector construction industry. About 1,40,000 civil engineers are employed in government departments and client organisations. About 1,20,000 diploma holders in civil engineering are estimated to be employed in the entire sector. The organised sector is estimated to employ 11 lakh employees of which 27 per cent are skilled and 73 per cent are unskilled.

The managerial level has graduate engineers and diploma holders; the skilled labour is only ITI trained, which train in trades of plumber, mason and painter. Only three trades related to the construction industry are covered by ITI. There is no other possibility of adopting any ITI course to construction workers. The levels of skills acquired by these trainees scarcely meet the requirement imposed by present day hi-tech systems (as applicable to the construction industry). The profile of unskilled worker is even more pathetic as they are mostly migrants from the farm sector. They normally go back to their villages during the harvest season and then come back for the construction activity during off-season. These unskilled workers constitute a formidable challenge to construction managers.

Unlike the IT industry that needs manpower at degree or postgraduate level; the construction industry needs highly efficient professional manpower at degree and post-graduate level and but also highly skilled workman at the lower levels.

Major problems relating to manpower focused by the experts during the 14th Engineering Congress of the Institution of Engineers (India) held during January 29-31, 2000 in New Delhi, are as follows:

(i) Lack of trained manpower.
(ii) Absence of certification procedure for skilled workmen.
(iii) Lack of interest of workers to take up the sector trades.
(iv) Indifference on the part of the government and industry to actively promote and pursue the manpower needs.
(v) Lack of trained and experienced teachers at education institutions and for training for skills building.

The experts identified that quality engineering education and training will be the basic requirement for meeting the challenge of the next millennium in the construction industry. Benchmarking of educational institutions with the best in the world; developing curriculum competitive to foreign universities and educational institutions and focusing on formal, non-formal, distance and continuing education have all been considered to create the requisite manpower to meet the challenge of the construction industry. Industry-academic interface was considered important for developing trained manpower, but such interaction can really be placed only through government support and motivation. The recent internal and external brain-drain has resulted in strong market pull on civil engineers to other sectors. Many of them are opting for jobs in banking and financial sectors because of the attractive compensation packages offered by these sectors. A general impression is that on one-hand the demand for engineers and workmen is increasing in the construction industry, but, on the other hand the availability of civil engineers is gradually decreasing. That is likely to cause serious problem to the construction industry.

Way Ahead for Manpower Development

To meet the challenge of the identified problems as given above, the experts at the 14th Engineering Congress broadly agreed on future course for manpower development to meet the challenge of globalisation, with specific reference to the construction industry, on the following lines:

Recommendations

1. Globalisation has projected the need and opportunity for improvement in engineering manpower skills through upgradation of education system as well as training procedures.
2. A National Policy on Engineering Profession should be developed.
3. A National Policy on Engineering Education and Training should be developed.
4. Accreditation and quality assurance should be mandatory for engineering education institutions. Benchmarking standards should be comparable with the best education system in the world.
5. The construction industry needs a focus on higher level professional education as well as on technician or workman level skills building.
6. Norms should be evolved on working conditions and incentives for bright engineering students to take up teaching assignment. As a first step, all vacancies in the engineering institutions should be filled up on priority. Their services should be recognised through awards and other means. More flexibility in working should be permitted for the industry so that they can play a leading role in promoting industrial development by integrating their academic output.
7. Private sector should be promoted to enter quality engineering education and training on a bigger scale. Necessary promotional packages should be developed. Strict norms for accreditation and regular monitoring should be enforced. Flexibility in operation and salary structure should be allowed.
8. Innovative schemes should be launched that will allow bright

engineering students to undertake R&D even when they are undergoing studies. These projects should be distinctly separate from their regular course work. The scheme should be applicable to engineering personnel in academics, industry and services to allow free flow and development of ideas. This can curtail internal and external brain drain.

9. Certification for workman in the construction industry should be insisted so as to maintain the quality of production. A target bound programme may be set up to have 100 per cent trained and certified workforce. The target date may coincide with the 2004 of WTO.
10. The government, in collaboration with the industry and academic institutions, should project demand and supply of engineering professionals required for 10 years. The same should be monitored regularly.
11. Innovative financing mechanism should be evolved to support manpower development. Successful models of different countries should be studied to evolve a national scheme. A certain amount of contract money should be allocated for workmen training.
12. The government should play facilitating role for promoting academic-industry link-up to facilitate quality engineering education suited to needs of the industry.
13. Professional Bodies like IE(I), IETE, CIDC and others should prepare and provide professional inputs to the government to facilitate manpower development. They should also develop their own programmes of teaching and training that should be implemented through their own centres.
14. The industry should develop in-house training programmes for different levels of technicians and technical personnel.

Conclusion

Globalisation has offered an opportunity for the Indian construction industry to improve its quality of workmenship and performance and thereby compete in the global market to the best of its advantage. The challenge can be met only by educating and training the required manpower of high quality and in requisite numbers. The situation indicates that there is no escape from improving the quality of construction industry manpower to face the future challenges.

14

Globalisation and its Impact on Engineering Innovation

Introduction

Globalisation of Indian economy has been under review ever since the first effort in 1991. There are strong proponents of this concept who believe it will help India get the necessary foreign exchange and earn its position in global economy. An equally strong opposite camp is critical of following this path as globalisation aims at removing subsidies, correcting prices and shifting the balance in favour of large and modern companies. They also believe that such an approach results in loss of employment opportunities. Critics would also give examples to say that globalisation and liberalisation has resulted in destabilising or damaging the R&D base and weakening India's scientific capabilities.

Liberalisation has given rise to new culture which follows a course different from planned economy. The critical difference between planning and liberalisation is that planning assumes that outcomes are predictable, while liberalisation facilitates the unpredictable. It does so by unshackling the energy of innovation of millions of people unknown to planners, of letting them play around with ideas unthought of Such unknown people and ideas have transformed other countries and will also transform India. It enables unknown to do the unthought of and become unstoppable.

Globalisation of Indian economy and its impact on Indian efforts at innovation need a dispassionate study.

Background paper for the 14th Indian Engineering Congress. Theme : "Human Capital Development in Engineering for Global Competitiveness", organised by the Institution of Engineers (India), Delhi State Centre, in New Delhi during 29-31 January, 2000.

Genesis of Globalisation

Globalisation is a phenomenon of atleast over a 1000 years when countries starting trading with each other. The earlier concept of globalisation was restricted to three basic elements:

(i) Physical capital in terms of plant and machinery;
(ii) Labour; and
(iii) Technology.

The concept continued well into 60s when theories in economics got prominence. Whereas the economic theory of Adam Smith continued to rule the world for over a century, it was Samuelson who really made a big difference by his definition of public goods as different from private goods. Subsequently, there have been a number of other elements that affected the international economic movement. New interpretations of globalisation of economy have also emerged. 1960s saw the emergence of information technology and its integration of capital market. This combination brought forth a new process of globalisation. This movement is often termed as financial capital. Thus globalisation starts with the concept of financial capital in terms of capital invested in the capital markets — mainly foreign direct investments in emerging markets. No doubt the other three elements continue to rule the economic sector. The globalisation process of the economy also has meant that with greater number of countries participating in the process, certain regulations are called for.

Major developments started after the World War-II in terms of the General Agreement of Trade and Tariffs known as GATT. This was followed by the Uruguay Round Negotiations of 1980s resulting in setting up of the World Trade Organisation, WTO, in January, 1995. So, today a more closely linked global trade is taking place and also a greater degree of regulation has been effected. Major trends are the lowering of tariff barriers to promote more trade. Further, due to satellite communication, people's aspirations are evolving uniformly throughout the world. Globalisation is also resulting in the development of the global consumer whether it is in terms of dress, music or consumer durables. A certain uniformity in desires is evolving all over the world. *Globalisation leads to closer integration between the economies of different countries and greater standardisation and an increasingly uniform approach in terms of the consumer markets for goods and services. Keeping this in view C.K. Prahlad has suggested evolution of consumer markets for the poor.*

One can also interpret this process of globalisation to have empowered people in the developing countries to take decisions for their consumer behaviour alike that of the developed world. There is possibly an irreversible power shift to the poor in all domains of public life, be it social, political or economic. The economic power shift is more pronounced in the past ten years. The growth economies of the 1990s are no longer the super powers of the past. About 10 years back Kenechi Ohmai, a Japanese Management Expert said that in the existing world economic order, only three countries mattered: US, Japan and Western Europe. The statement proved wrong which proves that as a matter of time the process of power shift is extended to each developing country. The focus now is on doing more with less over the whole product life cycle by minimising waste. Waste and emissions that result from poor environment performance are evidence of business in efficiencies and process failure.

Management Experts have also projected that today's business is characterised by innovation lethargy. *Innovation* is 'radical implementation', 'radical ideas' and 'application of available technology' to meet further needs. It is distinct from incremental improvement, which are reaction to current needs. The automobiles industry is quoted of an example of innovation lethargy. The basic model of automobile still resembles that of Ford Model. As per the records of the Touring Club of Switzerland during the last 25 years, the energy efficiency of the automobile has improved only by 18 per cent. We have seen how Toyota has been able to innovate through lean production and flexible manufacture system to produce 4 million cars with 37,000 employees against General Motors, 850,000 employees for 8 million cars; and bringing down the inventory levels from 2 weeks in General Motors to 2 hours in Toyota. Such quantum leaps could not be achieved in the field of energy efficiency, simply because our mindset are not tuned to its needs. The adverse impact of such major companies under globalisation is that the innovation lethargy is also passed on to their counterpart Indian companies.

Therefore, for most businesses the management should strive for quantum jumps rather than incremental improvement in the performance. There can be examples of a number of companies opposing or resisting new technology innovations. Globalisation is instrumental in moving the lazy so that they become partners in innovation.

Globalisation of Indian economy has resulted in effective competition on the global scale. The technology advancement has been the key element in deciding global mergers. Two important programmes involving technology have been 'Knowledge Management' and 'Environment Management'. Technology plays a big role in all knowledge management programmes but while technology serves as a critical enabler of management practices, it cannot by itself bring about a cultural change in the organisation. With the fast expansion of technologies supporting the implementation of information technology in organisations, knowledge management has come to assume greater significance. Knowledge management can be defined as a systematic way of leveraging information and expertise to improve organisational innovation, responsiveness, productivity and competency. It is the continuous activity involving acquiring, creating, packaging, distributing, applying and maintaining knowledge. The major success factors for critical knowledge management are defined as culture, leadership, incentives, measurements and technology.

Emerging Scene of Indian Economy

Emerging out of planned economy, the Bombay Club, headed by Mr.Rahul Bajaj, shouted hoarse that the ownership of major Indian companies will pass on to MNCs. Look at the market capitalisation at the end of year 1999. It will reflect that dynamic Indian companies are now leading the market. The market capitalisation (the stock market value) of WIPRO (Rs.68,000 crores) and Infosys (Rs.51,000 crores) has overtaken that of the traditional MNC leader Hindustan Lever (Rs.48,000 crores). Other upstarts in the information industry like NIIT (Rs.12,200 crore), Satyam (Rs.6,300 crore) and Pentafour Software (Rs.2,800 crore) have overtaken long-entrenched MNCs in India like ICI (Rs. 1,000 crore), Siemans (Rs.1,400 crore) and Proctor & Gamble (Rs.1,500 crore).

The traditional Indian business class including the Tatas, Birlas and Modis find difficult to fight the MNCs. It is appropriate to question if the traditional Indian business represented the talent. It did, but only a fraction and was lost in outdated business practices. Liberalisation gave a chance to millions of Indian talented, but unknown, people who were earlier kept out of business.

Let's look at the 1991 scenario at the initiation stage of on the era of introduction of economic reforms in India. Nobody in India could have predicted as to who the new giants will in 2000. Narayanmurthy of Infosys was unknown, Chandra was known mainly as the man who ran Essel World for kids near Mumbai; Raju of Satyam was a medium scale businessman going nowhere fast in Andhra Pradesh.

These business stars could see that IT and services were poised to sweep manufacturing into second place. The new business startups represent just the tip of the iceberg, India is full of talent, and thousands of unknowns will one day overhaul Narayanmurthy and Chandra.

Course of Liberalisation of Economy

The process of liberalising central government control over the industrial sector has advanced considerably. Industrial licensing has been eliminated for all but a handful of industries and the list of industries reserved for the public sector has also been sharply reduced. The remaining controls at the central government level need to be reviewed for further liberalisation. Indian industry must be unshackled from unnecessary bureaucratic and government interference. However, the major effort in future has to be to extend liberalisation to the level of state governments. Indian industry still suffers from a plethora of controls and regulations relating to matters in the purview of state government which cumulatively impose a heavy burden of delay and even harassment of our entrepreneurs. A thorough revamp of these controls and the procedures involved at the state government level would help to create a climate in which Indian industry can flourish.

Observations on Recent Growth Patterns (in the Era of Liberalisation)

The general impression is that the rural-urban divide is widening. The observation of the National Sample Survey on household consumer expenditure is an eye opener. There has been a significant decline of 6.7 per cent in rural spending and an accompanying 4.6 per cent increase in urban expenditure during 1991-98. Rural poverty has risen by 3.42 per cent since the beginning of reforms. Urban poverty, however, has declined by just over 1 per cent.

One should not get the wrong signal that the economic reforms have fuelled rural poverty. The 54th round of the NSS (data collected during January - June 1998) estimates an average monthly per capita expenditure of Rs.455. In urban areas, the figure is Rs.684; and in the rural areas it is only Rs.382). In villages, 61 per cent of the expenditure is estimated to be on food; in towns, it is 50 per cent. "The poorer the household, the higher the expenditure on food. It does not reflect intake of improved quality of food but only that the poor is being adversely affected by the rising prices." The share of expense on food has actually fallen. The survey shows that non-food expenditure increased from 35 per cent during 1987-92 to 39 per cent during 1996-98 in rural India, and from 43 to 49 per cent in urban centres.

The Planning Commission had indicated that the 80s recorded a fall in the poverty line by more than 10 per cent, the absolute numbers falling by 50 million. In the reforms period, however, poverty has risen by 130 million, and increase of 9 per cent over 1989-90. Experts point out a paradox: Despite a 5.6 per cent growth in gross domestic product (GDP) between 1990-91 and 1996-97, poverty increased by one per cent a year. In contrast, it fell by 3.1 per cent annually with a lower GDP growth between 1983 and 1990. In 1993-94, GDP grew by 6.9 per cent, yet poverty increased by 2 per cent. He argues, therefore, that reforms have reversed the process of poverty reduction.

But the irony is that poverty increased from 36 per cent in 1993 to 40 per cent in 1998. Yet, according to a survey by the National Council for Applied Economic Research (NCAER), urban income, which was 1.82 times higher than rural in 1975-76, had become 2.1 times more by 1994. Farm sector income declined from 37.9 to 20.5 per cent.

This observation only shows that the money allocated for rural development work has not been appropriately utilised. It is difficult to believe that the funds are not reaching the needy. In certain observations by a number of foreign aid agencies it has been observed that the aid allocations are not fully and effectively utilised because engineering inputs required for poverty alleviation programmes are not fully available in India. Local solutions for problems are desired. These agencies have interacted with leading R&D institutions — but of no avail. Such aid comes only from the government or international agencies and makes it obligatory for donors to approach only the government controlled or approved R&D institutions. Such agencies very often do not have appropriately trained manpower. As the local solutions are not found the possibility of job creation out of such donations is not utilised. Whereas the liberalisation has given higher growth rate of GDP, it has not led to higher employment opportunities.

The outright and gross negligence of the poor in urban and rural areas has kept them out of the market place. They do not get benefit of the liberalised economy and also contribute to growth of globalised Indian economy. The poor thus remain markets excluded. And the government is reducing subsidies and support thereby pushing the poor in deeper poverty trap.

Bring Poor Centre Stage in Market Economy

Dr. C.K. Prahlad, the Management Guru in his address to the CII Economic Summit, in New Delhi on January 10, 2000, has given a message to create a consumer market out of the poor (instead of only focusing on niche market). He called on the Indian CEOs to think out of the box and make more money out of the poor. Dr.Prahland advised that the Indian industry have to use its problems as advantages to build a globally competitive business. The challenge today is to target bottom of the pyramid consumer. He said, "you have to create a consumer market of the bottom layers of the Indian poor. If Indian entrepreneurs do not innovate, MNCs could capture the domestic markets. There is a strong possibility of turning water, food and primary education into a business model." In simple words he advised industry leaders to create avenues for new wealth generation by building consumer markets. comprising the poor. At present the poor are market excluded, because they do not have the purchasing capacity to enter the market. The advice given by Dr.Prahlad is very timely and indicates the urgent need to bring the poor into the 'market economy'. India and for that matter other countries cannot create islands of wealth in the ocean of poverty and still manage to survive successfully.

The first and the foremost important issue for the engineering community is to find options that will bring the poor into Indian market economy. This can be done through providing them better and newer engineering solutions for their problems, training them new technology and creating employment opportunities.

Impact of Globalisation on Innovation

Recent mergers of large industrial houses has been driven by technology advances.

AOL — Time Warner Merger

It is relevant to mention of the merger of America On Line with Time

Warner, the biggest deal of US$ 350 billion on January 10, 2000, in Washington. The new group, to be called AOL-Time Warner is aimed at revolutionising the way the people obtain information and communicate. The group would be the premier global company delivering branded information, entertainment and communication services across rapidly converging media platforms.

In 1923, Henry Luce and Britton Hadden established the news magazine, *Time*. For 50 years *Time* ruled the media world. Then, in the 1970s Luce's successor recognised that as important as print was, there were other media technologies that needed to be explored. Out of this initiative emerged the world's most profitable cable TV channel: Home Box Office (HBO). By the 1980s, HBO was making much more money than *Time* Magazine and *Time* incorporated decided to go the whole hog and to turn itself into a news and entertainment conglomerate by merging with Warner Brothers' who had movie and record interests. In the 1990s, *Time* incorporated recognised that Satellite News Channels now ruled the air waves and acquired CNN and Ted Turner's other interests. Reasoning behind this pattern growth, merger and acquisition was clear. In the media business, content is king but technology is the crown. The Internet is a younger, more informal environment and that dominates all Web based media offerings.

The Hindustan Times, in its Editorial, (dated January 12, 2000) has mentioned that it would be mistake to view the merger of AOL and Time Warner purely on business terms. The message has two unmistakable component. The first is that America's Savviest Media Company has recognised that the Internet is the medium of the millennium. And the second is that "no matter how advanced the technologies available to AOL, the Company nevertheless recognised that without the content of Time Warner, these technologies were media without any message." Time Group has kept pace with technology and remained market leader through mergers. Technology content as a product were both important.

Glaxo — Smithkline Beecham Merger

Another significant merger has been that of Glaxo and Smithkline Beecham announced in London on January 17, 2000. These companies have formed a conglomerate worth US$ 189 billion and a power house of research. They have announced that they would create the biggest Pharmaceutical Research Pool yet seen. They will control 7.5 per cent of global pharmaceutical market. Important aspect of the merger was the company's stress that no major research sites would be closed. This merger has been brought around to bring together the two organisation with complementary technologies and scientific knowledge. The new organisation will undergo rapid scientific and economic change.

This merger has also been enforced by the need of technology development globally competitive product.

The above mentioned mergers are representative of impact of globalisation on technology induced development.

Impact of Globalisation on Indian Scene

Public Funded Research

For the Industrial Sector: Immediately after announcement of economic reforms government took steps to initiate action on matching technology development. The Department of Science and Technology set up a Technology Vision-2020 for a longer term perspective to identify technology mission in different sectors of economy. The Reports was linked to the industry. The Adviser (Incharge) is also allowed to work concurrently with the Confederation of Indian Industries, with a view to transfer the government's intensive efforts to the industry.

In 1997, CSIR developed a Vision for 2001. That presented a plan of action as to how should the public funded R&D Institutions transform themselves. The Vision realised that the public funded research facilities, which were earlier thought to be only for creation of public good, need to be transformed into a system that would support and encourage private and public wealth in the country. At a time when the CSIR Vision 2001 was released the public looked at it with skepticism. With the passage of time the scientists at CSIR have brought around the change in the mindset.

CSIR followed the policy of science research with a new slogan 'Patent, Publish and Prosper'. This policy has now caught on all over CSIR. The Director General, CSIR has given an example of National Chemical Laboratory, NCL, as "A new body, NCL Research Foundation, funded through donations give away Medallions to all US patent holders every year. A healthy competitive spirit has developed, especially between the 'catalysis' and 'polymer' group at NCL. A few specialists were trained in writing patents. It was realised that patent writing is an art where you give away the least amount of information, while at the same time cover the flanks of your work so that others cannot easily by-pass your patents. In the last five years CSIR has filed about 350 international patents and NCL is the leader in US Patent Applications from India." It has been realised that there is a greater emphasis on exploitation of patents and income generated from them and not merely on the number of patents.

CSIR's open approach has helped in globalising Indian R&D. NCL has been often quoted as an example. It has carefully allocated resources between contract research and original work. NCL has been selling the R&D at a price that will be logically accepted by its customers. It has never sold R&D by 'man hours' but only by 'brain hours'. It has added the intellectual capital concept into whole concept of marketing of R&D. A pricing structure has been evolved so that a foreigner pays 5 times for the same R&D as the Indian.

NCL has also realised that the cutting edge work for foreign clients has many intangible benefits. It raised the quality of research of the whole lab. For example, GE ran its prestigious Six Sigma training course for NCL. Several scientists got their training that they would otherwise never have got. Time, quality, price and delivery are now internationally benchmarked.

The global orientation to R&D activities also had its impact on R&D laboratories and academic institutions. According to an internal study by CSIR, even though the number of scientific papers published between 1995 and 1998 remained more or less the same (1,500 — 1,600 every year), the citation index, which shows how many others are quoting one's paper internationally, has gone up by 60 per cent in the same period.

Dr.R.A. Mashelkar, Director General, CSIR is quoted as saying "Globally R&D and innovation have become a high risk game for all high technology corporations. R&D is becoming very expensive and is yielding diminishing results, when carried out under a single roof. On the other hand, without innovation and new technologies, one can lose one's business position very quickly. This dilemma has led to networking, outsourcing, strategic alliance and partnership in R&D. None of the Indian labs is in a position to develop a full-scale globally competitive technology by itself and then license it worldwide. Partnerships, where they assume a junior position initially can help them catch up with the rest of the world. So it is indeed a win win situation."

The fact that CSIR laid down the targets for 2001, shows confidence and conviction of scientists in CSIR in moving forward in a planned fashion. The assessments made in March 1999 have shown major breakthroughs in achieving targets and hopefully CSIR will be able to achieve their targets in a planned fashion. That has become a major achievement in science and technology management.

For the Agriculture Sector: It is not that the industrial research alone has been guided and funded so as to support research for creation of public goods. The achievements in agriculture are also reported on the same fashion. Dr. M.S. Swaminathan, the former Director General of Indian Council of Agriculture Research, while delivering the 31st Jawaharlal Nehru Memorial Lecture on 13 November, 1999 said, "the first Green Revolution was brought around in India through public funded research, aimed at improving the public goods like, water and electricity. The second Green Revolution will be brought around by providing public fund support to research that will be privately controlled and that will really be in terms of improving and maintaining the genetic improvements leading to higher production." Dr. Swaminathan said, "Our experience in agriculture has shown that synergy among science, public policy and social mobilisation can help us to leapfrog in accomplishments. I believe that unless we make rapid progress in both human development and gender equity, we will not be able to harness the fruits of both traditional wisdom and frontier science for building a sustainable food security system in the country during the 21st Century. Agriculture in the new century will be knowledge intensive and will be based on ecotechnologies which are not only environment friendly and economically viable but are also socially equitable both in gender and economic terms. Unless agriculture becomes both economically rewarding and intellectually satisfying, it will not be possible to attract and retain youth in farming professions in the years ahead."

It should be noted that the future growth in industry as well as agriculture will have to be "economically and intellectually" rewarding in a similar fashion. Public funding is desirable to facilitate larger generation of public and private goods and wealth.

Private Sector Funded R&D

Three examples are worth quoting where technology innovations have taken place in three different kinds of companies. The first one belongs to a large industry sector in manufacturing; the second to a medium industry sector in manufacturing and the third is a service sector industry. These companies were all given the National Golden Peacock Innovative Production/Service Award by the World Quality Council at its 10th Annual Convention at Bombay on January 17, 2000.

The first of these is the eco-friendly 4R 1040 diesel engine produced by Kirlosker Oil Engine Ltd., Pune. The engine has been indigenously developed. It conforms to European COM Stage-1 and US Tier-1 for exhaust emission norms as applicable to off-highway and industrial applications. The turbo charged engine meets European COM Stage-2 and US Tier-2 standards. The engine is fuel efficient with low emission values of Nox, HC, CO and particulate matter. It satisfies the norms for working in Europe until 2004.

The second example is of Usha Sriram Brita Pvt. Ltd. It has developed a UV based water purifier 70 per cent of water resources in India are contaminated, and 80 per cent of the population is inflicted by water borne diseases. The impurities are suspended particles, dissolved harder chemicals and microbiological matter. These cannot be easily removed by normal water purification methods. The innovation in the product emanated from the market research, which revealed that Indian household, have problem with hygiene and water quality. This has resulted in purifying water up to 99.9 per cent. The purified water has shelf life of 48 hrs. It does not need continuous water supply and does not need electricity. The water guard provides pure water at 27 paise per liter as against Rs.10-15 for a bottle of mineral water. The product is meeting the needs even of the poor.

The third example is of Satyam Computer Services Ltd. that has developed a multi-party teleconferencing service. The service has been developed solely for the use of the associates of Satyam Computers. This service is available at Hyderabad, Bangalore, Chennai, Pune, Bhubaneshwar, Japan, USA and UK. The main purpose of this service is to increase the effectiveness of the associates by avoiding or reducing travel time and making available the people and the information together on real time basis. The teleconference is established for 3 hours for which the company spends only Rs. 3200. Through this facility, geographically dispersed locations are benefited from real time communication. Participants from more than two locations can work together on the same conference.

Above are few examples of how the Indian industries and the R&D laboratories have geared up themselves to face the challenge of globalisatioin and liberalisation.

Emerging Characteristics of Indian Companies

Thus, it will be noticed that there has been a shift away from the traditional way of doing business and traditional way of learning. But, it does not mean that loss of traditional instincts and methodologies did not give rise to new approaches and new sectors. Following may be noted:

(i) Quality production conforming to ISO 9000 specifications was considered a major achievement in the beginning of the decade of the 90s. Even large public sector and private sector industries use to widely publicise their allotment of ISO 9000 certification. By year 2000, ISO 9000 certification has become a matter of routine and every industry tries to have this certificate.

(ii) Environmental consideration brought in environmentally sound concepts and compliance to ISO 14000. Industries are now opting for ISO 14000 in large numbers.

(iii) Information technology interventions are controlling and directing operations of all the major industries in the world and that is equally applicable to India. Traditional industries that were the leaders in the market place are losing their position and the small and medium companies with larger IT interventions are taking over.

(iv) E-Commerce and related service industries are gaining importance and most of the younger generation of engineering and management graduates are venturing into up-start companies.

(v) Entry of foreign and multi-national companies with latest technologies and processes provide a better salary option for jobs other than in R&D, and thereby stop migration of engineering personnel to other sectors.

(vi) Competition from foreign companies has improved skills in new and emerging Indian companies. They have opted for modern management practices and technology interventions governed by market forces.

Shift of Manpower in Innovative Technology

It is quite clear from the examples quoted above that the two major transformations have taken place as follows:

(i) Shift to qualitative R&D output and substantial improvement in product oriented R&D. Global acceptability of the Indian research work for its content and quality.

(ii) Realisation by entrepreneurs that exploitation of patents to create wealth was as important as doing R&D for attaining a patent.

These two changes have a fundamental impact on intake of students in higher research fields. Lesser numbers opted for Post-Graduate Courses in research work in engineering and science and a larger number of them diverted to either the management sector or else became up-start entrepreneurs. Liberalisation provided opportunities for new and unknown persons to show their talent and earn their position in the society.

Trends in Manpower Development in R&D Sector in India

R&D Statistics (1996-97) of the Department of Science and Technology has reflected the estimated stock of S&T personnel for 1991 and 1996. Table 14.1 indicates that the growth rate of 8.1 per cent in diploma holders in engineering was second to nursing graduates. The stock of engineering degree and diploma holders are estimated at 0.73 million and 1.2 million respectively, in 1996.

Table14.1: Estimated Stock of S&T Personnel in 1991 and 1996

Field	*Stock of S&T Personnel*		*Annual rate of growth per cent*
	1991	1996	
Engineering Degree Holders	546.7	726.9	5.9
Engineering Diploma Holders	873.9	1196.4	6.5
Medical Graduates	310.3	358.4	2.9
Agricultural Graduates	168.4	202.3	3.7
Veterinary Graduates	34.4	40.2	3.2
Science Graduates	2430.3	3154.8	5.4
Science Post-Graduates	482.0	626.1	5.4
Nursing Graduates	5.7	8.4	8.1
Total	4851.7	6313.5	6.0

Source: Research and Development Statistics, 1996-97, Department of Science and Technology, June 1999.

The data on the S&T personnel borne on the Live Register of Employment Exchanges gives some indication on the unemployment status of S&T personnel though the data reported do not refer to the actual number of unemployed. Table 14.2 indicates that this number was 1.9 lakhs in 1971, and 5.2 lakhs in 1981. The same has more than doubled to reach a figure of 14.6 lakhs in 1995.

Table 14.2: Break-Up of S&T Personnel Borne on the Live Register of Employment Exchange, 1995

Discipline	*Number on live Register*	*Percentage*
Science Graduates	704.1	48.1
Diploma holders in Engineers	421.0	28.8
Science Post-graduates	97.7	6.7
Engineering Graduates/PG	168.1	11.5
Medical Graduates	28.2	1.9
Agricultural Graduates	31.3	2.1
Others (Veterinary Graduates/PG Medical and Agricultural PG)	12.6	0.9
Total	1463.0	100.0

Source: Research and Development Statistics, 1996-97, Department of Science and Technology, June 1999.

Table 14.3 indicates that as on 1st April 1996, 3,35,072 personnel were employed in research and development establishments. Out of these, 38 per cent were primarily engaged in R&D activities. 32.5 per cent were performing auxiliary (technical supporting) activities and 29.5 per cent were providing administrative or non-technical support.

Table 14.3: Percentage Distribution of Personnel by Type of Employer/Activity as on 1-4-1996

Activity/Employer	*Percentage of Personnel employed*			
	R&D	*Auxiliary*	*Administrative*	*Total*
Institutional Sector	38	29	33	100
Industrial Sector	38	42	21	100

Source: Research and Development Statistics, 1996-97, Department of Science and Technology, June 1999.

Table 14.4 indicates that the Central Government continued to shoulder a major share of national R&D expenditure which was 69.8 per cent during 1996-97. In absolute terms, Central Government incurred Rs.5817.76 crores on R&D during 1996-97. Annual rate of growth for R&D expenditure at current prices for 1996-97 over the previous year was 11.9 per cent. The same in constant prices (Base 1993-94) was 3.6 per cent.

Table 14.4: Rate of Growth in percentage (Over the previous year)

Year	*Rate of growth in percentage (Over the previous year)*	
	At current prices	*At constant prices (Base 1980-81)*
1981-82	24.4	12.8
1982-83	26.3	16.9
1983-84	15.5	6.5
1984-85	35.0	25.7
1985-86	16.3	7.9
1986-87	19.7	12.0
1987-88	19.2	9.6
1988-89	13.4	4.9
1989-90	9.7	1.3
1990-91	4.2	(–) 6.0
1991-92	13.4	(–) 1.2
1992-93	5.7	(–) 2.6
1993-94	23.6	12.7
1994-95	4.0	(–) 5.2
1995-96	10.4	1.6
1996-97	11.9	3.6

Source: Research and Development Statistics, 1996-97, Department of Science and Technology, June 1999

Field of specialisation and qualification were reported only for about 0.28 lakh R&D personnel engaged primarily in R&D activities of institutional sector of Central Government. By field specialisation, Engineers (which include technologies) shared 51.8 per cent followed by Natural Scientists 33.0 per cent, Agricultural Scientists 9.3 per cent, Medical Personnel 3.2 per cent and Social Scientists 2.7 per cent. By level of qualification, they were comprised of 21.2 per cent of Ph.Ds, 37.2 per cent of Post Graduates and 13.8 of Diploma Holders and "other" qualifications.

It may be seen that Engineers and Natural Scientists dominate among the R&D personnel of institutional sector of Federal Government. The analysis of their educational qualifications are given in Table 14.5 reveals that more than half (59.8 per cent) of Engineers had graduate, diploma and "other" qualifications whereas 79.2 per cent of Natural Scientists had post graduate and above qualification.

Table 14.5: Percentage Distribution of Engineers and Natural Scientists in R&D by Level of Qualification in Central Sector R&D Institutions as on 1-4-1996

Qualification	*Percentage*	
	Engineers	*Natural Scientists*
Ph.D.	6.3	37.4
Post Graduate	33.9	41.8
Graduate	39.5	15.2
Diploma and Other	20.3	5.6
Total	100.0	100.0

Source: Research and Development Statistics, 1996-97. Department of Science and Technology, June 1999.

It may be seen from Table 14.6 that the field of science of Engineering and Technology dominate over all other fields of science in industrial sector as a whole as well as in the public and private sector separately accounted for 58.2 per cent, 79.2 per cent and 50.5 per cent respectively. Next to this comes natural sciences which accounted for 29.4 per cent, 13.8 per cent and 35.1 per cent respectively. It may be appropriate to conclude from the above analysis that R&D in industrial sector was more stressed towards applied sciences.

Table 14.6: Distribution of R&D Personnel in the Industrial Sector by Field of Science

Field of Science	*Public Sector*	*Private Sector*	*Industrial Sector*
Natural Sciences	945	6543	7488
Agricultural Sciences	35	726	761
Engineering & Technology	5417	9413	14830
Medical Sciences	113	1082	1195
Social Sciences	329	885	1214
Total	6839	18649	25488

Source: Research and Development Statistics. 1996-97. Department of Science and Technology. June 1999

It may be seen from Table 14.7 that out of 25,488 R&D personnel employed in industrial sector whose level of qualifications were known. 9.8 per cent were doctorates, 26.7 per cent were Post Graduates, 38.2 per cent were Graduates and 25.3 per cent were having Diploma or other qualifications and combined disciplines of natural, agricultural, medical, social sciences and engineering. The proportion of Ph.Ds and Post Graduates were more in private sector when compared to public sector.

Table 14.7: Qualification Mix of R&D Personnel in the Industrial Sector

Sector	*Qualification*				
	Ph.D.	*Post Graduate*	*Graduate*	*Diploma & Others*	*Total*
Public sector	576	1805	2742	1716	6839
Private Sector	1913	4991	7004	4741	18649
Industrial Sector	2489	6796	9746	6457	25488

Source: Research and Development Statistics, 1996-97, Department of Science and Technology, June 1999.

Table 14.8 indicates that based on the core databases in various areas of science and technology during 1989 to 1998 India's contribution to world publications was of the order of 2 per cent.

Table 14.8: Subject Area-Wise Number of Papers Published from India and World During 1989 to 1998

Subject	*Number of Papers from*		*India's Contribution to World Papers (Percentage)*
	India	*World*	
Agriculture	109093	1503061	7.2
Biological Sciences	89574	5329314	1.7
Chemical Sciences	1263499	6010154	2.1
Earth Sciences	11239	561318	2.0
Engineering	36027	1870103	1.9
Mathematics	15906	849692	1.9
Medical Sciences	43758	3657821	1.2
Physical Sciences	54836	2785116	2.0
Total	486782	22566579	2.2

Source: Research and Development Statistics, 1996-97, Department of Science and Technology, June 1999.

Table 14.9: Applications for Patents from Persons in India and Abroad

	1985-86	*1990-91*	*1991-92*	*1992-93*	*1993-94*	*1994-95*	*1995-96*	*1996-97*
India	999	1180	1293	1228	1266	1741	1606	1661
Foreigners Resident in India	--	1	--	--	--	--	--	--
Foreigners Resident abroad	2527	2583	2259	2239	2603	3589	5430	6901
Total	3526	3764	3552	3467	3869	5330	7036	8562

Source: Research and Development Statistics, 1996-97. Department of Science and Technology. June 1999

It is interesting to note that applications for patents from persons in India grew gradually from 1293 in 1991-92 to 1661 in 1996-97. This reflects thrust on applied R&D.

Status of Engineering Education

It has been observed that the higher education system has not been able to cope with the changing economic scenario. Education is not a static phenomena, it is an organise entity that recognised the changes in the environment, response to new demands and keeps growing with the society of which it is a part. The advance countries have responded adequately to the growing demands and new challenges; their education system has incorporated such changes, effected such improvements, made such departures and brought about such reforms as to serve the emerging requirements of a competitive world. The engineering education system has not incorporated the concept that progress depends on innovation and its application. Services and contribution of persons with expertise and exposure to developments in the field are needed in any area of activity. The education system is not open to changes at a pace that was called for by the economic reforms. The control of the UGC and AICTE leaves no possibility of a quick and responsive transformed education system which could really respond to the changing environment. The economic development is now a mere development in the economy but it also includes related social development, political development and economic development. The engineering education system has to respond and be responsive to the changing international needs and not live in isolation.

Way Forward

Market forces are to decide the future course of action. Market capitalisation of industries is a good indicator of the sectors that have largest appeal. IT sector dominates in every form. The Survey of Indian Economy conducted by the Confederation of Indian Industries (as reported on January 14, 2000) indicates that IT, cement, steel and automobile sectors are on the growth path, as reflected in the performance statistics for April – November 1999. TVs, refrigerators and other consumer durable have also shown remarkable growth. This indicates that construction industry – activities relating to housing and infrastructure – is growing and will continue to grow. That will also support the transport sector and ultimately larger surplus money supply to employees and entrepreneurs will mean growth of consumer goods sector.

However, a negative growth in capital goods sector — especially textiles and electrical machinery – has been reported. This is a serious concern and leads one to believe that the growth may not be sustainable.

Recovery of economy points out that in future engineering manpower requirement with proficiency in basic engineering faculties will also grow substantially. Therefore, the engineering education and training institutions will have to take this into account. A sustained growth can be ensured only by continuous facilitation of industry-institution linkage and interaction. The government can play its role in maintaining this facilitation.

Higher allocation of funds for R&D, from both the public as well as private sources is a must for India to take maximum advantage out of globalisation and liberalisation.

Following measures have been identified to strengthen India's engineering capabilities to sharpen India's Global Competitiveness:

(i) Globalisation has thrust the challenge on India to produce goods and services of international quality at a price lower than other countries. The process of market economy, developed in USA in 200 years, has to be put in place in a short period. This goal can only be achieved by acquiring and developing the best possible technology.

(ii) Globalisation has focused on modern engineering specialities that are characterised by concept of systems engineering.

(iii) Globalisation on calls for producing engineering manpower with knowledge of latest international engineering developments and opportunities. Formal, non-formal and distance teaching modes should be utilised. The laboratory work during teaching and industrial training, on completion of the syllabus, need to be emphasised in the curriculum.

(iv) Skills building training and retaining programmes needs to be introduced at all levels, especially at the technician level.

(v) Engineering manpower demand should be studied for at least 10 years, and developed as a rolling projection to be updated every year. This projection should be developed by a professional organisation like the Institution of Engineers.

(vi) Future areas for engineering manpower development should be clearly identified.

REFERENCES

CEO of CSIR Inc., *Business India*, New Delhi, June 28-July 11, 1999.

Corporates Get New Management Mantra, *The Times of India*, New Delhi, January 12, 2000.

CSIR, *Annual Report* 1996-97, New Delhi, 1997.

CSIR, *Annual Report* 1997-98, New Delhi, 1998.

Data on Post Graduate Enrolment, I.I.T, Delhi, January 2000.

Kulandiswamy, Dr. V.C., Higher Education in India – A System that Resists Change, Technorama (IEI), Calcutta, December, 1999.

Media and the Message (Editorial), *The Hindustan Times*, New Delhi, January 12, 2000.

Murty, M.N., *Environment and Trade: Developing Countries' Perspective and Indian Experience*, World Congress on Environment Management, World Environment Foundation, New Delhi, June 4-6, 1999.

National Peacock Quality Awards, World Quality Council, New Delhi, January 2000.

Ninth Five Year Plan (1997-2002), Planning Commission, Government of India, New Delhi, 1999.

Pearce, Robert D., *Globalising Research and Development*, University of Reading European and International Studies, Reading (U.K.), 1992.

Research and Development Statistics (1996-97), Department of Science and Technology, Government of India, New Delhi, June 1999.

Srinivasan, K.V., *Renewable Energy Sources*, Technology Development and Transfer, Paper at the ESCAP Expert Consultation, Bangkok, September 1999.

Subramanian, K., Leveraging Information Expertise, *The Hindu*, New Delhi, January 12, 2000.

Survey of Indian Economy, Confederation of Indian Industries, New Delhi, January 2000.

Swaminathan, Dr. M.S., *Science and Sustainable Food Security*, 31st Jawaharlal Nehru Memorial Lecture, New Delhi: 13th November 1999.

Thapar, Vishal – Reality Check: Poverty is Up, *The Hindustan Times*, New Delhi, January 16, 2000.

Vittal, N., *Challenges for Sustainable Development in a Globalised Economy*, World Congress on Environment Management, World Environment Foundation, New Delhi, June 4-6, 1999.

15

Quality and Value Engineering

This evening will be memorable in the history of the Delhi State Centre as it will be getting ISO 9001-2000 Certificate from the Hon'ble Minister of Power, Shri Suresh Prabhu. It is a matter of pride that this recognition comes in the Platinum Jubilee Year of the Centre. Probably the Delhi State Centre is the first Centre of any engineering professional institution in the country to have qualified for ISO 9001-2000 Certification. We hope that quality will be integrated into our centre's work culture.

There is a general curiosity as to why we opted for such a certification, when no other institution considered it necessary. I have pleasure in giving our explanation for the same. The Institution of Engineers (India) is the largest body of professional engineers with a total membership of over 4 lakh. Our product and services are: a sound examination system which helps in upgradation of skills and knowledge: library and referral services and conferencing opportunities for exchange of views and sharpening of skills. In all these sectors, the members have desired that the service they receive from the Institution should be of the top most quality, delivered in the least possible time and in the most cost effective manner. The Centre having a history of over 75 years (the parent body having been set up in 1920) the Delhi State Centre set up in 1927 have a long history of procedures, processes and systems. These are built on traditions and value system cherished by senior engineers during these 75 years. This is also reflected in terms of the age group of the Council Member of the parent body, which will average over 65. Their rich experience has helped in maturity of thought, well considered opinion and gradual and continual growth of the Institution. The last decade of the second millennium has changed

---

Welcome Address at the Quality Certificate Handing Over Ceremony organised by the Institute of Directors on March 22, 2002 at New Delhi.

the overall thinking and the members, old and new alike, expect that the product and services from the Delhi State Centre should be in keeping with the global competitive scenario.

The State Centre Committee therefore decided that create a system whereby this improvement is irreversible — rather continues to build on with the passage of time. Accordingly it was decided that the Delhi State Centre should opt for ISO 9001-2000 Certification.

The Finance Minister in his Budget Speech for 2002-03, said "provision of efficient and world class infrastructure is critical for our growth aspiration. A key issue that bears repetition is the imposition of appropriate user charges necessary to provide adequate returns on investments.

Efforts that have been made to attract private sector investment in the infrastructure sector to supplement public investment. The flow of investment has, however, been slow except in the telecom sector.

At the international level, a major conference on Financing for Development started at Monterry, Mexico on March 18, 2002 and will conclude later today to consider the next step forward after the Millennium Declaration and Doha Declaration for International Cooperation on Economic Progress, Development and Poverty Reduction. On the penultimate day, no consensus could be arrived on creation of a global fund or for larger aid and financial allocations for development in developing countries. The globalisation process introduced with great fanfare after the fall of the Berlin Wall in 1989 has been found to be not the ultimate solution for all developing countries. Under these circumstances, infrastructure creation remains the responsibility of individual countries mainly through their own capital markets and efficient and quality systems and processes.

As engineers play an important role in infrastructure creation, a discussion on improving quality infrastructure becomes relevant. Our effort this evening will lead to promotion of quality based value system in our operations.

16

Engineers and Food Security

This is probably the first occasion that a meeting is being organised by IE(I) in collaboration with the Food and Agriculture Organisation of the United Nations and on the topic that concerns every person on this earth for his own existence and that to support those who are deprived of basic minimum nutrition standards and face malnutrition and in certain cases hunger. FAO celebrates the World Food Day every year on the occasion of its Foundation Day, October 16. This year they have realised the interrelationship between hunger and poverty is intense. And, this relationship is two-way. If we fight hunger, we can reduce poverty. Normally the impression was that if you fight poverty then only we can reduce hunger. Accordingly the theme for this year is "Fight Hunger to Reduce Poverty" which underscores the need to re-focus attention on hunger. FAO asserts that fighting hunger must be the first step to reducing poverty. People are the engine of a nation's growth and food is their fuel. Engineers are the best delivery mechanism.

The Institution of Engineers (India) under its code of ethics has very clearly mentions the engineers' role in providing service to the mankind. The Institution has 15 engineering disciplines — including agriculture engineering — in its programme. It has three forums, viz., Water Management Forum; Rural Development Forum and Sustainable Development Forum. All the three have a direct role in fighting hunger and poverty. All the three Forum have been chaired by very eminent engineers.

Our country is passing through a peculiar situation of plentiful availability of food with overflowing stocks at Food Corporation of India under Public Distribution System and still one-third of the

---

Welcome Address at Panel Discussion on Engineers and Food Security organised by IEI and FAO on October 1, 2001 at New Delhi.

population is below poverty line and malnourished. Under this situation it becomes all the more important for all the communities in the country to come forward and provide support.

Our heads hang in shame when we read the news items in leading newspapers — children sold in the face of hunger situation. There is no way this situation can be allowed to persist. It is not only the government's responsibility but of all of us to see what we can do.

The fight against poverty cannot be won without eliminating hunger: it is the most critical manifestation of poverty. Hunger causes illness and death, robs people of their potential to work and cripples children's learning capacity. It traps individuals in a vicious cycle of poor health that is passed on from one generation to the next. Above all, it is a violation of fundamental human rights.

Unfortunately, most poverty reduction strategies fail to target hunger specifically. Policy-makers long assumed that if income levels rose and economies grew, the benefits would trickle down to the hungry. But malnutrition is both a cause and an effect of poverty.

Individuals suffering from hunger are caught in a trap of endless poverty and powerlessness. The damage caused by chronic under-nourishment begins early and follows people throughout life. A physically and mentally weak generation is doomed to pass the cycle of deprivation on to the next.

This is not to suggest that the importance of fighting hunger rests purely on economic grounds. The principle reason is a moral one: Every person on the globe has the fundamental human right to have enough to eat. In India, right to food is not a fundamental human right. This is recognised under international law. The covenant stresses the importance of creating an environment in which individuals can buy or produce food for themselves. But when they cannot, the State has a legal and moral responsibility to help them, with support from the international community, if necessary.

FAO therefore advocates a twin-track approach to fighting hunger, encompassing both short-term and long-term measures. Hungry people cannot wait for benefits of improved infrastructure, a more equitable distribution of resources, access to land and credit, and other elements of macro economic policy.

For them urgent help in the form of safety nets is essential, including school feeding programmes, supplementary food for pregnant and breast feeding women, emergency food aid and programmes that help people to become self-sufficient, such as employment or credit schemes. When well designed and targeted, these programmes not only meet immediate food needs but also put in place essential elements for future development, such as irrigation schemes and tree plantation.

Most of the work done by genetic scientists and support services have carried the message to improve food production at appropriate levels. What is now required is improving interventions that take care of the micro and local level foods that can bring in quick solutions to fast changing situation. Our horticulture produce is wasted up to 50 per cent and the remaining is sold at a lower price in the market for its perishable nature and local non-availability of right price. On the other hand, the input supply is not efficiently utilised for lack of efficient equipment and procedures. Now if the engineers are given the rightful place, they can do a lot to improve the situation and contribute in removing hunger and malnutrition, both under short-term measures and under long term measures. I am not going into details as we will hear these from our learned speaker.

It is in this context that I took the liberty of suggesting to the Chairman of the National World Food Day Committee (under the Ministry of Agriculture and Cooperation, at its second meeting) that IE(I) should organise such panel discussion and emphasise the role that the engineers can do in removing poverty and hunger. Duly supported by FAO, the idea was accepted by the committee and the Chairman gave us approval to discuss and suggest the measures for consideration of the government. We are glad that we are able to coordinate and organise this meeting at such a short notice.

17

Corporate Governance and National Resurgence

In its Platinum Jubilee Year, the Institution of Engineers (India) has the privilege to host jointly, with the Institute of Directors, the launch of the North India Chapter of the Institute of Directors and the Symposium on Corporate Governance and National Resurgence. Our joint meetings have enlarged the scope of coverage of field of activities. It is most appropriate that the North India Chapter of IOD is launched at the Institution premises as engineers have the main responsibility of implementation of economic development. Along with it the programme for Partnership for Sustainability is being launched today.

We are proud that the Guest of Honour Lord Swraj Paul is a Mechanical Engineer; the Chairman of IOD, North India Chapter Shri V. Suresh is also a Civil Engineer and the recipient of the Award for Excellence Corporate Governance, Shri Subir Raha is also an engineer.

Dr. Madhav Mehra is the distinguished President of the World Council of Corporate Governance, UK is the moving force behind the movement for good governance. Institute of Directors and the Centre for Corporate Governance are both his brain child. Dr. Mehra has not only advised in India, but also in many of the other emerging economies of Central Asian Developing Countries. Dr. Mehra advocates that interlinking corporate governance with environment and quality has to be the first step, and that should lead to sustainability. As this interlinkage is important, sustainable partnerships have to be created. Today's programme reflects partnership amongst IEI, IOD, CFCG and WEF. Other partners need to be identified and their joint effort needs to be reflected. IOD, therefore, launches its new initiative PIAC, the acronym for.

Welcome Address at the Symposium on Corporate Governance and National Resurgence organised by IEI, IOD, CFCG and WEF on April 2, 2002 at New Delhi.

Today's discussion on Corporate Governance and National Resurgence might appear to have nothing to do with the professional institutions of engineers like ours, that is not true. The Institution of Engineers (India) was established in 1920, when the role of engineers was found critical in national resurgence. The Industrial Commission, identified in 1916, to educate and train engineers. That followed the setting up of IE(I) on the pattern of the Institution of Civil Engineers, UK the Institution now has 400,000 members, making it the largest professional institution. Ever since its inception our members have played their role in national resurgence through service in governments/ corporates of social sectors.

The Constitution Reforms Committee, under the Chairmanship of Justice M. N. Venkatchaliah considered the three pillars of governance for development as — the Government, the Corporates and the Civil Society. Role of each one of them is considered equally important. Presence of Lord Swraj Paul is symbolic of the role of engineers in private sector and that of Mr. Suresh in the public sector. Engineers have recently proved to be all pervasive and have found themselves prominently in political as well as administration policy making seats. Some of the successful Ministers and Chief Ministers as well as the bureaucrats have engineering background.

The fall of the Berlin Wall in 1989 also led to emergence of the era of globalisation for the developing countries.

Even in developing countries with great appreciation for advancement through economic gains through the market based globalisation, economic measures were slow to catch on and difficult to replace the government supported and administered institutions of development. By the mid-1990s concern was effectively raised by the Civil Society groups worldwide and rudely shook the established multilateral and commercial financial institutions and forced all of them to have a re-look at the prophecy of market based globalisation. The Millennium Report (in 2000) of the Secretary General of U.N. clearly brought out the fact that globalisation is not a panacea. The Report said, "The crux of today's problem, where globalisation has to support build-up of economies of a large number of independent developing countries, is that while the post-war multilateral system made it possible for the globalisation to emerge and flourish, in turn, it has progressively rendered its designs antiquated. Our post war institutions were built for an international world, but we now live in a global world. Responding effectively to this shift is a core institutional challenge for world leaders today."

The International Conference on Funding for Development held at Monterrey, Mexico during March 18-22, 2002 clearly brought out that the process of globalisation has not attracted sufficient funding in keeping with the spirit of development in various countries. This has serious repercussions. Establishment and growth of corporates and of civil society has to be duly recognised and the role of the professionals like us has to be properly defined.

Rise of Corporates and Corporate Governance has always been a matter of concern as evident from the statement of the Past President of USA, Abraham Lincoln on November 21, 1864. He said, " I see in the near future a crisis approaching that unnerves and causes to tremble me for the safety of my country ..... corporations have been enthroned and an era of corruption in high places will follow, and the money power of the country will endeavour to prolong its reign by working upon the prejudices of the people until all wealth is aggregated in a few hands and the Republic is destroyed."

138 years later the developing countries, now with their emerging corporates in the administered markets (under globalisation), fear the same. The weak and developing capital markets, corporate operations without appropriate regulations in place and non-existent training facilities for skills building for various corporate stakeholders have forced the policy makers and institutions worldwide to consider a dynamic and living mechanism of structures and institutions to function in a responsive manner. If this process is unavoidable then the professional institutions have to play an important role for establishing good corporate governance for national resurgence.

I would like to specifically mention the role of professional engineering institutions as follows:

(i) First and foremost, they promote the advancement of their profession.
(ii) They protect the professional interest of their members and their acceptability in the society.

It is the second element that is important.

The emerging global economy, information, needs involvement of professional engineers on an ever increasing level. The recent setting up of the Engineering Council of India is a collective move of professional institutions that sends out a strong signal that with the maturity of professional institutions they are able to coordinate and evolve a mechanism of mutual interest. When all codes, practices and institutional arrangements are in place the ECI will certainly be able to play an important role with regard to development of corporates on professional lines and with the aim to achieving economic and social responsibility.

It is but natural that IEI should network with IOD and CFCG to arrive at better understanding on the role of corporates in national resurgence. Bharat Ratna, Sir Visvesvaraya, laid the foundation of national resurgence at the beginning of the last century, and today under his shadow we discuss strategy for national resurgence in the coming century.

I am privileged to welcome the Guest of Honour, Lord Swraj Paul, the Lord of Marleybone and an active member of the House of Lords, Britain. Lord Swraj Paul went to England in 1966 to seek medical aid for his ailing daughter. He founded Caparo, a Steel based engineering products company, employing over 3000 people in four countries. He was awarded the Padma Bhushan by the Government of India in 1983 and Granted Freedom of the City of London Award in 1988. He was conferred the Lordship in 1996. Lord Paul loves to describe himself as 100 per cent Indian and 100 per cent British. He did his graduation from the Punjab University and got his Master's Degree in Mechanical Engineering from the Massachusetts Institute of Technology.

His engineering background made him an ideal choice to be the Chairman of the World Council of Corporate Governance.

In an interview with *The Times of India*, Lord Paul described three lessons he learnt in his life and can be the guiding beacons for others as: First his father's discipline taught him never to shirk work, second his days at MIT taught him always to aspire and third that Indira Gandhi taught him never to abandon hope. Lord Swraj Paul, a visionary, has taken keen interest in improving the quality and status of higher education in UK, and has donated large funds. We were keen to have him to visit the Institution during our Platinum Jubilee year and receive his advice on how the Institution of Engineers can contribute more effectively in the globally competitive scenario. His presence is a matter of pride for all of us.

Mr. Vinod Dhall, Secretary Company Affairs, Government of India has the responsibility for establishing norms and guidelines for good corporate governance.

Dr. Sanjeev Reddy, the Director, Indian Institute of Public

Administration and the Vice-Chairman of the Centre for Corporate Governance has conceptualised the first centre for Corporate Governance in the country. Dr. Reddy has been closely associated with the activities of the Institution.

Mr. Ashok Kapur, is the Principal Secretary, Government of West Bengal and Secretary General of IOD. His insight into role of state level governance will be of immense value to the discussion.

Mr. Suresh, Chairman and Managing Director of the Housing and Urban Development Corporation will be taking over as the Chairman of the North India Chapter of the Institute of Directors. Mr. Suresh is an eminent engineer and Fellow of the Institution and heads the major habitat funding arm of the government.

18

Accreditation for Quality Engineering Education

The Institution of Engineers (India) is the largest body of professional engineers with a total membership of over 4 lakh. Our product and services are: a sound examination system which helps in upgradation of skills and knowledge; library and referral services and conferencing opportunities for exchange of views and sharpening of skills.

The aspect of quality is respected in the Institution. As you are aware the Institution was the first body set up to provide technical education through informal education system that now provides technical education round the country to improve qualification. More than 50,000 students appear every year. The quality of the education imparted by us is reflected in the fact that AMIE forms the 4th largest group that has provided successful candidates in the UPSC examinations for the year 1999. Such a large number coming out of AMIE education is a success story in itself. It does not stop here. Mr. Sanjiv Goel who stood first in the IES examination in 1999 was an AMIE. We are proud of the performance of the AMIE students and the quality of education imparted to them.

In all these sectors, the members have desired that the service they receive from the Institution should be of the top most quality, delivered in the least possible time and in the most cost effective manner. The Centre having a history of over 75 years (the parent body having been set up in 1920) the Delhi State Centre set up in 1927 have a long history of procedures, processes and systems. These are built on traditions and value system cherished by senior engineers during these 75 years. Respecting the demand of our members the Institution decided, in its Platinum Jubilee Year, to work for acquiring ISO 9000:2000

Welcome Address at Orientation Course for Accreditation of Engineering Institutions and Courses organised by the National Board of Accreditation on April 5, 2002 at New Delhi.

certification for establishing Quality Management Systems in our operations. Having been granted in January 2000, the Certificate was handed over to us by NQA-QSR on March 22, 2002. In the spirit of this qualification we aspire for better customer satisfaction; customer communication; transparency and continual improvement.

The Institution has a very important reason to be associated with the Quality Day. Everyone may not be aware that in 1917, the Government of India decided that the Institution, then under formation (established in 1920), should take the responsibility of Indian Committee of British Standards Institution (then known as British Engineering Standards Association). The Institution subsequently became the Indian National Committee of International Electrotechnical Commission, 1923.

Setting-up of a National Standards Organisation received attention at the Imperial Conference held in London in 1930; the Industries Conference in Bombay in 1940; the Industrial Research Planning Committee of the Council of Scientific and Industrial Research in 1944, etc. These developments promoted the Council of the Institution to appoint the Indian Standards Institution (ISI) Committee in 1945. The report was submitted in the same year and the formation of the ISI was approved by the Government in 1946. After the inaugural meeting of General Council of the ISI in 1947, responsibilities of the Institution were transferred to the ISI.

The Quality Council of India is also functioning from this building.

Thus, the Institution has shown appreciation for quality, and total commitment to quality management systems. We are obviously delighted to host this Orientation Course.

Last 18 months have seen closer cooperation amongst professional engineers institutions with the aim to promote and strengthen the two major functions of professional societies : (i) to promote the advancement of their engineering profession; and (ii) to protect the professional interest of their members and their image in society. They have also resolved to undertake the responsibility to ensure that their members follow a strict Code of Ethics in their professional dealings with the Society at large and offer the highest quality of service to their clients. It is in this context that an urgent need was felt for coordinating the activities and responsibilities of all professional societies in developing uniform code for regulating the conduct of Indian professional engineers both inside the country and abroad.

The outcome of concerted effort of all the professional societies was the formation of Engineering Council of India under whose umbrella the professional societies would collectively take all actions needed for the advancement of engineering profession; lay down norms of professional conduct; certify the competence of engineers for undertaking professional activities in India and abroad and ensure the competence of engineering organisations offering consultancy services. It is, but obvious, that I would like to mention of the effort of various professional societies agreeing to confederate themselves into ECI at this building of the Delhi State Centre of the Institution of Engineers, in its Platinum Jubilee Year and under the shadow of Sir M. Visvesvaraya. The resolve of all professional societies took shape on February 5, 2002, when ECI was formally launched.

With our deep involvement is quality education, the Institution of Engineers (India) offered its facilities to jointly conduct Orientation Courses. It is really heartening to note that the suggestion made a year back has resulted in NBA & IEI having conducted courses successfully at Ahmedabad and Hyderabad. This being the third in this series, and the first in North India, has its own significance.

The Institution was always apprehensive of the quality of education imparted by a number of small and remote engineering institutions. It became critical when the issue of mobility of engineers surface.

The concern for mobility of Indian engineers emerged when WTO started discussions on General Agreement on Trade in Services (GATS). The Ministry of Commerce, Government of India, in turn, got into discussion with various professional societies. The Institution of Engineers along with other professional institutions showed concern in dealing with the provisions of GATS. It is relevant to refer to WTO provisions and subsequent action.

The Working Party on Domestic Regulation (WPDR) has been established, by WTO, for development of domestic regulations for all services sectors, and engineering services figure upfront. While currently the work has started for developing systems on a horizontal basis, development of sector specific systems is not excluded. However, the general consensus amongst members has been, that it would be more efficient and less time consuming to develop such disciplines on a horizontal basis and supplement them if necessary by sector specific disciplines.

It may also be mentioned that such disciplines have already been developed by the Working Party on Professional Services (WPPS) for the accountancy sector. However, these disciplines are not mandatory and apply only to members, who have scheduled commitments in the accountancy sector. These are important because they provide an indication of the kind of domestic regulations that would be considered as compatible with the requirements of Article 6:4. The Government of India considered that our domestic regulations should be in line with such disciplines.

As part of the working of developing domestic disciplines for all sectors, the WPDR has identified the following issues with respect to the development of domestic regulations under WTO Regime:

(i) Necessity
(ii) Transparency
(iii) Equivalence
(iv) International Standards

The first two areas, 'necessity' and 'transparency', could help to develop rules on domestic regulations applicable to all types of measures listed in respective Articles relating to qualification and licensing requirements and procedures and technical standards.

The other two areas, 'equivalence' and 'international standards' could instead help to develop rules limited to some of the measures in Article 6:4. These are relevant to be discussed in relation to the orlentatlon course.

The Equivalence is an Important Aspect

In order to ensure that foreign service suppliers meet the qualification and other standards imposed on suppliers of national origin, regulators are often called upon to assess the equivalence of domestic and foreign qualifications. In many cases, they may require foreign applicants to obtain licences or other authority to provide a service or to undergo tests to demonstrate equivalence. Since such tests are imposed in order to ensure that a domestic standard is met, they may be regarded as domestic regulations. Article 6:4 disciplines, when they have been developed, would therefore, require that such requirements should be no more burdensome than necessary to ensure the quality of the service. Regulators in these situations could be obliged to take account of qualifications already earned in the home country of the Foreign Serv.ce supplier and to modify accordingly any additional requirements imposed upon them. This concept of equivalence has already been used in the qualification requirement section on the accountancy discipline and is being considered for other professions.

Every member state has to ensure that its competent authority take account of qualifications acquired in the territory of other member, on the basis of education, experience and/or examination requirements.

However, equivalence would not apply to all kinds of measures and to all types of services sector, and hence, would be restricted to professional services, where qualification and licensing requirements are important. This does not necessarily cover academic and government sectors.

The International Standards is Another Important Aspect

Article 6:5 indicates that domestic regulatory measures based on international standards could serve as benchmark pointing at the least paid restrictive measures, which are adequate to secure the policy objective in view.

The question arises whether international standards are necessarily relevant to the creation of horizontal disciplines. A few points are relevant to be considered.:

(i) Are the services standards "standardised at the international level"?

(ii) Are the developing countries able to participate fully in the creation of international services standards? If not, what are the specific difficulties?

(iii) Should we evolve international standards in the various services sectors?

(iv) Even after international standards have been evolved members may apply more onerous standards. Assuming that all members do not adopt the international standards, the question of evolving equivalence between standards of different members becomes relevant. How does one reconcile equivalence and international standards?

WTO's assertion to find all such equivalence and standardisation provisions in place by the end of 2004 has a direct impact on movement of professional engineers, more specifically for short term assignments.

Mobility of professionals (under the global market mechanism) enforcing 'equivalence in qualifications' and 'standardisation in their practices' attracted attention of professional institutions in some of the leading countries. In 1989, with a view to moving from international to globalised management practices—six countries UK, USA, Canada, Ireland, Australia and New Zealand initially set up, what is termed as the *Washington Accord* for accreditation of courses and institutions providing technical and engineering education. Hong Kong, China and South Africa were subsequently admitted. Japan was accepted as a provisional member and Malaysia would be applying formally for the provisional membership at the next meeting in 2003. India and Bangladesh are also expected to apply at the next meeting.

One must understand that the Washington Accord agreement effectively is a *quality assurance procedure* for the 'accreditation process' and the 'standards of the educational institutions' of the countries involved. As laid down in the ISO specifications, by its very nature, the Washington Accord agreement cannot, therefore, apply to anything in the past, but it is very meaningful for the present and the future. Any organisation as a full signatory therefore has been accepted as having programmes for the education of engineers that are equal to international standards. To *maintain the standard of education*, each member country has to ensure that the universities and institutions imparting technical education maintained those standards. Entering as a signatory to the Washington Accord, remain, therefore, a significant development for any country in its commitment that the standards in engineering education should meet international standards. Also, the admittance of any country institution into the Washington Accord would mean that the engineering degree programmes accredited by a government appointed/approved/recognised nodal agency will be recognised by other co-signatories of the Accord. Besides, the six earlier mentioned original signatories, who have been automatically accepting accredited degrees of one another for degrees obtained after 1989; they only accepted accredited degrees from Hong Kong and China from 1995 and that of South Africa from 1999. For degrees obtained prior to the dates of acceptance above, each country assesses the application on an individual basis.

It is apparent that there are some countries that will accept accredited degrees awarded prior to the above dates without much difficulty. In fact these same countries may even accept degrees that were obtained prior to the accreditation process but recognised by the accrediting body concerned. There are other countries, however, that apply the terms of the agreement strictly and will not accept the accredited degrees awarded prior to the above dates, let alone those that are recognised degrees prior to the accreditation process.

The National Board of Accreditation of India, set up under the AICTE Act, for carrying out accreditation of institutions and courses has approached for the membership under Washington Accord and was invited at its meeting in South Africa in June 2001. It is in this spirit today's Orientation Programme has been organised to expose the distinguished academicians and professionals who could support NBA in the process of peer review.

The *Engineers Mobility Forum* set up in 1999 has membership from Australia, Canada, Hong Kong, China, Ireland, South Africa, New Zealand, U.K., and USA. In addition Japan, Malaysia and Korea have also shown interest and India and Bangladesh are expected to apply for provisional membership of EMF at the next meeting in 2003. The Institution of Engineers (India) was invited as India's representative body to participate in the meeting of EMF in June, 2001 in South Africa. The Institution of Engineers (India) has sent its initial application papers in November 2001.

The aim of the EMF is to develop a system of mutual recognition at the full professional level to facilitate cross border mobility of registered practitioners. EMF, therefore, is striving to achieve this for present practitioners, whose educational qualification would not necessarily be accepted through the Washington Accord. In the light of the interpretation of the decision taken at the Sydney meeting in 1999, membership of the Washington Accord is not a pre-requisite for membership of the EMF.

As such the Institution of Engineers (India) can qualify to become a member of the Engineers Mobility Forum, irrespective of its membership of the Washington Accord. However, it will be desirable that NBA and the Institution enter respective bodies at the same time, so that the mobility of professionals becomes easier as their qualifications will be globally acceptable.

The agreement to establish and maintain an EMF International Register of Professional Engineers was formally signed by the member countries in June, 2001. The development of the understanding between various countries has involved a number of documents, *viz.*, the Memorandum of Understanding and the Agreement itself with its Schedule and the Draft Rules for the International Coordinating Committee.

The Coordinating Committee accepted all the assessment reports submitted by the 11 member countries, after presentation and discussion. This means that all signatories were provisionally authorised to prepare for the opening of the decentralised section of EMF International Register, which each country will launch at a date of their choice between 1 January and 30 June, 2002. Verification visits by teams over the next few years will be undertaken to each signatory to convert the provisional authorisation to full authorisation.

The burning question of "Right to Practice" has been raised, and each country has been requested to prepare a statement about this for their jurisdiction. It is expected that countries that have licensing systems not controlled nationally will have difficulties with granting of the Right to Practice. Indian professional engineers as on date are very vulnerable.

In parallel to the Washington Accord and the Engineers Mobility Forum the Sydney Accord has been established for Technologists which is equivalent to the Washington Accord for Engineers. The signatories are all the Washington Accord countries, except the USA who at this stage remains observer.

The Engineering Technologists Mobility Forum is similar to the EMF. A further intention of this Agreement will be also to recognise those professional technologists who have attained their professional competence through alternate routes.

I have mentioned about Sydney Accord and the Engineering Technologists Mobility Forum as these will also be relevant and important for the professional societies.

I am sure, the Orientation Course being conducted by the National Board of Accreditation will reflect the quality assurance process for accreditation to maintain international standards in the engineering education institutions. Worldwide, the engineering education quality assurance is carried out in the spirit of ISO 9000: 1994. It is necessary to move over to the Quality Management Systems Concept as recommended in ISO 9000 : 2000. That will also help in continual improvement in quality of education. Though, in keeping with the internationally practiced norms we may continue the present procedure it will be advantageous to move over to ISO 9000 : 2000 concept. I had long discussion even with Mr. Whtwel who has been helping such accreditation process and appreciated the idea. I wish we develop a Model that can also be presented to other Washington Accord Members to follow.

Before I close I would like to mention of the feedback from other

Orientation Courses where IEI was involved. The courses conducted in Ahmedabad and Hyderabad had participants from academics, industry and service sector who are in a position to spare time and their intellectual input to assist NBA undertake accreditation at a faster pace. I understand, some of them have already been empanelled by NBA are already assisting in accreditation process. IEI with its vast infrastructure at 94 centres has expressed willingness to contribute in this national effort to hasten up the process of accreditation to fulfil all provisions so that NBA becomes a rightful member under the Washington Accord.

Participation of the Indian delegation at the meeting of the Washington Accord and Engineers Mobility Forum in June 2001, has demonstrated close cooperation between NBA and IEI to project India's case for appropriate acceptance of their membership claim in Washington Accord and the EMF. The convergence of views witnessed at the Thornybush among the two organisations are being further cemented by such joint efforts. Stringent accreditation measures alone will provide quality engineering education; and continually improve its quality.

19

Building Materials and Technologies

I have pleasure in welcoming the Hon'ble Minister for Urban Development and distinguished guests. Members of IE(I) and participants to the 17th National Convention of Architectural Engineers being hosted by the Architectural Engineering Division and the Delhi State Centre of IE(I).

At the very outset I would like to convey the good wishes of the President IE(I) for the success of the Convention. He is out of the country and that is the reason he is not attending this convention. Dr. S. Maily, Chairman, Architectural Engineers Division Board also sends his good wishes as he had to cancel his visit at the last minute due to illness of his wife.

The Annual Convention is the most appropriate first activity in the Platinum Jubilee Year. It focuses on issues, which are extremely important to the Institution of Engineers (India) and the city of Delhi. The Delhi State Centre needs to focus all its attention on the built environment, in terms of appropriate design for aesthetics and structural soundness and low cost quality building materials. This focus only can ensure quality built environment. The Convention appropriately focuses on Building Materials and Technologies". By focusing on such an approach can the Nation have the Housing Policy and its implementation that is 'people centred' and 'sustainable'. This will also be in keeping with the thrust of Habitat-II+5.

The Habitat II-5 Conference, held in June tills year, reaffirmed that the human beings are the centre of concern for global sustainable development and people's welfare are the basis for your action taken for implementation of the Habitat Agenda. The Heads of Government stressed that this is a special moment in the development of human

---

Welcome Address at 17th National Convention of Architectural Engineers on October 29, 2001 at New Delhi.

settlement with half of the global population of 6 billion people expected to live in cities, by 2015, the world is facing an unprecedented growth of urban population; mainly in the developing countries. This applies as much to the city of Delhi. Decisions taken now will have far reaching consequences to the city of Delhi with population exceeding 14 million; half of the people identified to live in slums or unsatisfactory living conditions. Though the initial survey of the NSSO indicated that the urban poverty is at very low level in Delhi but that has not been accepted and the Government of Delhi is conducting another survey to identify the number of poor. Almost 30 per cent of our national population live below poverty line and does not have sufficient income to access the basic necessities of shelter, safe drinking water, basic sanitation facilities and sufficient good to eat. We are greatly concerned with this situation and the deteriorating condition in the city of Delhi. As the city of Delhi is considered to be amongst a prime mover of economic growth, it is necessary to allow rich to build their houses and to build houses for the poor that gives them shelter and a place to work. This has happened in the Leprosy Colony at Shahdara where 750 low cost tenements were built and each of the houses used as a work unit. The Leprosy patients have moved away from begging and are now earning their living.

While planning for the urban centres, we cannot ignore the locally available building materials. We have the option of either giving most efficient high rise, costly buildings only in the urban centres or also focus on semi-urban and rural areas with appropriate technologies and low cost materials and give a wide spread of comfortable living. Some of the building materials now developed out of the industrial and agro-waste are ideally suited to our conditions. But including them in specification and building architects' confidence to use them are still a low priority.

Building materials and technologies are important to housing as well as to infrastructure projects — but for different reasons. In the housing sector — low cost material and appropriate technologies allow larger numbers of quality houses to built; and in larger infrastructure projects — cost of the project can come down considerably making them bankable and acceptable to financial institutions.

Satisfactory observations can be made about the awareness creation programme that have focused on the needs to address in an integrated manner, unemployment, homelessness, poverty, lack of basic sanitary services, exclusion of women and children and of marginalised groups, including tribal communities and social fragmentation in order to achieve better, more livable and inclusive human settlement worldwide. Our housing policy will need to consider the issue in totality and in an integrated fashion. There is an urgent need to identify the gaps and obstacles in implementation. It is important to acknowledge the gap in shelter provision and urban policies that have limited the opportunities for 'participation and partnership' and have made it difficult to convert 'best practices' into 'good policies'. There is yet another identified obstacle associated with limited economic technological and institutional capacities at all levels of governance. There is a wide gap or absence of comprehensive and inclusive policies for capacity building institutions and their networking. HUDCO is looked upon be the financing agency, technology development and assessment agency, and the Building Centre Development and Networking Agency.

It is necessary to empower local authorities non-governmental organisations and professional organisations, like the Institutions of Engineers (India), within the legal framework and according to the conditions in the country. As the financial situation does not allow the government to setup a large number of capacity building Institutions, it is most appropriate that die intellectual and physical infrastructure of the Institution of Engineers (India), with its 90 Centres spread all over the country, be given the responsibility for coordination of technology development, implementation and evaluation of projects.

Management of urbanisation process requires strong and accountable public institutions that are able to provide effective framework in which everybody has access to basic services and the corruption is kept at the lowest level. Sustainable development is a process that needs continual improvement — that can only be achieved through quality at all steps — from government to project implementation.

I personally feel that there are two goals that we can, as engineers from the Delhi State Centre, can consider. Important inputs will be expected from this Seminar to develop our Action Plan.

The *first goal* is to work within the framework of Habitat call for 'Cities without Slums' initiative to make a significant improvement in the lives of at least one lakh slum dwellers in Delhi by 2020 (out of 100 million global slum dwellers identified in the habitat).

The *second goal* is to convert 'best practices' into 'good policies' and promote their application at the State, Municipal and Panchayat levels.

Hon'ble Minister Sir, the Institution also practices what it preaches. The Institution has developed a concept to build a new additional structure at the premises which will be a landmark in the skyline of Delhi. The design incorporates most efficient energy consumption practice; low cost quality materials; day lighting interventions and solar passive architecture interventions to keep the cooling and heating loads to a minimum. This building will provide you an ideal location to house your Habitat related networking mechanism. On behalf of the Institution, I have pleasure in presenting you the design of the New Building and request you to dedicate to the national cause.

TECHNICAL EDUCATION

20

Orientation of Technical Education to Meet Needs of Globalisation

Prof. S.S. MURTHY and Prof. B.P. SINGH*

Introduction

Technical education has undergone sea-change in recent years requiring adoptation coupled with new strategies and actions to face new situations. India is one country where the glamour for technical education is perhaps highest with the brightest of school-leavers opting for the same. Multiplicity of entrance tests has increased tension among aspirants. Varying standard of technical institutions from ITIs to IITs offers both opportunities and threats. Autonomy — administrative, financial and academic — has assumed significance. Finding teachers of whatever quality has become a herculean task. Resource mobilisation has become paramount for all categories of institutions with the state no longer able to support or subsidize higher education. Continuous upgradation of curricula has become essential due to fast obsolescence caused by rapid changes in technologies. Continuing education of practicing engineers and teachers need increased emphasis as part of the technical education system to face new challenges and to produce goods and services of international quality to face globalisation. Distance education has become a powerful tool due to Internet Revolution. Globalisation has thrown many challenges for technical education, which we may ignore at our own peril. Foreign Universities from USA, Canada, UK and Australia are luring Indian students to get their degrees sitting in India at a very high price through distance

* Professors, Department of Electrical Engineering, Indian Institute of Technology, Delhi

education mode although we may provide the same quality education at a much cheaper cost. Indian manufacturing base has considerably eroded due to dumping of foreign goods. To make Indian goods internationally competitive by value addition and quality control is a challenge for technical educators. This has caused dwindling of jobs in Engineering sectors with a great boost in IT sector which too has mostly non-engineering applications making the engineering training redundant. Post-graduation (M. Tech and Ph.D.) has become unattractive for bright graduates due to lack of challenging professional opportunities caused by reduced emphasis on indigenous R&D. Infrastructure in technical institutions — Class Rooms, Computers, Library and Laboratories — need quantum boost. Personality development and value education should be integral to technical education to produce technical leaders with foresight and humane face to ultimately guide the destiny of engineering profession, society and the country at large. Increased linkage with Industry and Alumni has become essential to achieve excellence in technical education through their support. This paper discusses the above factors and suggests some action plans.

Engineering Education

Engineering Education is pivotal to HRD for industrialisation. Quality of engineering graduates ultimately decides the quality of industrial output. India is endowed with largest number of bright school leavers opting for Engineering and this number surpasses all other countries including USA. The fact that more than 100 thousand students appear for IIT/JEE for coveted three thousand seats and several lakhs craving for state colleges through entrance tests reflects this National desire for engineering education. India can flood the world with Engineers by planning to produce largest number of English speaking International quality engineering graduates under globalisation. *Instead of globalising* India *we can Indianise the Globe*.

Indian Institutes of Technology System

The Indian Institutes of Technology (IIT's) have earned worldwide fame due to sincere efforts of faculty, students and administration to excel and their resolve never to sacrifice quality. The autonomy and academic ambience created in these campuses have attracted best faculty and students who have highest rating of professional excellence all over the world. IIT system is one of the few success stories of independent India. Eagerness shown by its very successful and distinguished Alumni from all over the world to help maintain its excellence under the present financial crisis caused by reduced government funding is noteworthy. Starving IITs of funds is a National disaster. But IITs have shown enough strength in raising additional revenues. Sufficient inputs in cash and kind coupled with increased financial, administrative and academic autonomy would only guarantee quality to face globalisation through HRD, R&D, CEP and consultancy. 3,000 IIT level graduates produced each year are too small for a country like India especially when they are in great demand abroad. We should plan for at least 10,000 IIT level graduates in next 5 years so that enough is available in India even after some exodus. This may be done by increasing inputs to existing IITs and by upgrading a few successful RECs as IITs. In fact the quality of school leavers taking IIT/JEE is so high that nearly 30,000 of them may have a quality on par with entrants to world renowned institutions like MIT, Caltech and Stanford. India should provide opportunities for such bright youngsters to have international quality engineering education. Out of more than one and a half lakh graduates produced every year only a small fraction (less than 3,000) come out of IITs. Recent decision of MHRD to convert University of Roorkee to IIT and to upgrade RECs to IIT level is a wise step.

Regional Engineering Colleges

Regional Engineering Colleges (RECs) too are providing quality graduates and attract high quality students. Many of their campus infrastructures are comparable to IITs to attract quality faculty. While a few of the RECs have done exceedingly well, fears are expressed on their steady general decline in not being able to attract good faculty compounded by financial crunch and deteriorating academic infrastructure. Following steps should immediately be taken to put them back on rails to produce good quality graduates to face globalisation.

(a) All RECs must be directly under MHRD of GOI with no state interference.
(b) Admission to all RECs must be made through IIT/JEE.
(c) All RECs must be fully autonomous and converted as deemed universities.

(d) Selection of faculty must have flexibility and liberal norms as in IITs to attract the best talent.

Government Engineering Colleges

Most of the Engineering Colleges funded by State Governments are doing quite well as they too attract good students. Recently they are finding difficulty in attracting good teachers and laboratories and building maintenance is in bad shape. In recent years teaching has considerably suffered with no classes taken, derailed semesters, outdated syllabus, absence of industry interaction and over-bureaucratisation due to undue interference from government. Urgent steps are needed to improve administrative structure of these colleges to provide quality education to such high caliber students.

Private and Self-Financing Colleges

Majority of Engineering graduates in the country are coming out of private and self-financing colleges whose conditions vary widely — from pathetic to outstanding — depending on the efficiency of the management and dedication of the Principal. Prof. Kulandaisamy during the Annual Convention of ISTE at Erode (2000) urged that all Colleges be granted academic autonomy and gradually do away with affiliated colleges to universities. As a first step all leading private Institutions must be converted as deemed technical universities. Market forces will ensure that only those maintaining quality will survive by attracting good students and faculty. All India Council of Technical Education (AICTE) should ensure that all private colleges maintain stipulated quality — present status in this front leaves much to be desired. Periodic monitoring and assessment must be carried out to maintain or continue their recognition/approval.

Technician Education through Polytechnics and ITIs

While Engineering Education has attracted sufficient attention in the country the technician education has received step-motherly treatment. Even after World Bank support and having TTTIs we are not producing world class technicians who can provide globally competitive products, processes and services. Polytechnics and Industrial Training Institutes are the backbone for producing this manpower, which are required in several sectors. There is dearth of good electricians, plumbers, TV repairers, motor winders, instrument mechanics, welders, auto-mechanics, telephone/communication, air-conditioning mechanics etc; in fact the list is amending. With the explosion in information technology we need new type of technicians to install and maintain hardware platforms and accessories — PCs, servers, LAN, Networks, Printers, UPS etc. Several problems pertaining to engineering colleges mentioned earlier are also applicable here needing appropriate solutions. Since placement of technician is mostly in the unorganised sectors there are acute unemployment or under-employment and mismatch of training with actual job. For successful globalisation this problem must be addressed squarely to produce best workforce to produce internationally acceptable goods.

Admission and Entrance Tests

In Western countries any person wanting to study engineering and having reasonable merit, motivation and financial resources can almost walk into an Engineering School. In contrast the number of aspirants in India is much higher than the available seats leading to tough competition and involved selection process. An IIT aspirant has to prepare for more than 2 years for JEE apart from his/her schooling for 10+2. In no other country a person has to prepare for 2 years to get into Engineering. JEE has become a rejection process and their standards are raised every year to effect rejection and increase drudgery of candidates. Some of my past students who passed from IIT in seventies have told me that they would fail in present JEE papers!

External coaching to face entrance tests has become almost a necessity. Based on my inquiry there was not a single first year Electrical Engineering student of IITD this year who had not taken such coaching. It is our recent experience that after so much grueling effort many students lose interest to learn after joining IIT. This is no way to produce innovative engineers. They tend to be interested in mostly non-engineering jobs in India or go abroad. Thus, the most brilliant are not available to engineering activity in India which is a threat to globalisation effort.

Multiplicity of common entrance tests is a bane of technical education system in India with several vested interests playing havoc unheard of in any other country, the scarcity situation being totally exploited at the cost of the aspirants and their parents. For example, for the popular Karnataka entrance test special trains are run to Bangalore from Delhi and Howrah with extra flights from several cities to Bangalore to meet the rush of lakhs of outside candidates and their parents. All Hotels in Bangalore are fully booked, black-marketing running rampant, with large number sleeping on railway platforms. Thus, crores of rupees of wasteful expenditure is incurred by the Nation. It is estimated that total annual turnover of all coaching centres preparing students for entrance tests is nearly Rs. 800 crores, paid by the parents. With this amount we may start an IIT each year! Even IITs cannot afford the type of newspaper advertisements put up by coaching centres. Bulk of the students prepare for 2 to 3 years through such centres, especially for premiere institutes like IITs, at the cost of their normal school/college education. They are at great tension throughout this period with no relaxation or extra-curricular activities with enormous dehumanising effect killing their creativity and urge to learn. As an IIT teacher for more than 30 years, I have observed many undesirable and mercenary qualities (increasing in recent years) in these 'bright kids' inflicted by the *torture* of JEE. Their concern/respect for the Nation, society, teachers and parents leaves much to be desired. Overall cynicism is rampant. Clashing of dates of different tests forcing students to miss some or rush from one to another (often needing to fly at huge cost) is another compounding problem. This chaos can be considerably reduced, if not totally eliminated, by taking following immediate steps –

(a) Conduct one common entrance test for admission to all colleges in the country.
(b) Reduce scarcity complex among candidates.
Of course (b) follows (a).

Single Entrance Test

It is heartening to note that MHRD has taken some action on one National test. IITs have volunteered to conduct this test (same as screening test of JEE) and make the result available to all other admissions. It is natural that any such drastic step will face opposition, more so from vested interests, some of which may be genuine. According to a functionary conducting such test for a university, it costs only Rs. 60 per candidate for the whole exercise, using multiple choice questions and optical evaluation method, while they charge

Rs. 500 per candidate. Thus Rs. 440 per candidate is the net profit to the university which they are not prepared to forgo. One may interpret this as an unfair trade practice, but the beneficiaries may not relent. Therefore, the government has to either convince them that this was unworthy money or give financial compensation to those who fall in line. Another argument against single test is the reduction of chances for candidates, especially if one is unwell on the day of the test. The solution lies in conducting two tests each year, say in November and May, so that the candidate has the opportunity to improve upon the earlier score and submit the better score along with the application for admission to any institution. Needless to say that we have to evolve a common and nationally acceptable syllabus for this test. Apart from Physics, Chemistry and Mathematics, it may be worthwhile to include an Aptitude-cum-General Knowledge test to test whether the candidate has aptitude for engineering. To begin with, the latter can only be a qualifying requirement. This has become necessary as it is found that many successful candidates have no knowledge of engineering developments in India. I have found Electrical Engineering students not knowing major Electrical Industries in India. In many leading Institutions in USA, apart from academic grade extra-curricular activities, leadership qualities and mental personality are considered for admission.

The score of the above National test must be given both in absolute and relative terms so that the admitting college may use them appropriately. In nutshell, each candidate applying to an Institution will submit the above score (similar to GATE score for PG admissions) with the application along with other certificates and grade cards. Each institution will prepare a combined merit list based on the above data as per their admission policy and effect admissions.

Reduce Scarcity

Scarcity of quality engineering seats is no doubt a cause for concern. Single test partly addresses this problem as more seats are now available for those appearing for this test. For example, only about 3,000 IIT and attached seats are now available for nearly 1.5 lakh JEE candidates (i.e. 1:50). But with single test, ideally a total of 1.5 lakh seats can be made available on All India basis for which total aspirants may be around 6 lakhs (i.e. 1:4). However, urge to get into premier institutes like IIT remains. Solution lies in increasing seats in such institutes. India needs at least 10 IITs with a minimum of 10,000 seats each year. Compared to reputed foreign technical universities intake of IITs is meagre for the same faculty strength. With suitable additional input it is possible to treble the B.Tech intake of IITs in 5 years. Other equally reputed institutes like Roorkee and BHUIT may be immediately converted to IIT. Reputed RECs should be given total autonomy as in IITs and converted to Regional Institutes of Technology. Efforts of MHRD in this direction need to be fully supported so that overall quality of technical education can be improved. If quality of students admitted to reputed foreign universities such as Stanford, CALTECH, MIT, UMIST, Imperial College is taken as benchmark, nearly 50,000 JEE applicants would be eligible for admission. If we create that number of seats in nationally reputed technical institutes, scarcity would be greatly reduced and unproductive coaching centres become redundant.

Autonomy Versus Affiliation

Ideally all institutions must be totally autonomous to bring out their best. In fact affiliating university system is prevalent in only a few countries such as India, Pakistan, Sri Lanka and Bangladesh and is universally considered as an outdated concept. Autonomy ensures both freedom and accountability. IITs have excelled only because of autonomy. Even private technical universities such as BITS Pilani have maintained good standards. In India affiliating college system must be treated as a necessary evil and not an absolute necessity and attempts must be made to give autonomy and deemed university status to more institutions every year by a quality control mechanism by AICTE. Institutions can be graded as A, B, C, and D as per their standards by AICTE. This ensures quality and competition to excel. Importance and control of State technical universities must be reduced. Academic linkages of different categories of Institution in a region and synergising their facilities and expertise would help in bringing up the overall standards.

How to Find Teachers?

Good teaching is a prerequisite to produce graduates of world standard. When IITs are finding it difficulty to attract competent teachers one can imagine the plight of other colleges. For a bright youngster the salary structure is less attractive compared to other competing options? Still it may be possible to attract some dedicated youngsters by providing suitable perquisites and academic ambience. Having children schooling and health facilities are found to be very attractive perquisites to lure them for teaching. Assured career growth through higher degrees and performance based promotional avenues is essential. Recently introduced AICTE scheme for early faculty induction by selecting bright final year students from colleges needs to be given impetus. Every regular teacher must ultimately acquire Ph.D. degree before the age of 40. QIP scheme for teachers must be enhanced and reinforced. Each IIT must network with at least four neighbouring engineering colleges to continuously monitor and help in updating curriculum, laboratories and teaching. Since IITs and some leading Institutes are still able to nurture outstanding teachers their recorded lectures may be made available to other colleges through video, CDs or Internet.

Recent economic reforms have focused attention on industry which also attracts bright engineering graduates. An effective linkage with industry can help in getting outstanding practicing engineers as faculty. Such industry-academic linkage makes engineering education more useful and current.

Finding good teachers for engineering colleges has become a critical problem. Teachers being the backbone for an institution, the system will collapse if we do not find appropriate solutions, as the bright students should not be exposed to bad or no teachers. I once asked the first year B.Tech students, while welcoming them to IIT, how many of them wanted to be teachers'. The response was nil. Teaching is no longer an attractive profession for bright youngsters, but we cannot reconcile to mediocre who will ruin generations. Early Faculty Induction Programme (EFIP) of AICTE is a right step, but some candidates even at the stage of joining for M.Tech are asking how to break the bond! While it is impossible to match the salaries with other competing options available to them, considerable improvement in salaries, perquisites, career growth and other facilities must be devised. IIT experience shows that campus housing is an important factor to attract good teachers. Children schooling, health and recreational facilities, liberal leave rules to take up visiting assignments in industry or abroad, consultancy facilities, encouragement for higher studies, contingency grants, loan facilities, support for higher education for children (including some reserved seats in those colleges), support to membership of professional societies are some major factors to lure and retain them. Even the revised AICTE scales are no longer attractive. Although IIT scales were revised long back, package of perks are yet to be announced. Even their Professor's scale is made at par with that of joint secretary, a reduction in status compared to previous one. Teacher's pay packet in most of the self-financing colleges is unattractive, situation being no better in many state colleges. It is no wonder that several teachers' posts are vacant throughout the country. We can ignore this problem only at our peril. At several departments at IITs standing search committees are in operation whose mandate is to search, chase and hunt good faculty. While we do not want to induct inferior faculty we make all our effort to lure ones if located. Autonomy helps in this effort as we can employ them as visiting or *ad hoc* faculty in the first place. Still it is hard to find good teachers. While all-out efforts must be made to recruit regular faculty, following additional schemes may be implemented.

(a) Using retired faculty
(b) Having adjunct faculty who are working in industries and other organisations in the neighbourhood.
(c) Short time visiting faculty from other universities in India or abroad.

Teaching can be augmented by using videotapes, CDs of popular teachers. Even live lectures of good teachers of other institutions in the neighbourhood can be transmitted to several colleges by distance education mode through Internet.

Resource Mobilisation

With dwindling government support fund raising has become an important function of all institutions keen on maintaining quality. Apart from government, major sources of funding are — Student fees, Alumni, Industry, Consultancy, and Sponsored research. We must realise that this is a worldwide phenomenon and all administrators and faculty are expected to raise funds to meet expenses of teaching and research. In India IITs are in the forefront — apart from a few reputed private institutions — in this effort which others may emulate to the extent possible. Alumni contributions, building of corpus fund, external funded sponsored research and consultancy, professorial chairs, enhanced fees and industry contributions are some of the sources tapped. Raising fees beyond a point would be retrograde due to poor paying capacity of parents. There should be increase in scholarships and part-time job opportunities for students like in libraries, computer centres, canteens, co-operative stores, alumni offices etc. as prevalent in foreign universities. Contributions can also be in kind, such as building student residences, library books, computers, laboratories etc. This requires tremendous drive, which only a few can exhibit. This author has written to all EE Department, Alumni of IIT Delhi to contribute for Scholarship fund, Lab development fund and Department development fund and we are eagerly awaiting response. Some accomplished alumni — Narayana Murthy (IITK), Kanwal Reki (IITB), Vinod Gupta (IIT Kh) and Gururaj Deshpande (IITM), Vinod Khosla (IITD) — have made significant contributions. This trend should increase. Even large number of small contributions would yield substantial sum. While marketing of expertise is welcome, pure commercialisation should be avoided. In India contribution of industry to promote technical education is very insignificant. They can do much more.

Impact of Globalisation and IT

Globalisation is a double-edged sword as it can be a boon or a bane depending on how we use it. Instead of *globalising India* we can *Indianise the globe*. So far the effect on India is mixed tilting more towards negative. Manufacturing base has diminished. Jobs in Engineering sector have dwindled except in IT, which will have a major impact on technical education. R&D and design base has reduced with most of the Industrial R&D units in dismal state. All landed goods from China are cheaper than local ones forcing local industries to close and increasing unemployment. Impact is seen even in farm and rural sectors, as imported food items are cheaper. Drastic reorientation of technical education to produce international level manpower aimed at making Indian goods globally competitive is urgently required. Action is needed across board from technicians to designers, as we cannot impart training on obsolete technologies. We must remember that globalisation is not reversible and we have to work out strategies to protect national interests. Entry of multinationals to India with direct foreign investment is inevitable and may be desirable. An encouraging trend is the opening of Research Centres in India by several multinationals — GE, Marconi, GM, Intel, HP, Lucent — which increases the need for Indian researchers with its positive effect on education. Jack Welsh of GE has declared that he may need 8,000 post-graduates and Ph.Ds for the research centre in Bangalore. But we must ensure that these units will not confine to providing design, software and R&D support to parent companies but expand into manufacturing sector to increase local jobs resulting in growth of Indian economy.

Schemes of foreign universities to offer degrees in India through distance education mode at enormous cost is a new challenge to technical educators in India as we should be able to provide the same quality degrees at much reduced cost and save foreign exchange. With got teaching expertise we should reverse this trend and offer Indian degrees in foreign countries. We can certainly target Middle East, Far East and African countries. We must emulate organisations like British Council that are successful in marketing British Universities all over the world. Brand equity IIT degrees will certainly be popular in Middle East and Far East with considerable NRI presence. This will not only help in resource mobilisation but open enormous opportunities to develop new expertise in pedagogy and create teaching-learning materials for global use through Video, CD and Internet.

Information Technology (IT) will have an important bearing on technical education, in view of enormous demand for IT manpower. India has rightly declared its intention to be an IT super power. AICTE has taken proactive effort to increase seats in IT related courses in Engineering Colleges. However, quality has to be maintained keeping in view the scarcity of teachers. With the bulk of jobs in IT and scarce opportunity in other engineering disciplines, an undesirable unbalance is created, with the students neglecting other disciplines. Jack Welsh, the Chief of GE declared while inaugurating the Bangalore Research Centre that India cannot succeed in IT if infrastructure such as *power* is not established to international standards. Electricity should get preference over IT he said. Thus, if we have to succeed under globalisation and IT environment, our infrastructure such as roads, airports, power, communication, and railways must be of international levels. This requires proper prioritisation, resource allocation and manpower training for infrastructure. Engineering institutions have a major role to play in this direction.

IT can be effectively used for technical education. Apart from e-governance, e-commerce we must have e-teaching encompassing the use of IT for lectures, tutorials, laboratories, library, teaching-learning materials, office automation, data bank and web-site of institutions and instructors etc. This requires a totally new thinking in technical institutions to become paperless, efficient and globally competitive.

Distance and Continuing Education

Globalisation and IT have thrown new challenges and opportunities for distance and continuing education. Since lectures can be delivered through Internet *online* to different locations simultaneously, we can reach technical knowledge to largest audience with minimum cost. Teleconferencing would enhance interaction through interface. India should give major thrust in this direction by employing expert teachers. Presently education centres at IITs and TTTIs have established facilities and produced video lectures of expert teachers. This activity must be expanded to be on the lead.

Continuing education of practicing engineers and teachers has become paramount to catch up with new technologies and transfer to the classroom. But industries and colleges must be liberal in deputing their staff to short term courses or higher degrees. Many experts are reluctant to deliver lectures in short courses due to poor emoluments; this needs re-look as an honorarium of Rs. 1,000 per lecture appears reasonable considering the effort involved in delivering capsule talks.

Another facet of distance education is the globalising of education through latest tools of education technology including Internet. India is bestowed with large pool of experienced teachers whose services can be utilised for globalising education for offering courses to other countries. Universities in England, Australia, Canada, Germany and USA are making all out efforts to lure Indian students who often pay hefty fee. Some foreign universities have centres in India under a franchise scheme through which Indian students sitting in India can get foreign degrees. This process must be reversed so that foreign students can get high quality Indian degrees. University of Roorkee recently attempted one such arrangement with Malaysia. In all these arrangements only merit and excellence can survive, which stipulates that our educational institutes must maintain very high standards.

With the demand outstripping the available seats in formal educational system Distance and Non-Formal education have to be resorted to. Professional Societies such as Institution of Engineers have a crucial role to play in HRD to face globalisation through updated syllabus and quality teaching and learning materials. Internet has revolutionised the concept of distance education through enlarged opportunities. President of the Canadian Association of Polytechnics delivering the Karnataka Memorial Lecture during the ISTE Convention in December 1999 at Erode mentioned about the phenomenal growth of registration to several courses in North American Universities through distance education *via* internet where student need not live in the location of the institute. India should siege this opportunity to educate large number of persons in engineering, technology, management and other skills through tools of Information Technology. Quality teaching and learning materials using videotapes, CDs and software may be produced using expert teachers.

Continuing Education of practising engineers through regular short term courses conducted by leading institutions need to be vastly enlarged to upgrade their skills and to adopt and absorb new technologies.

> It is retrograde that many industries do not depute their personnel for such short courses. Recently some tailor-made sponsored M.Tech programmes for NTPC; L&T and Micro-electronic industries have been started at IIT Delhi. These can be trend-setters to plan more such post-graduate programmes in leading institutions. This concept can be marketed in other industries too.

Post-Graduation and Research

M.Tech and Ph.D. programmes are generally in doldrums due to various factors. With attractive job options, mainly in IT sectors, bright graduates seldom opt for post-graduation (PG). Apart from a dozen top institutions quality of PG training in the country leaves much to be desired. Even GATE has not helped much in getting quality inputs as M. Tech itself is considered unattractive due to poor job options except in teaching which in turn is not much sought after either. Most of the M. Tech placements in IITs are in software sector and not in hard core engineering. But, the flip side is that industry sponsored M. Tech programmes are found to be successful. IIT Delhi has several such programmes sponsored by L&T, NTPC, Microelectronics Industries, DRDO, Navy etc We must increase such relevant programmes. Fresh Ph. D. aspirants even in IITs are rare and generally of poor quality with little motivation for research. Engineering research scholars have become *vanishing species*. But deputed college teachers are motivated and form backbone of Ph.D. programmes in such institutions. QIP programme needs further strengthening to facilitate more teachers to acquire higher degrees. With multinationals establishing research centres in India need for PGs will increase. PG programmes will flourish only if the country needs design and R&D personnel who are essential to upgrade technologies to face globalisation.

Sponsored research and consultancy provides philip to research activities. With negligible spending by Indian industry on research and reluctance of multinationals to sponsor research in India, academicians have to seek government funding through DST, CSIR, AICTE, UGC etc. Even the funding by government sector is either lukewarm or negligible. Research grants of several ministries are not found to be effectively utilised towards achieving new product or process. With mainly bureaucrats involved in selection of Head of research institutions leadership to guide nationally relevant R&D has become ineffective. Industry-Institute consortium schémes such as PATSER of DSIR and TIFAC, although very attractive, have not picked up in a big way. Bureaucratic procedures for processing and funding of projects turn off genuine researchers. Effective and sustained support is often missing to take the inventions to the field, many of them therefore do not see the light of the day. On the other hand Indian researchers have also not come out in flying colours due to poor outcome of majority of funded research which calls for introspection. While funds are utilised, almost nothing is delivered. Thus their credibility has suffered in the eyes of the public. Major corrective actions are required by all players.

Post-Graduate Education

Post-graduate engineering education is crucial to produce manpower for innovation, R&D, design and develop expertise in relevant areas so as to create a strong technology base. Except in IITs, IISc and a few leading technical Institutions/Universities the general quality of PG education leaves much to be desired. Quality of input is generally poor and non-motivated and consist of those who could not find placement. There is no proper auditing of courses. The report of the expert committee on PG education submitted to AICTE needs to be considered urgently.

High quality post-graduates can form backbone to Indian Technology. We must give a big push to this programme for global competitiveness. Industry can play a major role by sponsoring candidates and supporting relevant projects. IIT M. Techs are effectively contributing to Indian technology through research, design and academic pursuits. However, there is a disturbing trend recently of their drift towards non-engineering software jobs totally irrelevant to their PG training. Therefore, most of our PG programmes must be industry related and supported. Our experience with industry and defence sponsored candidates indicates that they are highly motivated and successful in spite of initial hick-ups.

Curriculum Development

Curriculum development for engineering education must be a continuous and regular affair due to fast obsolescence of subjects and need for upgrading. Sometime back AICTE undertook a massive exercise involving leading institutions to prepare model curricula for different degree programmes. This author was the coordinator to prepare model curriculum for Bachelors degree in Electrical Engineering, which can be a benchmark for all colleges. AICTE has to take follow-up action to prescribe such a model syllabus as a national pattern. As a first step these model syllabi need to be printed and widely made available to all institutions. A more pressing need is to standardise laboratory courses with a set of experiments and equipment which would be a useful guideline for setting up new laboratories or to modernise the old ones. This helps in better utilisation of funding under MODROB. It would be very useful if model laboratories are set-up in select institutions with AICTE funding for others to emulate. Industry may be persuaded to donate state of art equipment for such laboratories. Use of IT for computer interface and data-acquisition and processing can make the experiments really interesting. IIT Delhi is working with NIIT to have some model experiments for Basic Electrical Engineering Laboratory.

Infrastructure

A modern infrastructure in an institution considerably enhances the quality of education within available resources. Classrooms need to have latest audio-visual facilities. For some core courses with large number of students, a few big classrooms with suitable gadgets — OHP, LCD projector, video projector, slide projector, large screen, microphone and speakers etc. — would be required which may also be used for popular lectures or seminars. Internet, geographically distributed cyber facility and networked computers with servers and generic software have become essential for any campus. Fast obsolescence of PCs is a matter of concern and mechanism to recycle PCs must be evolved. With high cost of foreign books networked library system would save scarce resources. Internet has revolutionised this sector too and we must exploit to our advantage.

Laboratory is a matter of prime concern, their status in most of the colleges is appalling. No wonder the students find most of the laboratory classes *boring*. Apart from resource crunch very few teachers take interest in laboratory development. Fast obsolescence, dishonest and unreliable suppliers, poor maintenance, archaic purchase procedures are problems to be addressed. Laboratories in most of the colleges are storehouse of obsolete and useless equipment occupying precious space. A major thrust to tackle this problem is called for to provide a quantum boost. Although virtual laboratory is suggested as a remedy, it is doubtful if engineering training can be imparted without equipment. IT can no doubt help in making laboratory training interesting, but we have to evolve suitable schemes.

In an article in IEEE spectrum an American professor had remarked that laboratory training of Indian Engineering graduates was weak although they had good theoretical background. Our laboratory training is deteriorating over the years and IITs are no exceptions. Engineers with good laboratory training are very essential to face globalisation. Industry and government should support setting up of model laboratories in leading institutes to be replicated in other colleges. Installation, upgradation and modernisation of laboratories must be an important function a teacher with full support from management. Dearth of trained and dedicated technicians is another matter of concern. Use of IT in laboratory training must be explored with virtual laboratories and instrumentation. Industry-academic interaction can help in supporting laboratories to be funded by local industries. Model laboratories must be created in leading institutes for others to emulate. AICTE may support this venture.

Inter-Institutional Linkages

In each geographic region it is natural that different institutions of varying standard and inputs co-exist. Synergising a cluster of institutions as regards faculty expertise, laboratories, library and computer facility is desirable to optimally use the resources. Reputed institutions like IITs should take lead in helping less endowed institutions in the neighbourhood on curriculum planning, establishment of laboratories, general guidance to teachers/students etc. Network scheme of MHRD attempted a few years ago did not yield the desired result. AICTE may evolve suitable schemes to effect such interaction with appropriate funding.

Industry-Institute Interaction

It has already been mentioned in earlier sections how industry and alumni can assist technical education. In industrialised countries, industry helps universities in a big way, but the same cannot be said about India with a few exceptions. Quality of an institute must be judged by the extent of industry interaction indulged by its faculty. There is no dispute that Industry-Institute interaction must be strengthened, but *how* is the question. Typical modes of interaction are as follows.

Industry to Institute

(a) Student training and visit to industry, (b) student projects in industry, (c) industry help in laboratory modernisation, (d) lecture by industry personnel, (e) adjunct faculty, (f) participate in curriculum planning, (g) fabrication support, (h) institute chairs, awards/medals, scholarships, and (i) campus recruitment.

Institute to Industry

(a) Consultancy, (b) sponsored research, (c) design and software support, (d) deputation of faculty to industry, (e) product development, and (f) continuing education and specialist lecture.

Alumni Interaction

Dr. Gururaj Deshpande one of the richest persons in USA and an IIT alumnus mentioned in a TV interview recently that leading technical institutes in USA such as MIT, CALTECH, Stanford have stayed in forefront mainly due to their alumni support. This aspect is totally missed in India in planning technical education. According to Indian tradition *Guru-Shishya* relation is eternal. The famous saying '*Ma vidwishavahai' (Let us not dislike each other)* reflects the eternal bondage between the teacher and the taught. Relation with alumni is not commercial but emotional. But still alumni associations in India rarely exist for most institutes and even those active are confined to social activities oblivious of the issues of their *Alma mater*. Recently IITs have taken proactive steps to reverse this trend and some of the successful alumni have come forward to donate substantially. Each institute should devise effective schemes to increase alumni interaction, which is beneficial to both. We must bear in mind that any interaction succeeds in a *Win-Win* situation. Alumni can help in resource mobilisation, laboratory development, scholarships, library upgrade, sponsoring projects etc. Institutes must reciprocate in offering their facilities to alumni such as guesthouse, sports, recreation, and organising social events to make them feel they are welcome. Alumni office in leading universities like MIT are really massive and it is a worthy investment. It is necessary to keep in touch and to handshake regularly. Their goodwill is very precious.

Campus Recruitment

Quality of an institution is judged by the number of firms it attracts for campus recruitment and the number of students thus recruited. Placement units of IITs are busy throughout the year. It is a public relation exercise all institutions must do. While reputed private firms and multi-nationals excel in headhunting through this mode, government and public sectors lag behind due to outdated procedures. This explains the poor performance and service of these sectors. Since large number of engineering graduates will be produced each year with continuous addition of new colleges, national effort for their placement is in order. While we need not bother about the brain drain, which seems inevitable, we must evolve schemes to gainfully employ those staying back whose number is not insignificant.

National Security

Technical education has an important bearing on national security to create technological self-reliance on crucial sectors through R&D and manpower support. Space, atomic energy and defence are crucial sectors where our weakness will make the country vulnerable. But excellence in civilian sector is also important. In a seminar held recently at IIT Delhi, one speaker commenting on setting up Microhydel units in border areas mentioned that India must demonstrate technological superiority in such areas so that our people should not feel that the system on the other side of the border is superior. Technical institutions must get actively involved in promoting technologies concerning national security — both civilian and defence sectors.

Personality Development and Value Education

Engineers we produce must have leadership quality with high self-esteem and overall personality. They must be people with a vision capable of contributing to development of society and country at large. If we observe most of the work places inhibited by Engineers (others are no exception) inter-human relations are not satisfactory with individuals exhibiting weak qualities such as ego and jealousy at the cost of the output. Many of their decisions are emotional and not rational influenced by personal factors. Team spirit so essential for an engineer is missing which results in derailed projects. Technical education must have a component to develop personality and leadership qualities in students. H.R. professionals are available to impart such training for teachers, students and administrators.

Complementing the above is the value education to impart basic human and universal values to make the student a good human being. Although population density of Japan and UK are higher compared to India their quality of life is higher because of good values expected of a citizen. Although historically India is endowed with great thinkers, philosophers and spiritual teachers preaching universal values of respect for nature, parents, teachers and guests with emphasis on truth and righteousness, these are not effectively passed on to young generations through education to make them good and responsible citizens who, as John Kennedy said, should not ask what the country can do for them but ponder what they can do for the country. While humanities courses were expected to impart such values, the effect is not visible among the youth who are exhibiting more mercinery qualities of 'Self before everything'. The decision of MHRD to open a centre for value education at IIT Delhi is therefore a right step. But the training must be comprehensive combining theory with practice through field experience. Internationally, some of the traditional Indian knowledge such as *Yoga*,

Meditation, *Pranayama* has been accepted as useful and relevant for good physical and mental health and we should not deprive our youths of such wealth. This is an area requiring considerable thinking and planning before implementation.

Conclusions

India is at crossroads in technical education with events overtaking faster than we could imagine. Major critical issues are listed and comprehensively discussed in this paper. Admission procedure, bane of multiple tests, teacher scarcity, impact of globalisation and IT, Resource crunch, Alumni and Industry linkage, PG and Research, Distance and Continuing Education, Infrastructure and Value education are relevant factors. Irreversible process of globalisation and IT revolution will make major impact on technical education and intelligence lies in converting threats to opportunities to make India a leader by effectively harnessing human and material resources. There is no alternative to strengthening indigenous technology base, a challenge for technical educators.

21

Distance Education in Engineering

C.V. RAMAKRISHNA* and ASHOK GUPTA**

Introduction

Distance education is an ideal solution where the teacher and students are separated by physical distance. Technology (video, data and print), often in concert with face to face communication is used to bridge the instructional gap. Open universities with a mandate to reach out students who are disadvantaged by limited time, distance or physical disability in attending a regular programme have in the past developed programmes in certain special areas, liberal arts and sciences. The implementation of an engineering degree programme has been treated with a certain amount of scepticism since these involve mastering of complex concepts, understanding professional practices and extensive work on instruments and equipments in addition to the execution of professional projects and industrial experience. Rapid strides in computer networking and web technologies have resulted in a totally new outlook on higher education (McArthur, 1997). An elaborate model of a learning network for engineering education was presented by Bourne *et al.* (1997). A brief current state of the out and futuristic trends were presented by the authors Ramakrishnan and Gupta (2000).

In this paper, we specifically address the role of distance education in engineering in a developing country like India with limited financial resources but a globalised open economy.

---

* Professor, Department of Applied Mechanics, ** Associate Professor, Department of Civil Engineering, Indian Institute of Tecnology, Delhi.

Importance of Distance Education

It is now well recognised in developed countries that Distance education involving extensive use of Internet and web technologies is extremely cost effective on account of the following reasons:

- Ability to reach a larger student audience at moderate cost.
- Availability of limited funds for formal classroom based education.
- Need for continuing education and constant upgradation of skills with flexible timings for professional engineers in the information.
- Need for specially tailored professional course to suit manpower requirements.
- Increased international competition in attracting students for high quality education.
- Availability of learner friendly interfaces.

Thus a large number of US universities have introduced DE programmes at the graduate level and many universities have introduced undergraduate programme in Computer Science, Information Technology and Electrical Engineering and Electronics. UK is about to start a major e-university with the participation of Open University, Imperial College of Science and Technology and Medicine. Several universities in Canada, France and Spain have set up education programmes based upon distance education.

It was highlighted in an earlier article by the authors that presently there are four categories of Universities/Higher Technological Institutions offering tertiary level engineering education.

(i) General University in which engineering faculty is a small
(ii) Special Technical University (Government or Private)
(iii) Open University
(iv) Private/profit oriented Institutions (Self-financing engineering college)

We also find that the following types of private institutions already exist and attract a large number of students.

- Self-financing engineering colleges offering regular classroom based education affiliated to General/Technical University Instructions may be for full-time or part-time students.
- Self-supporting Institutions offering regular classroom education in India affiliated to well known US/UK/Australian Universities with partial inputs from foreign institutions.
- Self-supporting Institutions offering distance education with local learning centres catering to laboratory and tutorial classes and affiliated to US/Australian Universities.
- Self-supporting Institutions offering full-fledged diploma/ professional certification programmes (NIIT, Aptech, Ssi, STG etc.) full-time/part-time. Short term training/certification programmes offered by small enterprises using CAI and CBT.
- Web based e-university programmes, on-line Training Institutes (Microsoft).

All the above ventures are profit-oriented and the benefits may not be truly optimal for the progress of the country. It is also a fact that the institutions belonging to the last three types do not belong to the conventional higher-education model but involve very innovative use of information technology for essentially corporate training of employees and also cater to the continuing education needs of knowledge seekers. But the difference between the two is becoming hazy and university programmes tend to be very rigid slow to change and are insensitive to student requirements. Further with competition from foreign universities and private corporations increasing, many of the engineering programmes based on old fashioned curricula and constrained by general university regulations and lack of high quality faculty may lose out. It is therefore necessary that we initiate action to

(i) Motivate high quality technical institutions like IITs, RECs and selected well-known engineering colleges to increase intake and also implement strong DE programmes for continuing education and post-graduate education apart from part-time programmes. This will be the best way to ensure that tax payer supported public institutions retain their competitive edge while ensuring equity and social justice.

(ii) Set up a high quality high band-width state of the art. IT network infrastructure with a reasonably robust administrative support to ensure good connectivity between premier nodal institutions RECS and participating state institutions and district level learning centres with a mandate to operationalise many strong DE programmes or e-universities. It is worth noting here that the reputation of an institution of learning will enhance only if the DE programme administrated by it is good in quality. However a conservative approach may mean that we lose out completely.

(iii) Set up a Digital library for sharing of resources use of new media and new services (National Digital Library, USA). Also active research is necessary in the development of tools and software agents with which such libraries can be effectively searched by all.

(iv) Build a strong education community consisting of institutions, students, facilitators, administrators and industry. Although the community is virtual, the administrative and other support models are still evolving. It is quite possible to make the responsible industries as stake holders in the venture. In US, the ventures evolved by Microsoft, Oracle, Cisco and SUN are wonderful models but it is not clear if the Indian industry used to subsidised manpower, limited experience in education and training, borrowed technology facing global competition will be able to rise to the occasion. At the international level, it is not clear what approach the higher education institutions will follow — fight, flight or friends.

(v) Provide encouragement to innovative teachers scholars to become digital publishers. This may result in the availability of high quality educational materials in the form of different media but the copyright law may have a serious impact since there is no clear acceptable definition for "fair use" of copyrighted digital material.

A pragmatic approach to the whole issue will be to set up a moderate high band-width network infrastructure with committed participation from the partner institutions and industry with a clear vision statement and well defined goals to be achieved within a reasonable time frame ensuring long term economic viability. It should also be recognised that the set-up even in its fully developed form will be able to provide larger reach at reduced cost without seriously impairing effectiveness but the teachers will have very little scope for research.

Thus having recognised the fact that distance education/training in various forms will inevitably compete with formal engineering education in the near future, we discuss below in great detail various aspects of distance education.

Distance Education Technologies

The essential components of distance education are

(i) High quality content development and delivery of information through voice, video, data and print.

(ii) A high band-width computer network of servers and clients with appropriate Web Technology tools and audio/video devices.

(iii) Effective educational administration complying with security, examination scheduling and evaluation, electronic commerce, IPR matters etc.

(iv) Digital Library, Web based Virtual Laboratory, Intelligent Agents etc.

Conventional distance education tools like printed notes, audio conferencing and short wave radio and tapes for voice, instructional video tools like slides, video recordings and video conferencing etc., will continue. However computer network and web technologies have totally revolutionalised DE. The above listed technologies are put together by the participation of students, faculty, facilitators, support staff and administrators. The role of all categories of human resources is extremely critical in the successful implementation of a DE programme.

High Quality Content Development — Authoring Tools

Recent advances in multimedia has brought new teaching media. Apart from the obvious advantages of providing realistic audio and visual effects, multimedia education can be interactive and self-paced. The development of good computer based technology packages is a key element in the development of net based distance education through pedagogical improvement on the traditional lecture-tutorial-laboratory paradigm. The interactive multimedia software allows the students to explore in a sequential manner or to move about different topics receiving several topics if necessary and stripping others. The courseware can be designed keeping in mind the level of knowledge of the student audience. Multimedia takes away the boredom of passive lecture notes and brings in diversity through the interactive nature. Thus making multimedia rich courses which can be accessed over the internet is an attractive and creative option for faculty while it serves the dual purpose by enhancing the learning experience for the resident students and opening the educational experience to distance students.

The following objectives are to be kept in mind while authoring a computer based courseware

- The system should be user friendly. If the students have to be trained how to use the system, it will probably never be used.
- The students should be able to use the system at their own pace and level of understanding.
- The system should be intelligent and interactive and not merely a fancy electronic page-turner. The students should be able to solve problems interactively and if necessary guided intelligently.
- The system should be intelligent enough to mimic the actual tutoring by providing helpful hints to the students in solving the problems.
- The system should be easily portable and accessible.

In the past, the teacher delivering courseware had to be conversant with HTML and several other tools. However several authoring tools like Authorware from Macromedia are available in the market now. The executable version does not require Authorware on the client computer and the system requirements are extremely modest. A sample interactive online course is available at site http://www.iitd.ac.in/civil. The course is on Engineering Mechanics — Statics. The courseware acts like a virtual tutor providing hints and guiding the students towards the correct solution. The course was earlier offered to the first year Engineering students of NTU, Singapore.

It is desirable that a distance education institution has a staff team which can generate very attractive courseware. While the teacher provides the inputs, the complementary skill sets on the state of the art technologies such as Java and Javascript, Shockwave movies along with their plug-ins, CGIS, forms, web page-database interactions, frames, layers, image maps, archived and real time streaming audio and video etc.

Table 21.1 shows some of the service providers for Authoring Tools, Course Management and Delivery and Assessment tools.

Table 21.1

Course Management and Delivery	Learning Corporation, ACTV, Aleks, Contiego, Asymetrix Learning Systems, Imagin On, Invest Learning, JDH technologies Knowledge Soft Inc. Lotus (learning space) now owned by IBM, McGraw-Hill Learning Architecture, SCT, WBT, WebCT, White Pine Software
Authoring Tools	Macromedia Inc., Asymetrix Learning Systems
Assessment Tools	ALEKS Corporation, Intellimetric Knowledge Soft

Network and Internet Infrastructure

While it is obvious that even with existing technologies in Networking and WWW, excellent Distant Education programmes are being made available, the future possibilities are even more exciting. The important hardware components for effective DE programmes are–

1. Extensive availability of Client Systems in Learning Centres or affordability of web access equipment for learners.
2. Reliable web access with reasonable bandwidth (upgradable to support video streaming).
3. Collection of reliable servers with server system software — web servers, video servers and Audio server operating on appropriate Operating Systems.
4. Reliable equipments for video and audio capture along with appropriate hardware and software in the client/server systems for recording, archiving or streaming at the studio/classroom.

Engineering institutions generally have sufficient funds now to earmark for the creation of Computer and IT infrastructure and with the availability of cheaper and more efficient technologies, the first two may not be major hurdles. However total confusion prevails on the use of the right technology for getting the institutions or learning centres wired. Although computer ownership and internet access is growing rapidly, it is fair to expect that individual student ownership of PCs and their affordability for the maintenance of the hardware and software may not be achievable over the next 10 years excepting elite institutions. However planning for sufficient dedicated bandwidth for each user in institutions and cyber-cafes in dormitories is a viable solution. Students also learn substantially while working in these locations through interaction with their peers. This argument is particularly relevant in the context of asynchronous learning centres.

The development in the field of high bandwidth fibre optic networking is mind-boggling. With the dismantling of controls, it is anticipated that the development of network infrastructure will be driven by commercial interest in the field of entertainment, data communications etc. The availability of alternate technologies like cable TV, DSL for internet access also opens up new opportunities. While this capacity expansion means that educational material flow crowded out. DE is likely to become extremely effective when two-way video streaming becomes a reality within the available bandwidth. Such a day may not be too far as rapid strides are being made in data compression technology (this can shrink movies so that they can be streamed through ordinary telephone lines) and high bandwidth communication technology (cable modems which can provide bandwidths upward of 2 Mbps). Thus it should be technically possible to set up good quality video conferencing using PCs and Internet and using software like Netmeeting.

The experience of University of Florida at Gainesville is described in Fig 21.1. For effective delivery of audio and video contents, Real Audio and Real-Video systems from Progressive Networks was utilised. Existing Educational Technology studio was integrated with the Internet capabilities using a video digitizer card and a sound card on a P-I 200 MHz machine. An industry standard 16 bit sound card was used. The digital audio + video is streamed at 20 Kbps to the server while ensuring high level of synchronisation between the streams and low latency. At the server, these streams are delivered upon request from web browser. Sixty simultaneous streams are supported. The sequence of events is as follows.

The Web browser points to a page with a link to the audio metafile. The user clicks on the metafile link and the web server sets the MIME type to audio/x-pn-real audio. The web browser looks at the MIME type and starts the real player as a helper application.

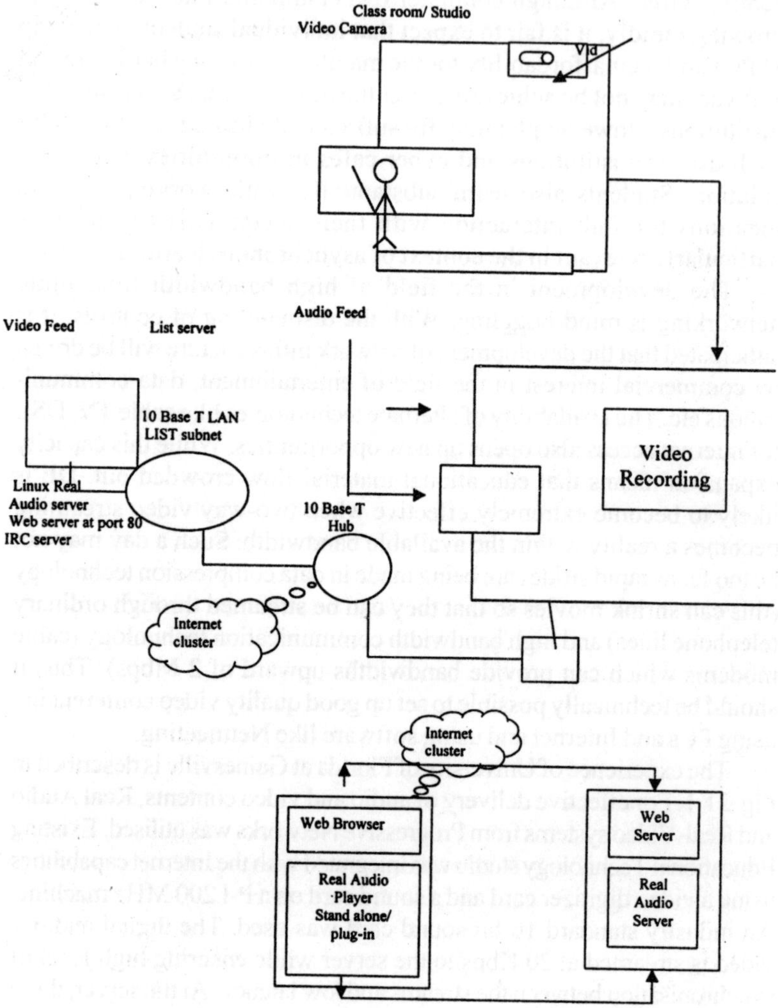
Class room/ Studio
Video Camera
Vid
Audio Feed
Video Feed
List server
10 Base T LAN
LIST subnet
Video
Recording
Linux Real
Audio server
Web server at port 80
IRC server
10 Base T
Hub
Internet
cluster
Internet
cluster
Web Browser
Real Audio
Player
Stand alone/
plug-in
Web
Server
Real
Audio
Server

Fig. 21.1

- The Real Player reads the URL from the metafile and requests the real media file from the Real server. The Real server and WWW servers may be hosted be the same system or multiple servers.
- The Real audio server starts streaming the audio/video files to the Real Players using the UDP streaming protocol.
- The live lecture is also simultaneously achieved.
- Real time interaction from remote students is achieved using electronic conferencing software.

The organisation of windows on a colour graphics writer for an asynchronous lecture session is shown in Fig. 21.2. The individual windows are

1. Audio-video window
2. Textual + graphics window
3. Links to chat room
4. Mailing lists.

The audio-video window depicts the video picture of the lecturer along with the spontaneously written material. An auxiliary web camera is used to capture the written materials as a WWW image. An online WWW chat window allows interaction by remotely located students.

Audio/Video Stream	Class notes
Chat window	Hand written notes

Fig. 21.2

Conduct of Laboratory Sessions

One of the essential components of the regular classroom engineering education is the organisation of laboratory sessions. Presently these are organised during off peak sessions in reputed engineering organisations by sharing the facilities and if necessary the faculty also. However the web technology has thrown up an exciting option to carry out the experiments online over the Internet.

Computer and Electronics technology have been available for a long time to control equipment using Computers. For this, the development of device driver and interfacing this device driver to the computer with suitable electronic card is necessary. The signal from the equipment is also interfaced with the computer for processing data. Appropriate device driver software written in a high level language is essential. In the past, such software used to be proprietary. However LABVIEW developed by National Instruments is very widely used to develop the programme in a user friendly manner. Once such a facility is available for controlling the equipment, web technology can be utilised to access the equipment through the network. A large number of virtual laboratories are being utilised for laboratory experiments in Chemistry and Electrical Engineering. While the technology has been demonstrated the actual offering of laboratory classes has been limited due to problems of bandwidth, latency, userfriendliness etc. Experiments pertaining to Oscilloscope, Control systems and Robotics have been demonstrated and are operational at NUS, Singapore and IIT, Delhi.

Digital Libraries

The libraries of future will essentially be resource centres. They will store information /data in electronic form. They will also

- Concentrate on services to help students and faculties find and organise information.
- Plan to aggregate virtual holding info more encompassing and complete and up-to-date collections.
- Catalogue new multimedia documents.

Michigan Digital Library project envisages providing services to search, filter and manage information in the field of earth and space sciences and economics. They use intelligent agents based software. It is also possible to aggregate single libraries into Mega-Libraries.

Other Policy Issues related to Distance Education in Engineering

It is obvious that the DE technologies are still evolving and there is no specific "the best" option for the implementing Distance Education. It is also obvious that the size at which one needs to operate needs to be carefully chosen. The reputation and commitment of the people to the project is also very essential. A co-operative nature is desirable but to begin with the institutions working together must have some reasonable experience in non-traditional teaching/training systems. The participation from industry could also be added improvement to the programme particularly in the leading edge technologies.

The following modes of Distance Education (DE) are feasible:

1. Regular in-campus students participating in virtual class room asynchronous in space. This may become useful if large classes are to be handled by teachers. However, there is nothing more ideal than one to one interaction in a class room between the teacher and students. However with the establishment of high bandwidth internet and all dormitory rooms wired up, students can participate in the class room. Some universities have attempted this but the availability of information outlet in each hostel room needs to be debated. However establishments of cyber cafes in the hostels is a very positive step.
2. Regular off-campus students asynchronous in space. Such students have limited interaction with the teacher and fellow students. Their utilisation of university resources is also likely to be limited. Further internet services quality may impose restrictions.
3. Regular off-campus students asynchronous in space and time but administrated by a strong local university sub-centre. Such students have reasonable interaction among themselves but if local administration and lecturers are sufficiently motivated, the system works positively. However limited physical access may result in the stymification of the level of education imparted.
4. Students belonging to a university sub-centre take courses asynchronously in time. This is highly desirable form of DE even if offered with the help of tutors etc., since the access to the university resources is better.

5. Self-learning programme where students proceed at their own pace with the use of archived course materials including actual lectures.

As mentioned in the earlier article, logistic issues, teacher related issues, students' approach related issues and other issues to the conduct of examinations, continuous evaluation etc., need to be addressed with care. Planning of laboratory sessions and introduction of web based laboratory classes wherever possible are important.

Suggestions

- Reported engineering institutions like IITs and leading institutions should initiate suitable DE courses to begin with which can be formalised into a coherent programme later.
- Distance Education strongly based upon new web technologies is very promising. Evening programmes with archived lectures and local tutors in sub-centres are likely to be cost effective.
- Other modes of DE should be extensively experimented and studied.
- Encouragement to teachers to generate innovative course delivery materials ensuring IPR protection is essential.
- Training of support and technical staff for administration and technical services is essential.
- To begin with, the university DE programme may hire learning centres for the administration of the programme and use strong network and web technologies for effective implementation and administration. Highest level of quality in evaluation/ certification need to be maintained while adhering to strict time schedules.
- The university may subsequently network with other institutions and offer joint programmes.

REFERENCES

1. MacArthur, D. — *Untangling the web: Applications of the Internet and other Information Technologies to Higher Education*. http://www.rand.org/publications/DRU/DRU1401/index.html

2. *Distance Education at a glance.* http://www.uidaho.edu/evo/dist1.html
3. Ramakrishnan, C.V. and Gupta, Ashok (2000) — *Non-formal Education in Engineering using New Information Technologies* — Proceedings, Seminar on Human Capital Development in Engineering for Global Competitiveness, Fourteenth Indian Engineering Congress, Jan.
4. Bourne, J.R., Brodersen, A.J., Campbell, J.O., Dowant, M.M., Shiavi, R.G. (1997) — A Model for On-Line Learning Network in Engineering Education, *JALN,* Vol. 1,1,73-96.

22

Information Technology *Versus* Technical Education Synergy: The Need of the Hour

Prof. J. R. ISAAC*

IT: What is the Problem? and, What is IT?

With the growing acceptance of IT as a major economic tool for the country, there is a tendency for IT to detract from other crucial national needs. It is certainly true that IT, in its incarnations as software and Internet-based technologies, has the potential to capitalize on India's main strength — the availability, the competent, well-trained human resources. However, apart from this task of earning much-needed foreign exchange; the country has its own internal developmental problems. When developed countries turn to IT, they know that other developmental needs have already been met. However, in a developing country such as ours, it is essential that all developmental essentials be prioritised and met. So IT has to be viewed not only as a foreign exchange earner, but also as a vital tool in development.

Has IT been defined in precise terms? Is the notion of the computer being an "information processor" understood? If IT is to lead us into the Information Age, have we understood the main paradigms of this age? In fact, has the very notion of "information" been given a common understanding? Before Computer Science was accepted as a scientific academic discipline, the issue was debated over years by the world's leading experts. The term IT has been a sort of "back-door" entry! The notion that it is concerned with computing and communications — in

* Adviser, NIIT Ltd., New Delhi.

vague uncertain terms, conveniently leaves out all reference to "information" ! So IT has come to mean many things in many contexts, and has been used as the basis for even policy formulation. It is the word "information" — which is not a technology but essentially a human commodity — that enables IT to be thought of as a "human technology". So IT is more a social phenomena, than a technological one.

The "Pull" of IT — Harmful Effects?

We are aware of the fact that IT has the potential to greatly enhance all developmental initiatives. But this requires the understanding and research into IT as a catalytic multiplier of all human activities. But perhaps the most important role that can be played by IT is in the generation of more effective human resources. The critical role that can be played by computers and the internet in education and training has not been understood.

In fact, almost the inverse is taking place. Historically, India's strength in the generation of human resources in science, engineering and technology had been commendable. Science and mathematics have been highly respected, and India has an established and commendable university system. In particular, from the developmental angle, the engineering institutions have been effective generators of human resources.

However, India had to first face the "external brain-drain" caused by the Western pull, first for engineers and then for software specialists. But with the advent of the universal interest in IT in the country, there is the possibility of a more insidious "internal brain-drain" taking place. There is the possibility of the "remuneration-pull towards IT" drawing away scientists and engineers. As it is few have genuine interests in the existing college courses. The general trend is towards "conversion to IT". If the present trend is allowed to continue unabated, in ten years the development of the country will be severely handicapped due to a serious shortage of scientists and engineers.

Further, too much reliance on the current "export-oriented" IT thrusts may not pay off in the long run. It is evident that the foreign demand for IT products will tend towards being more and more science and engineering based. Embedded systems call for high level techniques. Then there is the looming potential of genetic engineering as a future thrust.

With these impending dangers, the country has been lulled into complacency due to the rosy picture presented by the current export-oriented IT initiatives.

Towards What Future?

Should this trend be permitted to continue?

Should students be allowed to take less and less interest in engineering and science (not to mention all other present disciplines)?

What would be the quality (and quantity!) of human resources generated through the years?

Can India's educational systems offer a viable alternative to this dilemma?

Will the current trust in Indian IT human resources be sustainable — or will it dwindle through the years?

Is there a Solution to this Educational Problem Caused by the Over-heating of the "IT pull"?

The possible solution lies in understanding IT in its larger perspective — not just as a "foreign exchange earner". IT has been classified as "one of the greatest social change agents", and India as is well known, cries out for social change. Yet there are only a handful who consider IT to be a possible solution provider to this dilemma.

Computers and IT in Education

Falling interest in science and engineering studies is our prime concern, aggravated by the fact that there is a general drift towards IT. Is there a synergistic bond between science/engineering and IT? With the advent of computers, there was a great interest in computers as powerful tools in education. This synergy been computers and education has been manifested in Computer Assisted/Aided/Enhanced/Enriched Learning/ Education, etc. Computer based/managed Education has had a close relationship with educational specialists. Many attributes of the computer — its programmability, interactivity, memory, speed, etc., make it an ideal educational media. But perhaps "simulation" is the most potent of the tools, as it yields educational insights into physical phenomena. Adaptability to user needs on an individualised basis, is another advantage. Intelligent Computer Assisted Instruction (ICAI) and Intelligent Tutoring Systems (ITS) included the power of Artificial

Intelligence into the processes of teaching and learning. The Industrial Age set the stage for the "Instructor-Driven Paradigm of Education". However, the Information Age introduced the more potent notion of the "Learner Driven Paradigm". In any case, rapidly changing technologies made the "learner" central to the educational process.

The advent of the Internet, with its principal power of "dispersion", education took on more "open" initiatives. With the developments, "technical education" and "IT" became true synergistic partners as the generators of effective human resources.

"IT" and "Education": Towards a Synergistic Future?

It is through this strategy that the dwindling interest in technical and engineering education, and the general drift towards IT, can be meaningfully synthesised. It is essential that the country take steps towards incorporating IT into all its educational systems. Not only into its science and engineering programmes, but also into other areas such as law, medicine, art, etc. IT should become an inherent part and parcel of all education. This would not only increase a true appreciation of IT among students but also enhance their interest in disciplines of their own choice. IT should be instrumental in enhancing the students understanding and interest in the discipline of his/her own choice. This meaningful exposure to the student — of IT as an integral part of his/her educational process — would gradually minimise the unnecessary "IT glamour" of present days. Also this would be essential for the higher level scientific/engineering hardware/software development of the country for the future.

Based on this strategy, the synergy between "IT" and "education", will generate a truly strong human resources workforce, which can meet the higher challenges of the future. It should not be "IT" or "Education" that defines the required higher level human resources, but rather the synthesis of IT and Education.

23

Educational Reforms in Technical Education
Major Issues and Concerns

Prof. P.B. SHARMA*

Introduction

Fifty years of Indian Republic have witnessed tremendous growth of technical education in this country. From around 60 institutions of engineering at degree level in 1950, today we have around 800 institutions offering degree and post-graduate programmes in addition to around 1250 polytechnics. The intake at the degree level in engineering and technology today stands close to 2 lakh while at diploma level, the intake is around 2.2 lakh indicating a rapid growth of degree level programmes in India.

Technical education in India has emerged as one of the major areas of strength for our nation's economy. The advent of Information Technology revolution has enabled India to occupy a front seat in the arena of IT education and software export and it is the outcome of the sustained efforts in India in technical education in the last few decades. However, with the rapid advances in Information Technology, technical education in India is facing a serious challenge of significant upgradation and coupled with this is the challenge of motivating the engineering phenomenon of cross over from engineering to non-engineering disciplines has become a major concern in this country.

* Vice Chancellor, Rajiv Gandhi Proudyogiki Vishwavidyalaya, University of Technology of Madhya Pradesh, Bhopal.

This has largely eroded our engineering technology strength in the industries as well as in the service sector organisations. The net result is that the engineering and technology education in India is still, by and large, service the interests of the developed countries through brain drain and human capital flight. Integration of the ethics and values of engineering profession is still a desired goal in engineering education in India. The agenda for education reforms in technical education has, therefore, to focus on the following major issues:

- Revitalising teaching-learning processes through enhanced inputs of Information Technology.
- Meeting enormous shortage of faculty by innovated teaching-learning methodologies such as teaching comprising of self-learning modules supported by expert academicians, and finally value-added by intimate contact with the faculty.
- Reforming work culture in the institutions — tuning it to the requirements of quality, productivity and service.
- Establishing synergetic partnership with the industries and promoting entrepreneurship.
- Integrating ethics and values in engineering education.

The paper discusses the above issues concerning reforms in technical education. Strategic framework to meet the challenges in hand within a short span of time is also presented with a view to provide a meaningful strategy for rapid track transformation of technical education in the next few years in the new millennium.

Our Strength

One of the main strength of our engineering education is that it has retained its bias for merit-based admissions, thus encouraging competitiveness. Degree programmes in engineering and technology — disciplines have remained a prime attraction for school leavers in this country, ever since Independence. The enthusiasm with which the student community turns towards engineering and technology courses I can be witnessed in a large number of applications that are received for the entrance tests in engineering — such as JEE for the IITs wherein over 1,00,000 applicants compete for approximately 2,500 seats. The same is the case for the highly competitive entrance exam for the Delhi College of Engineering (DCE) (and other premier institutions, such as the University of Roorkee, BITS Pilani and the Regional Engineering Colleges. Secondly, engineering and technology education in India has constantly nurtured — the science base of modern engineering, alongside with core engineering courses. This has equipped our students with necessary competence for a meaningful integration of science with engineering and technology. Modern technologies heavily lean towards scientific analysis for continued improvement in process efficiency, for a cost effective product innovation and for an overall increase in efficacy of a system. A strong component of industrial training and project work forms an integral part of engineering curriculum. In addition to laboratory exercises, this promotes problem-solving capabilities in our students.

With the above backdrop, it is not surprising that engineering education in India has received widespread recognition from the advanced nations. In fact, the engineering education in the IITs and in some select institutions such as the University of Roorkee, BITS Pilani and the DCE, is considered superior to many well-known universities in the advanced countries. This superiority is primarily because of the focus on quality and strict adherence to merit in admissions. The competitive edge which the Indian engineering institutions have developed in engineering the technology education, has attracted foreign universities from America, England, Canada, Australia, France and Germany, to come to India, to seek student for their post-graduate and research programmes. This reflects positively on the competence of our engineering graduates and on the capabilities of higher technical education system in our country.

Our Weakness

But then the IITs, University of Roorkee, BITS Pilani and the DCE are not the only institutions in Engineering and Technology in this country. We have, as of today, around 800 institutions at degree level affiliated to around 200 universities in this country. A wide variation of competence and calibre is produced in these institutions. While the IITs and other reputed institutions are able to market their produce in India and abroad, a large portion of engineering graduates in the country specially in conventional disciplines remain unemployed immediately after leaving the institutions. In fact, many are under-employed while some are even labelled as unemployable.

One may wonder, however, that despite having world recognition for the quality of our graduates and post-graduates, why is it that the Indian engineering institutions such as the IITs, University of Roorkee, Madras University, and Anna University, do not actively engage themselves in attracting foreign students in great numbers in these institutions? Perhaps we are allowing our territory to be visited by outside universities to take advantage of the competence, which we generate in our students. Our own institutions which impart high quality under-graduate and post-graduate education are not currently having any policy initiative to take advantage of equally bright students in other developing and developed countries, who could receive quality technical education at an affordable cost in India. Such an initiative will also reduce the burden of fees on Indian students. Thus, there is a genuine need to consider this aspect in our future policy plans. Marketing of Indian technical education abroad is an important agenda for policy markers in India.

Another point of concern is the multiplicity of entrance exams, which prevails in this country. Even in Delhi, one has to appear in JEE for the IITs, CEE for DCE, and another entrance examination for Jamia Millia Islamia in addition to combined entrance examinations for the state level colleges in various states of the country. The multiplicity of entrance examinations is in fact breaking the back of energetic school leavers who turn towards engineering education in great numbers. The students are nearly exhausted while taking admission in an engineering institution. The urge to pursue engineering as a career on completion of the degree programmes gradually disappears, giving rise to an intense desire to cross over to non-engineering professions.

R&D in Educational Institutions — Need for a Paradigm Shift

Teaching alone or teaching and research both as the responsibilities and job functions of teachers in engineering institutions are a matter still being debated in our country. There is a feeling, which persists in academic circles that diversion of efforts of a teacher towards R&D usually sacrifices teaching interest. There are teachers who are highly devoted to teaching and spent much of their spare time for preparation of teaching material and innovate in teaching to sustain interest in the class. They obviously do not have much interest in research and development, which besides being time consuming deprive them of the intellectual freedom, which they enjoy as teachers. R&D being time-bound and result-oriented demands that the teacher devotes his considerable time to the success of the work, which often involves managerial functions besides expert guidance. Bring financially rewarding and a means of recognition in the profession, R&D acts as a catalyst to sustain one's interest in innovation and creative research.

The students in engineering institutions are to be taught by those who take pains in sustaining the interest of the students by constantly updating their teaching material while at the same time commanding a high reputation as practicing technologists, something similar to what is done in medical colleges. This requires a paradigm shift from the R&D for career prospects to R&D for national prosperity and for nurturing excellence in technical education.

Another point of interest here is in respect of funding of R&D in India. The government is the major financer of R&D expenditure in engineering institutions and R&D laboratories in India. The private industries only contribute less than 1.0 per cent to this vital component of economy. In any case, the R&D expenditure in India is only 0.9 per cent of GNP while the developed nations spend upto 6 per cent of GNP on R&D to create a competitive edge for their innovative products. The poor spending on R&D speaks for the miserable position in respect of intellectual property generation in India. While a higher allocation on R&D is essential, the higher technical educational institutions must perform a lot better in respect of effectiveness of their R&D activities. A clear focus on relevance is essential to produce the desired impact on our economy.

Curriculum Innovation — Immediate Steps Needed

With rapid advances in science and technology, the fast decrease in half-life of knowledge acquired and with the emerging demands for flexible human resource development, it has become absolutely essential to restructure the course curriculum, design course structure to in-built flexibility as also to strengthen the inter-disciplinary component in engineering and technology courses. At the same time, a sound science base of modern engineering is to be provided. Care and concern for society and environment has to become a core component of the engineering curriculum so that the engineers of today as well as the engineers of tomorrow become more responsible to the society to which they belong. They, then, in true sense, will be the pillars of strength of the economy and will be the prime movers of techno-economic growth and development of the country.

In order to succeed in our efforts of providing the much needed improvement in the course curriculum, it is absolutely essential that the dons in the educational institutions recognise the need for assessment of skills, aptitudes and knowledge requirements of the industries and organisations, which recruit their products. Currently, there is a total absence of such a feedback system.

Because of the visible compulsions of global competitiveness, the industries foresee the technology and human resource requirements faster than the institutions do. In fact, the industries are conscious of their requirements and they gear their management to meet the challenges, which the market driven economy assign to them.

Institution Industry Linkages — Need to Create Synergetic Partnership

The academic environment in an engineering institution is to be enriched both by the analytical as well as practical aptitude. Such an environment can be effectively created if the linkages between institution and the industries are strengthened. Such linkages should provide a dynamic environment in which the expertise from the R&D could be effectively utilised by the industries and the real life problems and prospects of the industries are taken as challenges both by the expert faculty and the students.

The effective linkages between industry and the institution could take the form of MOUs allowing each other to take advantage of and to support each other's activities. Greater participation of students in solving the industrial problems can be ensured by designing project work in consultation with the industries. Such projects will provide a meaningful opportunity for the students to express their innovative and creative skills. The project work will thus induct the students into the research methodology even at the undergraduate level where the mind if often highly innovative and creative. It is also highly desirable that the students are provided with much greater contact hours with the experts from the industries and R&D organisations so that they can effectively interact and perceive the value of their studies. Such visits can become more meaningful if a more direct linkage is established with the selected industries and organisations. The idea should be involve the student in the real life situations while they are still in the institutions. Special courses with a committed intake designed specifically for the industries can also help develop the relevant human resources. The training and re-training of engineers can also be ensured through such linkages.

The linkages between the institutions and the professional societies are also highly important. Such linkages shall help inculcate an attitude of professionalism in the young minds and such help the students community aspire for a contribution to the profession to which they shall rightly belong to on completion of their studies.

Style of Management — Need for Re-orientation

The style of management of higher technical education in India has by and large lacked the appreciation of the role of the teachers, its faculty in the overall development of the institutions. It has lacked emphasis on people's development least it has cared for nurturing an environment for the development of an individual. The quality improvement programme of the 70s and 80s has, no doubt, improved the qualifications of the faculty but this programme has not largely benefited the institutions. The management and the teachers still remain at loggerheads in most institutions in respect of their expectations and aspirations. There is no meeting of the minds between the objectives of the institution and the growth and development of the faculty members.

The global economy scenario requires world class people who, besides being globally competitive, must practice a quality and productivity linked to work culture. The educational institutions in the higher technical education sector have to ensure that they have in their faculty and staff, people who are world class having calibre and competence to remain knowledge workers throughout their working life. To cater for these requirements, the study of management has to undergo a clear re-orientation in respect of

- Recognition of achievements.
- Empowerment of an individual.
- Identification of talent.
- Respect of one's capabilities.
- Motivation for continuous upgradation of knowledge and skills.

In essence, this calls for re-engineering the system of administration and management of engineering institutions.

Framework for Rapid-Track Transformation of Technical Education

Rapid track transformation of technical education in India should be the desired goal of educational reforms in technical education if we have to retain the global competitive edge, which, we have today. The proposed strategies for success in this regard are:

Policy Reforms

Prepare a Policy Document on Technical Education in India in the next twenty years. In the absence of a well-defined policy for technical education, unplanned growth of technical education has created institutions without teachers and technical education to create national prosperity.

Create Mechanisms for Quality and Productivity Audit of Institutions engaged in technical education — current accreditation policies are not adequate. Bring Q and P revolution through rigorous campaign and by attractive incentives for the institutions showing constant improvement.

Revitalise Technical Education in affiliated colleges by strengthening University of Technology of the state. Ensure that these universities become facilitators of rapid track transformation of technical education in their state.

Canalise central funding from AICTE and Government of India through the Universities of Technology. This way, we shall be able to ensure productive utilisation funding for modernisation of laboratories and thrust area and development.

Curriculum Reforms

Carry out major reforms in curriculum to make it more suited to today's requirements of the industry. The industry requires engineers having knowledge and skills to hand today's technology systems, possessing interdisciplinary competence and capabilities to handle modern IT driven equipments and systems. The industry requires engineers to possess high managerial skills and skills of handling changing work requirements. The industry needs engineers committed to excelling through worship of work having high moral and ethical commitment to the profession. The curriculum is to meet these requirements in addition to preparing its students to become global players.

Create synergetic partnership with the industries: set up mechanisms to facilitate such a partnership. Both the policy for technical education as well as the industry policy of the country must focus on strengthening the partnership between institutions and the industries.

Massive overall of management of technical education is to be carried out to create structures supportive of nurturing innovation and creativity alongside serving the cause of quality technical education and research.

Rapid track transformation of technical education requires that the agenda for reforms be implemented with speed while at the same time ensuring that the reforms yield the desired results.

Concluding Remarks

- The management of higher technical and management institutions in India has so far lacked its emphasis on quality of the system or monitoring of its productivity. Compared to this, quality culture and productivity movements are the backbone of the success of the modern industries. Time has come when engineering institutions, which contribute one of the most important resources, *i.e.* the human resource, adopt and practice Total Quality Management (TQM) as the management philosophy.
- The productivity in higher technical institutions is seriously affected by the quality of teachers. Teachers must, therefore, be highly motivated and committed to the cause of teaching, research and industrial liaison. Attracting talented youth to join the faculty is a monumental challenge to the management of these institutions. There is an urgent need to review the personnel policies in this respect.
- Teachers in engineering and technology institutions have to enhance their activities beyond teaching. They have to perform a triple role — the role of an expert teacher, a sincere scientist and a practicing technologist simultaneously. It is only then that their profound wisdom will be an instrument of social change and will undoubtedly be the guiding spirit for the improvement of quality of life of the people at large.

- Technology development, technology transfer, increased R&D and product innovation are to be given an added impetus in engineering and technology institutions to meaningfully utilise the expertise of the faculty and the infrastructure.
- Heavy expenditure on modernisation of laboratories, library books and journals, and high-speed computational facilities necessary demands resource sharing between the institutions, R&D organisations and the industries. A part of the solution to resource crisis lies in networking of resources and facilities. A more productive utilisation of infrastructure, laboratories and the talented skills of the faculty and staff is an essential aspect of resource generation.

Thus, educational reform in technical education are to focus on the issues and concerns raised in this paper so as to ensure that the programme of action is carefully formulated to pave the way for rapid track transformation of technical education in India in the next 8 years.

REFERENCES

Sharma, P.B. (1994) Management of Engineering Institutions — New Challenges, *International Jr. of Engineering Education, USA*.

Sharma, P.B. (1996) "Excellence in Higher Technical Education — Issues Involved", *Planning and Management of Technical Education in India*, AICTE, New Delhi.

Sharma, P.B. (1999) "*Financing R&D in Engineering Institutions in India*", proc. of AIU National Seminar on R&D in Universities, RRL Bhopal, September 20-21.

Sharma, P.B. (2000) "*Libraries and Information Systems in the New Millennium*", Keynote address at National Seminar on Libraries and Information Systems at Cross Road, Bhopal.

24

Revamping Engineering Education and Training in India to Meet the Challenges of Globalisation and Poverty Reduction

S.S. CHAKRABORTY*

Strengths

India can legitimately take pride in the progress made in many fields of science, technology, education, agriculture, health etc. over the last 50 years. Food grain production has increased four-fold. Per capita income had doubled. Life expectancy has significantly increased; infant mortality has declined, literacy rate has gone up to more than 62 per cent. Technical education institutions have increased considerably from 38 institutions at the degree level in 1947 to more than 500 institutions at the degree level today. Correspondingly, from 53 diploma level institutions in 1947, there are more than 1100 technical institutions at the diploma level today. Indian professionals have made a mark in the Information Technology field world-wide.

Weaknesses

These achievements over the last 50 years should not obscure the facts that

- India has more than one billion people to feed.
- More than 26 per cent of the people are below the poverty line.

* Managing Director, CES, New Delhi.

- On UNDP Human Development Index (HDI), which is a composite measure of three basic dimensions of development
  (i) health and longevity,
  (ii) knowledge and skills, and
  (iii) income generating capacity, India stands at 128th position out of 175 UN member countries.
- Regional disparities have persisted in India; levels of achievement in education, health and income generation vary between and within states, as well as between social groups.
- Quality of education and training particularly in areas of skill development and professional growth, has been indifferent and falls far short of international expectations and standards.
- In the field of Civil Engineering, which is one of the oldest and largest groups of skilled professionals engaged in infrastructure development, curriculum and teaching methods have remained unchanged by and large.
- Quality of education and training in civil engineering and other disciplines of technical education are often unsatisfactory and irrelevant to the needs of the industry.
- Industry and education do not co-operate effectively to modernise curriculum, or provide training of teachers and sharing knowledge of modern technology.

Opportunities

- Globalisation has opened up unprecedented new opportunities and risks in India.
- The globalisation process is finding its bearing in a slow but steady manner.
- India's present climate of trade liberalisation and privatisation, which started with reforms in 1991, opens up opportunities to integrate Indian economy with the global economy and promises, employment expansion and poverty alleviation.
- Education and skill level of technical workforce need to be developed to seize the opportunities offered by the process of globalisation and liberalisation.
- Technical education and training is root and branch of global competitiveness and vital factor in attracting Foreign Direct

Investment (FDI) and the transfer of technology, which it may bring.

- Government of India has embarked upon an ambitious plan of infrastructure development in transport, communication and other sectors, implementation of which will require large number of high quality "global" technical manpower. This will lead to rapid economic growth and reduce poverty in rural and urban areas.
- India's rising private sector industry, strong institutional base, growing science-based secondary education system provides additional opportunities for revamping engineering education and training to meet the challenges of globalisation and poverty reduction.

Conditions

To revamp engineering education to turnout 'global' workforce for the 21st century, the basic requirements are:

- Capacity building and strengthening degree and diploma level technical education institutions.
- Linking technical education system with international professional bodies and industries.
- Establishing strong industry-institute partnership within and between countries.
- Developing continuing education and professional upgradation programmes for engineers.
- Develop national consensus on the strategy to be adopted for development, and the priorities to be accorded to the different branches of Engineering Education.
- Developing a strong partnership for technical and financial support from multilateral, bilateral agencies, and international professional organisations, national policy making bodies and the private sector organisations showing interest and concerns for human resources development for infrastructure development.

A Five-year Approach Twards Revamping Engineering Education

To deliberate on the issues involved and develop sustainable strategies for revamping engineering education in India, a beginning could be made through:

- Organising four regional level workshops attended by professionals, policy makers, experts in technical education and private sector players.
- Four regional level workshops to be followed by a National Seminar on the key issues identified and recommendations made on the Regional Workshops.
- A national consensus is to be arrived at.
- A plan of action and implementation over a period of 3 to 5 years to be developed.
- Beginning may be made through the 4 workshops organised for revamping Civil Engineering Education. It is the profession creating infrastructure of transport, sanitation, energy, health etc.
- Some of the key players have already expressed keen interest in this area and it occupies a critical place in the context of the GOI's commitment to develop vast network of roads and highways as well as other communication facilities.
- Linkage to be established with appropriate programmes of DFID, IEI, ICE, WB and ADB to augment internal resources.

Focus

Civil Engineering is the practice of improving and maintaining the man-made and natural environment to enhance the quality of life for present and future generations. Focus for this section on Civil Engineering as the starting point for revamping engineering education in India. IEI, CEL and CES are deeply committed to revamp civil engineering education in India.

Objective

- To enhance professional efficiency, work ethics and standards in civil engineering profession for effective and economic development and global competitiveness.

- To enhance the capability of civil engineers in planning, designing, construction, maintenance and management of infrastructure.
- To enhance the potential of civil engineers in the process of globalisation to improve their international mobility and competitiveness.
- To improve the image of civil engineering as a profession in the society and ability to work in a cross-cultural team environment and in partnership with the community.
- To play an active role in development policies, investments and infrastructure management.
- To act as a leader in development planning, infrastructure development and management of natural resources and maintenance programmes.

Issues for Discussion in Workshops

To identify constraints faced in civil engineering education, the profession has limitations including the following:

- Not always able to contribute effectively due to lack of basic practical training and experience in different aspects of work.
- Shortage of experienced personnel to solve the problems of planning, designing, organisation, management and supervision of civil engineering works.
- Shortage of sufficiently trained engineers to supervise maintenance of roads, irrigation systems, sanitary and health facilities and other infrastructure activities in India.
- No organised institutional training for Continuing Professional Development (CPD).
- Lacks organisational and management techniques as part of formal civil engineering education.
- Quantitative assessment of demand and supply of civil engineers in India.
- Ways and means of improving the quality and efficiency of the engineers through Continuing Professional Development (CPD).
- CPD can be structured *via* workshops, talks, seminars, meetings, newsletters and open learning programmes.

- Enhancing professional standards through appropriate accreditation and certification.
- The process of accreditation and certification needs to be standardised to international levels meeting internationally quality standards.
- Strategies to improve the image of civil engineering professional including becoming signatory-member of Washington Accord, and the Engineers Mobility Forum.

Collaboration of National and International Agencies to Achieve the Objectives

- The core group may be composed of DFID, CES/ICE and some state governments. This group could be expanded.
- DFID in partnership with State Governments in India would be requested to finance the project since they are committed to elimination of poverty and support the process of globalisation.
- IEI/CE/CES would be responsible for accreditation of civil engineering courses as per international standards. They would work together for accreditation from appropriate bodies and would be responsible for imparting professional training in a coordinated manner including IT enabled services.
- CES would identify organisations for training of workforce at the grassroots level and facilitate the work of IEI and work and act as the Nodal Coordinating Agency.

Proposal for a Discussion Group

- This concept paper may be discussed in a small group meeting of 8 to 10 persons to highlight the issues and thrash out the problems.
- This discussion should lead to the preparation of a definite project proposal for submission to appropriate agency(ies) and initiate time-bound action for Revamping Engineering Education in India for poverty alleviation, sustainable development and globalisation.

25

Technical Education in India

BALA KRISHNA K. NAYAR*

Inordinate Stress on Humanities

India has the second largest education system in the world, next only to that of the United States of America. The total number of students at the tertiary level in India was about 64 lakh in 1996-97 consisting of 60.6 lakh in the Universities and 3.2 lakh in Polytechnics.

The number of tertiary level students in the Russian Federation was only three-fourths of that in India. Japan had about two-thirds our number, and China about half the Indian figure. France and Germany had only about one-third of the number of tertiary students while Mexico and Brazil had about one-fourth of our number.

University Education in India is characterised by the inordinate stress on Humanities. Of the 13 countries with tertiary enrolment exceeding 15 lakhs listed in the UNESCO Statistical Year Book 1999 (Table 25.1). India had the highest percentage of 48.5 in Humanities. None of the other countries listed had even 20 per cent of their tertiary students specialising in Humanities. The number of students pursuing Humanities in the Indian Universities in 1996-97 would appear to have been larger than the total enrolment in Chinese Universities.

The inordinate emphasis on Humanities leads to the diversion of scarce resources needed for the pursuit of technical education.

Comparative Neglect of Natural Sciences and Medicine

Natural Sciences, including Engineering and Technology, accounted for over 53 per cent of the tertiary enrolment in the case of China and

* Vice President, Indian Association for the Advancement of Science.

Table 25.1: Percentage Share of Different Fields in Countries with Tertiary Enrolment exceeding 15 lakh

Country	*Year*	*Enrol-ment (lakhs)*	*Hum. per cent*	*Soc. Sc. per cent*	*Edn. per cent*	*Nat. Sc. per cent*	*Med. Sc. per cent*	*Others per cent*
India	96-97	60.6	48.5	20.7	3.9	24.6	2.0	–
Russian Fed.	94-95	44.6	7.3	22.3	10.2	48.5	8.5	3.3
Japan	94-95	39.2	18.1	37.9	7.9	22.9	8.1	5.0
China	94-95	29.3	6.4	9.4	16.4	53.2	8.9	5.6
Korean Rep.	96-97	25.4	16.5	25.2	5.9	34.1	5.1	13.2
Indonesia	95-96	23.0	6.4	46.3	17.2	28.2	1.9	–
Germany	96-97	21.3	15.8	30.5	5.8	30.7	10.8	6.4
France	95-96	20.9	15.0	39.6	4.2	24.7	10.6	6.0
Italy	96-97	18.9	15.4	41.9	3.4	27.7	8.7	3.0
UK	94-95	18.1	14.9	30.8	9.4	28.7	16.2	–
Spain	96-97	16.8	9.9	42.2	8.0	30.5	7.1	2.3
Brazil	94	16.6	9.0	44.0	11.8	22.5	9.3	3.7
Mexico	96-97	16.1	2.0	40.0	14.2	31.1	8.3	3.5

Source: UNESCO Statistical Year Book 1999.

48.5 per cent in the Russian Federation. It exceeded 30 per cent in the case of the Korean Republic, Germany, Spain and Mexico. Natural Sciences accounted for less than 25 per cent in the case of India. Only Japan and Brazil had a lower share, among the top dozen or so.

The percentage going in for Medicine was only 2 in India, compared to 7 per cent or more in 10 of the 13 countries listed. The other two exceptions were Indonesia with 1.9 per cent and Korean Republic with 5.1 per cent in Medicine. Indonesia had 5 qualified nurses per doctor and Korean Republic had 2 per doctor compared to only 1 nurse per doctor in India.

Taking Medicine also into account, India had a total of 26.6 per cent of her University students in Scientific and Technical fields. India is the only country in the top list in which the combined total in these fields was below 30 per cent of the tertiary enrolment. The loss of emphasis on Education in Science and Technology, in a country immensely proud of its long and glorious heritage in these fields, may appear an unmitigated tragedy.

Striking Decline in Share of Enrolment in Technical Education

Most of the students in scientific and technical fields in India have been pursuing pure science. The share of technical fields was only about 10 per cent in 1996.

University enrolments had increased six-fold from 2,28,881 in 1947 to 13,68,803 in 1967. In the meantime, enrolment for technical educational had increased nearly ten-fold 45,643 in 1947 to 4,32,686 in 1967. As a result of the concerted action taken by the Nehru Government, the share of technical education increased from about 20 per cent in 1947 to about 32 per cent in 1967.

Table 25.2: Growth of Enrolment in General and Technical Education

Year	*Enrolment in*		
	Tech. Edn.	*General Edn.*	*Total*
1947	45,643 (19.9 %)	1,83,238 (80.1 %)	2,28,881
1957	2,00,100 (23.2 %)	6,61,975 (76.8 %)	8,62,075
1967	4,32,686 (21.6 %)	9,36,117 (68.4 %)	13,68,803
1977	5,03,134 (14.7 %)	18,29,801 (85.3 %)	23,32,935
1987	5,49,669 (9.9 %)	49,83,329 (90.1 %)	55,32,998

Source: K.B. Power, Higher Education in India since Independence Retrospect and Future Options, AIU 1997 (Table 3).

Note: Figures in paranthesis indicate percentage.

The engineering unemployment crisis of 1964 dealt a severe blow to the rapid growth of technical education in India. During 1967 to 1996, the overall enrolment had increased nearly four-fold from 13.7 lakh to 55.3 lakh. But the enrolment in technical education had increased only marginally by 25 per cent from 4.3 lakh to 5.5 lakh. The share of technical education had come down from 31.6 per cent in 1967 to 9.9 per cent in 1996.

Talented Body Losing Interest in Technical Education

A closer examination shows that this increase of 1.17 lakh in enrolment in technical education in India between 1967 and 1996 was largely due to the increase in women taking up technical education.

Of the increase in enrolment of about 70,000 between 1967 and 1977, as many as 32,000 was contributed by female students. Between

Table 25.3: Enrolment of Male Female Students in Technical Education

Year	*Enrolment*		
	Male	*Female*	*Total*
1947	3,92,751	39,935	4,32,686
1977	4,31,051	72,083	5,03,134
1987	4,27,931	1,20,951	5,48,882
1996	4,27,126	1,33,543	5,49,669

Source: K.B. Power, loc. cit. (Table 5).

1977 and 1987, there was a fall of over 3,100 in the number of male students. Between 1987 and 1996, there was a greater fall of about 12,600 female students who had joined technical education.

Thus, between 1977 and 1996, there had been a fall of about 15,000 in the number of male students taking up technical education in India at the degree level, against an increase of 61,000 in the number of female students.

Poor Pass Percentages

Out of 40,665 students who appeared for the Bachelor's Degree in Engineering/Technology, 12,482 failed to get through according to UGC data. They formed more than 30 per cent.

The pass percentage of males and females in the subjects are given in Table 25.4. The performance of female students is distinctly better than that of the male students in all the cases listed.

Table 25.4: Pass percentage at degree level in Engineering and Technology

Subject	*Male*		*Female*	
	No.	*Pass per cent*	*No.*	*Pass per cent*
Civil	14.256	57.3	1,172	73.3
Mechanical	6,159	63.9	22	83.3
Computer Sc. and Eng.	2,663	51.1	689	80.0
Electronic and Comm.	2,424	65.6	628	78.5
Chemical	1,938	65.8	68	91.2
B.Tech	1,768	84.3	211	93.8
Electronic and Inst.	1,180	65.7	189	88.4
Architecture	888	84.0	164	89.6
Production	804	73.9	30	93.3
Elect. and Electronic	295	28.1	64	34.4

Source: Based on UGC Data.

The pass percentage of male students in Civil Engineering, the subject with the largest intake, was close to that of BA students with over 56 per cent. The performance at the Bachelors degree in Computer Science and Engineering by male students was much worse—closer to that of B.Sc. students with a pass percentage of about 53 than that of even Arts students.

Whether this large-scale failure is due to our inability to attract talented students to pure and applied science, or our inability to provide appropriate training is a matter for serious consideration.

Low Outturn from Institutions for Technical Education Compared to our Competitors

The outturn of engineers at the diploma and degree levels in the mid-1990s in a few leading countries is given in Table 25.5.

Table 25.5: Outturn of Engineers at Different Levels (Mid-1990s)

Country	*Year*	*Outturn*		
		Level 5	*Level 6*	*Total*
Russian Federation	95	1,80,979	1,32,874	3,13,853
China	94	1,39,490	1,28,813	2,68,303
USA	95	1,12,479	90,961	2,13,440
Japan	96	90,450	99,457	1,89,907
India	96	94,554	75,450	1,70,004

Source: UNESCO Statistical Year Book 1998 and IAMR Data.

Russian Federation had the largest outturn of non-graduate engineers (Level 5 according to UNESCO) amounting to about 1,81,000. China with an outturn of about 1,40,000 came second, closely followed by USA with about 1,22,500. The outturn of diploma level engineers in Japan was about half of that in the Russian Federation. In the case of India, the diploma level outturn in 1996 was about 95,000, two-third of that in China.

At the graduate level also, Russian Federation, with an outturn of 1,33,000 led the field in Engineering, closely followed by China with 1,29,000. Japan with an outturn of about 1,00,000 graduate engineers was clearly ahead of USA with 91,000. India had an outturn of about 75,000 according to data available from the Institute of Applied

Manpower Research. This was only a little more than half the outturn of graduate engineers in China, and about three-fourth of that in Japan. It may be recalled that Japan had a University enrollment of about two-thirds that of India, and China about half that of India.

On the whole, Russian Federation had an outturn of over 3 lakh of fresh engineers a year, China about 2.7 lakhs, USA about 2.1 lakh and Japan about 1.9 lakh compared to only 1.7 lakh in India in the mid-1990s.

Training of Post-Graduate Engineers

The relative emphasis given for Post-Graduate specialisation varies from country to country.

Table 25.6: Outturn of P.G. Engineers

Country	*Year*	*P.G. Outturn*	*Per cent of Grad. Outturn*
USA	95	40,780	44.8
Japan	96	24,775	24.9
China	94	11,605	9.0
UK	95	11,605	32.0
India	95	6,500	8.6
Russian Federation	95	3,798	2.9
Canada	96	2,915	26.5

Source: UNESCO Statistical Year Book 1998.

USA had the largest post-graduate outturn of Engineers numbering over 40,000. Japan came second with about 25,000, China and UK had outturns of about 11,500 each. India had an outturn of about 6,000 at the PG level in Engineering. Russian Federation had about 4,000, at the second degree level. Canada had an outturn of about 3,000.

As a percentage of the graduate outturn, USA ranked first with about 45 per cent, UK was second with 32 per cent. Canada and Japan had about 25 per cent each. Outturn of PG engineers in China corresponded to about 9 per cent of the graduate outturn while it was about 8.6 per cent in India.

The high figure for the outturn in USA, UK and Canada is due to large number of international students, mainly from Asian countries. The high figure in the case of Japan is due to substantial number of students from China and the Korean Republic, who have to return to their mother countries after studies. China and India have a large number of Graduate Engineers, working for their Master's Degree in USA and UK.

The Report of the Review Committee of the AICTE on Reshaping Post Graduate Education and Research in Engineering and Technology (IACTE 1999) propose "to double the present output of post-graduate and doctorates" from 7,000 to 14,000 in the case PG during a five year period, and from 375 to 750 in the case of Ph.D., in the course of 8 years.

The sanctioned intake capacity for PG in Engineering in December, 1994 was 19,180. The actual outturn was less than 50 per cent of the sanctioned capacity, or about 60 per cent of the actual intake.

The sanctioned intake at the beginning of 1995 as a percentage of the graduate outturn in 1996 is given in Table 25.7.

Table 25.7: Sanctioned P.G. Intake in Engineering

Subject	*Outturn of Grads 1996*	*Sanctioned P.G. Intake January, 1995*	
		Number of Outturn in 1996	*As per cent of Grad.*
Civil	8,875	4,295	48.4
Structure		105	1.2
Mechanical	13,582	3,339	24.6
Electrical	8,160	2,384	29.2
Electronic and Telecommunication	18,160	1,204	6.5
Chemical	2,411	36	41.0
Petrochemical			1.5
Metallurgy	788	324	41.1
Mining	508	163	32.1
Aeronautical	102	36	35.3
Agricultural	354	192	53.5
Production	2,132	126	5.9
Industrial		115	5.4
Instrumentation	1,924	82	4.3
Textile	581	277	47.7
Computer Engineering		841	
Others	17,685	4,590	26.0
Total	75,450	19,180	25.4

Source: IAMR and IACTE data.

The sanctioned intake for the PG courses in Engineering represent about 50 per cent of the graduate outturn in the case of Civil

Engineering, Agricultural Engineering and Textile, 40 per cent in the case of Chemical Engineering and Metallurgy, 30 per cent in the case of Electrical Engineering and 25 per cent in the case of Chemical Engineering. With the proposed elevation of the Regional Engineering Colleges to Deemed University status and their restructuring, Post Graduate Education in Engineering is likely to get a substantial promotion.

A graduate engineering with two year experience in USA and UK gets a higher salary than the starting salary of a Post-Graduate in most fields. USA and UK are finding it increasingly difficult to find adequate number of students for their existing PG programmes.

It may be mentioned that the number of persons who took a Master's Degree in Engineering in China in 1989 was about 15,000. It had come down to 11,600 in 1994. There had been a pronounced shift in favour of the non-degree whose outturn had increased by over 83,000 during the period. (There was, however, a steep rise in the number of engineers sent abroad by China for Post Graduation. Most of the Indian students going to USA used to opt for PG in Engineering. More recently, there has been a marked shift towards management).

Can we afford to carry forward lightly the present wasteful gap of about 10,000 between the number of seats sanctioned for PG Courses in Engineering and the actual outturn?

Non-Utilisation of Engineers

The growth in the number of qualified engineers is related to their need in industry, teaching, research and development on the one side, and popular demand on the other. There is admittedly a shortage of teaching staff to the extent of 15 per cent to 20 per cent. Yet, the number of job seekers appeared to be unconscionably large.

Table 25.8: Job seekers among Engineers at the end of December, 1995

Level	*Live Register*	*Registration during the year*
Post Graduates	4,870	609
Graduates	1,63,196	15,279
Diploma Holders	4,21,029	35,728

Source: Data from DGET.

The number of PGs on the live register represented about 75 per cent of the outturn in 1995. The registrants during the year do not include about 6,500 who qualified that year.

In the case of graduates, the number of registrants during the year was about 20 per cent of the size of the outturn. But the number of graduate engineer job seekers on the live register at the end of December, 1995 was the equivalent of about two year's outturn. Granted that all of them were not unemployed, it represents a large body of graduate engineers looking for fresh employment. The number of diploma level engineers on the live register represents the outturn of about 5 years.

Graduate Engineers looking for jobs constituted about 23 per cent of the estimated stock slightly over seven lakh of Graduate Engineers in the working age group in 1995 and diploma level Engineers about 37 per cent of the estimated stock of 11.4 lakhs.

Unused knowledge gradually becomes extinct. In an era of rapidly changing technology, refurbishing the knowledge of those no utilising it is a major challenge of technical education.

The possibilities of the IT revolution have to be appropriately geared for the retraining and updating of our technical personnel not gainfully employed, so that they can be enabled to play a positive role in the resolution of our technical, industrial, social or educational problems, especially in the rural areas where technical talent is at a premium.

Training of New Aspirants

"Most aspirants to engineering colleges and IITs want to pursue only IT related disciplines", says Prof. S. Sadagopan, Director, IIIT, Bangalore, "Wherever possible, efforts must be made to accommodate the requests of young aspirants of knowledge to pursue options of their choice, instead of being forced into disciplines that are well established. It is important for institutions to rise to the occasion and meet the challenge of IT — enabling all engineering disciplines rather than cry hoarse about youngsters ditching other disciplines. Adequate opportunities have to be provided to non-IT students to combine IT skills with other disciplines. Adequate opportunities have to be provided to non-IT students to combine IT skills with their domain knowledge so that our youngsters would not wish to run after IT blindly." Greater interdisciplinary interaction is essential for ensuring that this change takes place successfully. Talented students have to be attracted to every field of technical education essential for the progress and well being of the country.

Instead of running after IT as the new goddess of wealth, we have to treat it as a hand maiden in the effective solution, or resolution, of our developmental problems, IT has to become an increasingly important Instructional Tool in meeting the challenges of Technical Education. For this, there is need for an intellectual transformation in our academic to ensure adequate inter-disciplinary interaction.

26

Technical Education in India

S.M. CHATTERJEE*

What are our expectations from technical education in India? The basic expectation is Human Resources Development through professionalism, Skill Technical Manpower Generation for Socio-Economic Growth/ Development and hence, contribution to national economy and thus sustainable development along with R&D. Unfortunately, the existing systems of technical education has not met the expectation as forecasted, the reasons for this are fairly apparent, the chief of which is defective planning and programming. Planning and programming are essential for any sustainable development of a system. The demand the supply must tally each other. Demand of industry and other sectors are changing as per social, national, global demands particularly with technological revolution. Hence, the priority lies with data collection, analysis, removal of imbalances, mismatches followed by planning, forecasting and programming. Unfortunately, NTMIS was either not available or not consulted for plan growth of technical education. As a result, technical education in India has expanded very rapidly in the last four decades after Independence, because emphasis on industrial growth was given top priority in successive Five Year Plans. Thus, there are tremendous quantitative expansion in technical education. In the subsequent plan period, emphasis was given to other sectors but not only the existing Institutions continue to produce technical manpower but also a large number of technical institutions were allowed to establish on self-financing basis under private sector. Since supply is more than demand, it was unplanned quantitative growth and hence,

* Adviser, West Bengal State Council of Technical Education, Government of West Bengal.

it neither contributed to national economy nor to sustainable growth, as a result there are huge unemployment and under employment as reported by NTMIS, particularly in the traditional and conventional branches of engineering.

As reported above initially, demand is more than supply, quality was compromised with quantity, subsequently emphasis was given on quality because quality was compromised with quantity, subsequently emphasis was given on quality because quality was not as per expectations of all sectors not to speak of global expectation. Here again, there are huge unemployment and under-employment. On analysis, it was revealed that there are serious imbalances, distortion, mismatches in the growth of technical education. The courses and programmes were not relevant as per current demands of manpower, future demand for manpower, demands changing with globalisation of industry. It has caused mismatches and imbalances in the growth and advancement in technical education, resulting in huge unemployment and under-employment on one hand and acute shortage of knowledgeable skilled engineers on the other for developing and developed sectors.

There are Sectorial, Occupational imbalances that are still existing in Technical Education. All along, emphasis was given to formal organised sector that to the heavy/large, medium sectors of Industry, which account only 10 to 15 per cent, on the other hand, little emphasis was given to informal sector like service, domestic, small-scale industry, cottage industry, rural etc. There is a huge shortage of technical manpower in the informal sector which is 85 to 90 per cent. Here again, it resulted in unemployment and under-employment in formal sectors and on the other hand, shortage in informal sector. Consequently, it has caused progressive sickness and hence unhealthy development in informal sector.

Since inception, there are existing cadre imbalances. Most of the attention was given for top level but little to middle level. There are also existing courses/programs/discipline imbalances. Traditional and conventional courses in existence are not need-based and industry-oriented. They are mostly uni-disciplinary and rigid in structure. Re-structuring and phasing out of outdated conventional courses are essential, multidisciplinary courses are most suitable in the present context of industrial growth.

Technology and development are made for each other. It has been seen that either GNP or DGP or rate of economic growth is dependent on technology development. Unfortunately, there are technology gaps in the present education system. Sustainable, effective development of technical education and industry and other sectors were ignored. Technological development is very fast whether industrial technology — product and process or education technology. The lifecycle of one generation of technology is hardly four or five years.

R&D culture is almost nil in either Government Technical Institutions or Private Self-Financing Institutions, particularly in UG, label. Except in IIT, ISC, REC and University Department, Research and Development and Technical Education are supplement to each other. Thus, for sustainable and effective development, priority should be given:

(a) National/International Industry
(b) National/International Technical Institutions
(c) National/International R&D Organisations
(d) National/International Professional Organisations
(e) Alumni Associations
(f) Society, Community and others.

The selection/admission of students through entrance examination test is not out of shortcomings. Usually, admission test are elimination test and, hence, it cannot claim foolproof system. Text knowledge test, Technical attitude test, skill and habit test, Physicometry test are either not available or to a little extent. The selection are not in conformity with the attitude of the students. It has caused mismatches and hence national loss.

Carrier counselling and guidance are either not available or to a little extend. This is the greatest drawback in technical education. This has resulted in mismatches and imbalances in the growth of carrier and, hence, national loss.

The curriculum and syllabus is vital for sustainable development in technical education. The basic requirement/identification in technical education large knowledge/information, skilled aptitude and attitude, innovative and creative, analytical and problem solving etc. Accordingly, manpower requirement theory to practice is to be given weightage. In additional, social cohesion value addition, humanities and social science, economics, commercial accounts and costing, basic sciences—their history and development, engineering sciences—their history and development, human rights and intellectual property rights etc. are essential, for balanced technical education. So far, engineering curricula is concern, relevance, thrust and emergent areas in technical evolution, techno-entrepreneur, leadership and IT-oriented. Infrastrutural facilities and their obsolesce are also greatest drawbacks. Upgradation of technology is very fast and, hence, removal of obsolesce is a must, which involves huge capital requirement.

Probably, the foremost important is the Faculty. At present, except few institutions, there are huge shortage of faculty. Faculty cadre, Faculty requirement criteria and policy, Faculty appointment condition etc. are very vital. Obsolesce Faculty requires Faculty Development Programmes, which is either not available or at a little extend. Faculty Development Programme such as short/long term QIP, Summer and Winter School, Consultancy, R&D, Industrial Collaborative Project. Paper Publication, Book Publication etc. must be encouraged for quality education.

The teaching and learning system has undergone tremendous changes internationally. Unfortunately, the modern technology in teaching such as ET, TETE etc. are not adopted. Top priority should be given for adoption for the same in technical education.

Instructional material development and educational aid development are very weak in technical education in India. Instructional materials development is the responsibility of the faculties such as preparation of lessen plan, handouts, desk works, lab, manual etc. Educational aid development is the concern of educational management. Video, Audio, Multimedia, CD, OHP, Slide Projector etc. are essential. Web education, Internet education and teaching software etc. will further enhance the quality of education.

Accessibility of students to the library, computer centre, workshops, laboratory and other are limited both in number and duration. Student should be allowed, in my opinion, 24 hours for consultation, study, project work and others.

The facilities available in most of the libraries are not at all satisfactory. The number of text books, reference books, monographs, particularly journals are inadequate. Reading rooms, library accessories and equipment etc. are also not available. Library should be automated with the facility of networking with IIT, IISC, National Library along with internet.

The placement and training is weak. Without shop-floor training, the students cannot develop skill. With little exposure to industry, students are not acquainted with the problems of shop-floor, culture of industry where he has to work after graduation. Shop-floor experience in 5 Ms are essential for professional development.

Flexibility, diversity, autonomy etc. are almost absent in most of the technical institutions of India. This is essential for the healthy development of technical education in India.

Accreditation, bench marking etc. are not up to the standard event to national, not to speak of international. Washington Accord and WTO obligations are essential to compete internationally.

Technical education is different from other sectors of education because it has some specific objectives such as professionalism, academic requirements, technical upgradation, sustainable development, manpower development, social obligations etc. Technical education in India has to be given more emphasis on global expectation than national expectation such as on quality, emergent/thrust areas, multi-disciplinary, flexible, innovative, creative, value-aided, effective, equity, efficient, accreditation and bench marking etc.

27

Technical Education at Cross Roads in India

N.V. ARUNACHALAM*

India rightly has opened the gate to globalisation and liberalisation; otherwise it is likely to be left behind in the mainstream of the countries that are running to reach supremacy in one field or the other. Hence, it has become imperative that we open the door to globalisation and liberalisation so that we can also be equally reckoned.

Engineering has entered into every area — Administration, Information, Agriculture, Medicine, General Education, Insurance and many more. Without assistance from Engineers, none of the department can function effectively.

When foreigners arrive to compete in all spheres in our country, due to liberalisation and globalisation they are either going to bring their own workforce or employ nationals of equal competence. If we are not prepare to meet this need, we are likely to be trailing behind and this may affect our job potential as well.

Under the above circumstances, are we ready to face the challenges? Has our technical education modified its approach to face this uphill task. Really, the technical education is at the cross roads.

Many policy making bodies are involved in the expansion and improvement of quality in technical education in our country. The foremost among them are Federal Governments, All India Council of Technical Education (AICTE), University Grants Commission and Universities.

Due to globalisation and liberalisation, there will be imperative need for more technically qualified manpower as well as quality, comparable with that of international level.

Federal Governments, AICTE and UGC are involved in planning

* Chairman, IEI, Tamil Nadu State Centre.

and so they are fully responsible in producing the required number of manpower whereas the Universities are responsible for the quality of technical education.

However, to produce better quality technical manpower, minimum requirement of infrastructural facilities is to be made available in Universities and in Technical Institutions.

Let us see the roles each agency has to play in facing these challenges.

All India Council of Technical Education (AICTE)

As of now, there is not an equitable distribution of technical educational institutions in India. Education is a state subject. Hence, in this task, the state governments also have to cooperate. Due to policy differences and priorities, each State will have their own planning. Hence, this equitable distribution is very difficult to achieve.

However, one can observe that all the branches are also not given equal importance. This can easily be seen from the fact that every college has Computer and Information Technology branches and branches like Civil, Electrical, Chemical are provided in many Institutions. AICTE may take an excuse stating that students do not prefer the branches. The common statement is that as the branch is not offered in the Institution, the students do not join.

Hence, AICTE should see that all branches are offered in many colleges so that these engineers are available for building up the required infrastructural facilities.

In order to improve the quality, three things are essential:

1. Qualified and well-trained teachers;
2. Updated and up-to-date syllabi; and
3. Well-equipped laboratory and libraries.

The Institutions are growing in numbers, thanks to the policy of the Government. Do they have qualified staff? Are they following syllabi which cater to the need of the hour? Are the laboratories and libraries well-equipped? Unfortunately, the answer for all these questions is a big "NO". They how can one expect a quality engineer coming out of these factories, *i.e.* the Institutions?

What is the basic problem?
Insufficiency of funds!

Trusts and societies with the amount available on hand buy the prescribed extent of land and set-up the minimum requirement of building space and minimum laboratory equipments so as to get the AICTE approval. Once approval is obtained, they think they can run the institution based on the fees collected from the students.

Once on the job, a reality dawns on these people that it is not practical and may not work, when they start balancing the fees and expenditure. The result is inadequate infrastructure and ill-equipped laboratories.

Immediately, one will ask a question they "why should we allow more number of institutions at this condition why not close down these?"

It is not possible since opening of many technical institutions is the need of the hour. We have to produce more technical manpower to develop our nation and compete with foreign nations who will be entering our country due to globalisation and liberalisation. Hence, there is only one way and that is to improve and develop. Is it possible?

Yes, it is possible. The only requirement is money. But who will provide? Government is not in a position to provide as it is already burdened with more number of social obligations to the society.

In a Round Table on "Internationalisation of Indian Higher Education" at the University of Mysore in February, 2001, the participants — Senior Educationists, Planners and International Educational Experts have advocated a setting up of International Education Development Bank. This bank can provide "soft loan" to educational institutions wishing to develop the facilities and also to well-qualified and meritorious students wishing to go abroad.

In this effort, AICTE can play a major role. It is collecting huge sums as endowment from every institution. It will be in the order of billions of rupees. A part of it can be set apart as seed money for starting this "IED Bank".

As regards the trained teachers, AICTE has already identified the developed institutions to which prospective teacher candidates, proposed by needy institutions, are admitted for higher degrees. After completion, they are expected to go back to those institutions to work. It is a very bold and innovative step. This effort should continue and more candidates should be selected and deputed to augment the shortage of qualified teachers.

Developed institutions must identify strong areas wherein there are well qualified and motivates staff and well-equipped laboratories with modern instruments are available. They should develop international contacts through participation of their staff in many international seminar, symposium and workshops. These contacts may eventually lead to "Twinning" arrangements with foreign institutions and later this relationship can be firmed up through Memorandum of Understanding (MoUs).

This is one method by which Institutions of Excellence can be established.

These institutions can produce engineers of eminence comparable to foreign engineers.

This also can be a forerunner to the underdeveloped institutions to identify its strong areas and develop itself keeping the former as its roll model.

Last but not the least, we would like to inform the practice of forcing the students to select a branch which he does not like to study because of the mark he has obtained in the qualifying examination or to satisfy the social order of the government. This is currently prevalent.

This, in no way, will produce engineers of eminence. If the choice is left to the students, one can be pretty sure that India will produce engineers who will out beat the engineers of other world, both in quality and in rational forward thinking.

28

Technical Education in India
Some Prominent Issues

I.K. KHANNA*

Technical manpower is the main stay supporting the economic development of any nation. It is quality of this manpower, which divides the nations into developed and developing nations. India is known to possess the third largest force of technical manpower, but is rated low in the scale of development. Whereas Japan, with a fraction of technical manpower in comparison to India, ranks among the top developed nations of the world. The difference clearly lies not in quantity but in the quality of technical manpower. Therefore, if its quality has to improve, we have to look towards the institutes where this manpower is groomed.

Overview of Growth of Technical Education in India

Though the seeds of technical education in India were planted before independence, but its real growth started only after 1950, when the government decided to establish few premier institutes of technology in the country, namely IITs and IISCs. These institutes were established with the help of foreign aid, therefore, they not only had huge finance to build their infrastructure, but also had access to sophisticated instruments and trained faculty. As a result, they could provide the nation with some of the world's best technical manpower. But the output from these institutes was insufficient to meet the ever-growing developmental requirements of the nation; therefore, many more institutes were added in subsequent years, mainly with the government's

* Chairman, IE(I) Jabalpur Local Centre, Jabalpur (M.P.).

assistance. These institutes fell broadly under three categories, namely Regional Institute, State Institute and Private Institute. Regional Institutes were better than the other two in terms of facility, infrastructure and the quality of students they produced.

The above situation prevailed largely till the fag end of 80s and beginning of 90s. But with the liberalisation of economy, there came a drastic shift in government policies towards technical institutes. Government started curtailing its funds and wanted them to become self-sufficient and financially autonomous. At the same time, government also became liberal in granting permission to private sector technical institutes. As a result, the latter half of 90s saw mushrooming of technical institutes in the country. Sadly, the overriding consideration of these institutes was to make profit, which pushed quality consideration to the back seat.

Concept of Quality

Quality of a product depends upon the quality of its building blocks and the skill of the person who puts them together. In other words, the quality of a product does not solely depend on the reasons that lie within it but also depends on the reasons that lie outside it.

This simple concept applies to technical education also, *i.e.* to instil quality in technical education; we have to take for the reasons that lie not only within the system but also outside it. To do this, first, all those factors have to be identified which have a direct or indirect influence on technical education, then the relationship between them and the way in which they affect the system have to be understood. Then, only corrective measures can be suggested for improving the system in a realistic way. The whole system has been divided into three sub-systems, namely Faculty, Institute and Government/ Management and their interactions shown. A very careful and pragmatic approach is needed to analyse the effect of these factors on the quality of technical education.

A Pragmatic Approach to Improve Quality

Any attempt to improve the quality in technical education first requires as a prerequisite a clear understanding of the system. It opens up a completely new perspective in understanding the working and the factors influencing the system. A step by step approach of analysis of various sub-systems and variables operating therein is followed, which will eventually lead us to the key factors responsible for quality in technical education.

Faculty

Faculty plays a pivotal role in influencing quality in technical education. But unfortunately, it is not getting as much attention as it deserves to get either from the government or from the management. As a result, most of the technical institutes in the country are facing an acute shortage of trained faculty. The problem is further compounded by the fact that this profession is fast loosing its sheen amongst the prospective job seekers which effectively keeps away bright and meritorious students from joining this profession. Is it not a great irony that on one hand the number of pass-outs from these institutes is raising every year and on the other hand, the number of students opting for this profession is decreasing? Clearly something is going wrong somewhere, and if it is not checked and rectified immediately, then undoubtedly, the technical education in India is doomed to see even worst days ahead.

Attractiveness of a job is the primary criterion, which influences the decision of a job seeker to join a particular job. Therefore, in technical education also an endeavour should be made to search for the factors which will make it more attractive in the eyes of a job seeker and, therefore, lure good and meritorious students to join it. Fortunately, a slight beginning has already been made in this direction. A limited survey was conducted amongst the faculty members of Engineering College, Jabalpur to find the factors, which influence the attractiveness of technical education. Faculty members were asked to first list the factors they deem are important to improve the attractiveness of their profession and then rate them on a ten point scale. Analysis of the survey findings revealed some very encouraging facts. It was not the salary but the interaction with the industries, which was rated as top factor affecting the attractiveness. Promotional avenues, salary, class size, welfare programmes were some other factors which came high on the rating. A detailed survey on the similar lines may be conducted on All India basis and more representative view obtained from a bigger sample size. High rating for industrial interaction indicates the need to develop a symbolic relationship between industry and institute, which will not only benefit both of them, but also give students a much needed industrial exposure to stand out in this global competitive environment.

Institute and Students

Quality in technical education can be built only on the solid foundation of basic facilities available with the institute, like land and building, well-equipped labs, good classrooms, library etc. It is, therefore, absolutely essential for any institute to have those requirements fulfilled before it even thinks of imparting technical education, rest aside the question of imparting quality technical education. No accreditation agency should ever allow any institute to function without ensuring the availability of these basic facilities. Any compromise here will lead to deterioration in quality, which is amply supported by the fact that the institutes of repute have excellent basic facilities with them.

Other quality important factor, which can make or mar the quality technical education, is the quality of students at the entry level. Again, it is a well known fact that institutes of repute conduct an elaborate, screening test to ensure that only the best stuff gets in, because they know honing an iron can never make it glitter like gold. But, at the same time, it is very unsettling to note that the new institutes, which have grown up like mushroom all over the place, are at times severely compromising on this account for monetary gains. When there are seats remain vacant, they advertise in newspapers and admit even those students who could not qualify the screening test, even worst admit those who even did not appear in the screening test. If such is the degradation at entry level, then it is a folly to think of improving quality in technical education. Government institutes are also no better placed, in this regard. Lowering of cut-off marks in screening tests is done to such an extent that the screening test itself becomes irrelevant. One mark out of nine hundred students get admitted in the college! Is it not a complete mockery of screening test? Slackness here reflects as slackness of quality in technical education. It is, therefore, absolutely necessary that the accreditation agency also sets strict guidelines for maintaining the quality of students at entry level and see to it that these guidelines are not flouted either by government or private institutes to gain political mileage or monetary benefits.

Government/Management

They can play a very important role in instilling quality in technical education because they are at the helm of affairs regarding everything concerning institute, faculty or the student. It is they, who make plans and policies regarding the governance of the institute, and also provide vital financial support to execute it. Therefore, their policies and decisions have a direct bearing on the attractiveness of the profession. For instance, institutes with good policies for recruitment and promotion of its faculty attract better-trained manpower as compared to the institutes, which does not have it. Good governance gives contentment to the faculty and motivates him to do his best for the development of the institute and the students, thus automatically ensuring improvement of quality. AICTE has already laid down elaborate guidelines regarding these matters and by any standard, they are good enough to lure good and meritorious students in this profession. But unfortunately, these guidelines are not implemented in the right earnest in most cases. Some unscrupulous institutes pay meager salaries to their staff, which acts as a deterrent for the talented person to join them. Government institutions are also not free from this blot; they tend to manipulate these norms as per the whims and fancies of the ruling party, thereby making a complete mockery of the guideline. Promotional policy is one such area, which has suffered greatest wrath of government's callousness, with no clear-cut promotion policies, even the qualified staff is left to stagnate in the post for years. It creates an apathy in the mind of the sufferer towards the job which ultimately demoralise and demotivate him to work with his optimum efficiency. A person should get what is due to him in time and at the same time, be rewarded for the extra efforts he puts in for the development of his institute by way of doing research and consultancy or any productive work. Unless such schemes are implemented in right earnest, the quality of technical education may continue to suffer.

Student's quality at the time of entry is the other factor which suffers heavily in the hands of Government/Management. Private institutes do not maintain the standard for monetary gains, government institutes lower standards for political gains. AICTE is doing a great service to the cause of improving quality in technical education by setting guidelines for quality of new entrants and seeing that they are rigorously implemented.

From the foregoing discussions, it can be concluded that the two important factors which can bring about some quantitative improvements in quality of technical education are: attractiveness of the profession and quality of students at entry level. Improvising its attractiveness will not only bring talented and meritorious students in this profession but also keep the existing faculty contented, which will go a long way in improving its quality. Second factor is equally important and needs to be addressed with even more sincerity and caution because its implementation may face some stern opposition from both government and private institutes at it hits directly their narrow vested interests. But for the cause of technical education, somebody will have to show courage to implement it. Otherwise, the ship of technical education will sink under the weight of its quantity and want of quality.

INDEX